CLASS 11

INSIDE THE CIA'S FIRST
POST-9/11 SPY CLASS

CLANDESTINE SERVICE TRAINING
CST CLASS 11
VICTORIA
PERSEVERANTIA SACRIFICUM
ANSWERING THE CALL

T. J. Waters

DUTTON

DUTTON
Published by Penguin Group (USA) Inc.
375 Hudson Street, New York, New York 10014, U.S.A.
Penguin Group (Canada), 90 Eglinton Avenue East, Suite 700, Toronto, Ontario M4P 2Y3, Canada
(a division of Pearson Penguin Canada Inc.); Penguin Books Ltd, 80 Strand, London WC2R 0RL,
England; Penguin Ireland, 25 St Stephen's Green, Dublin 2, Ireland (a division of Penguin Books
Ltd); Penguin Group (Australia), 250 Camberwell Road, Camberwell, Victoria 3124, Australia
(a division of Pearson Australia Group Pty Ltd); Penguin Books India Pvt Ltd, 11 Community Centre,
Panchsheel Park, New Delhi—110 017, India; Penguin Group (NZ), cnr Airborne and Rosedale
Roads, Albany, Auckland 1310, New Zealand (a division of Pearson New Zealand Ltd); Penguin
Books (South Africa) (Pty) Ltd, 24 Sturdee Avenue, Rosebank, Johannesburg 2196, South Africa

Penguin Books Ltd, Registered Offices: 80 Strand, London WC2R 0RL, England

Published by Dutton, a member of Penguin Group (USA) Inc.

First printing, April 2006
10   9   8   7   6   5   4   3   2   1

This material has been reviewed by the CIA. That review neither constitutes CIA authentication of
information nor implies CIA endorsement of the author's views.—Publications Review Board, CIA

REGISTERED TRADEMARK—MARCA REGISTRADA

LIBRARY OF CONGRESS CATALOGING-IN-PUBLICATION DATA

Waters, T. J.
   Class-11 : inside the CIA's post 9/11 spy class / T. J. Waters.
      p.   cm.
   ISBN 0-525-94929-1 (hardcover)
   1. United States. Central Intelligence Agency—Officials and employees—Training of.
   I. Title: Class eleven.   II. Title.
   JK468.I6W37   2006
   327.1273—dc22   2005034372

Printed in the United States of America
Set in Minion

To Cathy,
For understanding why I disappeared
for the first year of our marriage

CONTENTS

INTRODUCTION

THREE LARGE U.S. GOVERNMENT BUSES sit in the parking lot of an otherwise empty strip mall outside Roslyn, Virginia. It's five-thirty on a cold Thursday morning in November. Students arrive one by one, half awake, with their coffee or diet cola in hand. I pull my suit-case out of the trunk and pat myself down one last time. We are conducting this exercise in alias. I can't have anything in my pockets that reveals my true name. Experienced interrogators will strive to break down our cover identities, family histories, and jobs. If anyone learns my true name, it means arrest. Handcuffs. Jail.

Satisfied I'm not carrying anything that can expose me, I board the bus and sit down next to a fellow student named Jay. We engage in a little ner-vous chatter, trying to forget about the approaching drill. Our conversation turns to the sweeping changes in the intelligence community over the past five months. Al-Qaeda, an enemy unlike any this country has ever known, is still trying to kill as many Americans as possible. Dawn breaks as the bus pulls away to take us to the interrogation site. Reflecting on the moment, Jay looks out the window, and with characteristic understatement notes, "It's no longer a gentlemen's game."

It most certainly isn't.

The trade of espionage is no longer professional intelligence officers working against one another in a practiced and civilized manner. The old methods for recruiting foreign nationals during diplomatic parties are now part of Cold War history. Terrorists aren't on the diplomatic circuit. They quietly toil in towns and villages, away from the capital cities where the United States maintains an official presence. Commercial cover operations, paramilitary action, and covert influence programs have replaced embassy parties. Unfortunately, there's a shortage of qualified field officers to do the work. That's where we come in.

We are the CIA's Clandestine Service Training Program Class 11. We are the volunteers who entered the CIA after the September 11 attacks—the largest training class in CIA history. The exercise we are conducting today is only the beginning, a peek into the main instruction conducted at the Agency's legendary training facility in Central Virginia, commonly known as the Farm.

This isn't a story about tuxedos, martinis, or fancy gadgets. This is the real world of espionage. But it isn't exclusively about tradecraft. It's about people. A group of people who took dramatic turns from career and family to answer a nation's call.

This is our story.

PREFACE

EVERY TWENTY YEARS OR SO an unimaginable tragedy befalls our nation. Beautiful sunny days are suddenly and irrevocably tainted. In every instance, people never forget where they were standing when they learned the terrible news. Witnessing these events makes them even more horrific. The invention of television brought terror to our living rooms in heretofore unthinkable ways. Pearl Harbor in 1941. Kennedy's assassination in 1963. The explosion of the space shuttle *Challenger* in 1986.

On September 11, 2001, I was at home packing for a business trip that afternoon to Montreal. I was watching live when the second plane, United Airlines Flight 175, struck the south tower of the World Trade Center. Like many people, I thought I was watching the first plane being played back on tape. Only after an offscreen engineer corrected the news anchor, saying the images were live, did the full scope of the event begin to dawn on me. Or on any of us.

Al-Qaeda succeeded where emperors, dictators, and tyrants failed. It attacked the mainland United States, successfully striking multiple targets in broad daylight. Evading law enforcement and military defenses, it conducted the ultimate sneak attack. It was, for most Americans, completely inconceivable.

I contacted the CIA a week after the attacks. I'd been recruited several years earlier and still held a top-level clearance. I sat down for a serious discussion with my girlfriend, Cathy. Though I had not yet proposed, I'd already purchased the ring and was just waiting for the perfect moment. How would this affect us? I wasn't willing to go unless she was fully on board. She didn't hesitate. With her support we entered a phase of our relationship neither of us truly understood. I bent down on one knee at a quiet little restaurant in North Tampa, promising her a life unlike anything she could imagine.

More than 150,000 people applied to the Central Intelligence Agency in the weeks following the attacks. The agency typically accepts less than one-tenth of one percent of the applications received. After September 11, the CIA brought in retirees and reassigned existing staff from other offices to handle the incredible mountain of applicants. Highly skilled, highly motivated professionals were applying by the thousands. But these weren't twenty-year-olds without appreciable skills. These were lawyers, consultants, investment bankers, scientists, and a myriad of other professionals. Not just witnesses to the terror in New York City or Washington DC, the applicants came from military bases in Georgia, law firms in Texas, and software companies in California. From sea to shining sea résumés poured in, asking one simple question: What can I do?

Terrorism was no longer something that happened elsewhere. It now had a local face, a local presence. Cathy and I were strolling through a local mall one Saturday night when her father called wanting to know if we were OK. A local teenager had stolen a plane and slammed it into the Bank of America building, the tallest structure in downtown Tampa. Police found a note stating his support for Osama Bin Laden and the attacks of 9/11, but found no direct link to al-Qaeda.

This copycat attack was neither supporting radical Islam nor protesting U.S. policy in the Middle East. He was simply a lonely young man who had lost his way. This incident made us ask ourselves lots of question: How many more such young people are out there? How many like him had we known at that age? What other threats to our national security and the safety of our own hometown awaited us? This fortunately isolated incident served to underscore our commitment to the career, family, and life choice we have since made.

Normal processing time to enter the Clandestine Service is about eighteen months. After September 11, that processing time was shortened to just over six. In this abbreviated period a class was selected, approved, notified, and relocated to the Washington DC area. The logistics involved were staggering.

Each student was required to complete a battery of exams and approvals. Each was interviewed repeatedly, by phone and in person, by a number of different staff officers. They explained why they wanted to join the Agency and what they expected to offer. What work did they feel most suited for? The information gathered was evaluated, along with a security investigation conducted by an outside agency. Any discrepancies or incomplete information was thoroughly evaluated before the process moved forward.

Each applicant underwent a rigorous medical examination. Unlike military exams, Agency medical evaluations were not open for discussion. Those who did not pass were not advised of the condition or circumstance that caused the failure. They were simply declared medically unfit and removed from further consideration.

Those who continued processing were moved through the medical office's mental evaluation procedures. A variety of psychological instruments were administered and strenuously analyzed. While test results were never directly shared with the applicant, separate sessions with psychologists and psychiatrists polished any rough edges identified by the exams and weeded out another group of applicants. Finally, there were the infamous polygraph exams.

Few parts of the entry procedures for the Clandestine Service are as legendary as the so-called lie detector. The examination doesn't actually test for lies. It measures physiological changes in an applicant's breathing, heart rate, and galvanic skin conductivity as they respond to questions from the examiner. The value is not in the test itself. It's in the professional utilizing it. As many applicants soon learn, Agency polygraph examiners are experienced, and they've heard it all.

The applicants who made it through these hoops had arrived at a pivotal date: their conditional offer of employment. Pending final review of their entire file, the Agency was tentatively extending a job offer. Was the applicant, after all this time, still interested? For the September 11 applicants, the answer was a loud and impassioned "Yes!"

During this same time my engagement to Cathy was in full swing. We simultaneously made wedding plans in Tampa and travel plans to Washington. The problem was getting it all done without drawing undue attention from family, friends, and my current employer. Caterers, DJs, and florists in Tampa were balanced with appointments, tests, and polygraphs in Washington. Only on the way home from our honeymoon did the call come from the investigator, finalizing my clearance. He would meet us at home only a couple of hours after we arrived.

Two weeks later, the actual offer letter arrived. After one last discussion with Cathy to ensure she was still with me, I contacted the Agency and accepted their offer of employment. Having just made one huge leap of faith, we were preparing to take another. But like the former commitment, the question was were we ready?

Were we ready to live our lives undercover? Were we ready to lie to family and friends about what we were doing day to day? Were we ready to disappear to complete the Agency's secret training program? It is one thing to say it. It's quite another to actually do it. For those who accepted the conditional offer of employment, follow-up notices were sent out a few weeks later. Enclosed with the various security details was an enthusiastic welcome to the CIA. Then it was real.

For logistical reasons the students did not all arrive at once for training. Instead, our arrivals were staggered over a several-month period, giving the Agency and us time to absorb what was happening. We were the best and the brightest the United States had to offer, and we were all coming to the nation's capital. It was the largest training class ever assembled. There was no precedent. We didn't know it, but we were members of what has since become the most talked-about spy class in CIA history.

The chapters that follow offer an insight into what this year was like. It will mainly focus on the people—my colleagues—who answered a wounded nation's demand for justice. We have little in common other than a desire to serve. Yet we forged a bond so great that spouses, family, marriage, children, and all of life's other priorities had to temporarily accept secondary status. Even now it is difficult to put into words.

Many officers have preceded us. Many more will follow. Every class has its traditions and legends, but Class 11 carved out a unique niche in Agency folklore. I leave it to you, the reader, to decide if it was fate or good fortune that brought such an odd mix of people together.

Each chapter is a month's mix of training, class bonding, personal reflection, and world events viewed through one officer's perspective. There are good times and bad, moments of triumph and periods of despair. We shared these events like brothers and sisters.

When military cadets make mistakes, it's common to punish the entire squad. Our experience was similar in many ways, but still distinctly different. When one of us stumbled, we all felt the pain, not from our superiors but from our own need to be the best. We refused to disappoint our families, fellow students, or our country.

The September 11 victims deserve our best.

CLASS 11

Gathered Around the Seal
July 2002

THE MAP ARRIVES ANONYMOUSLY, with no return address and no attached note of any sort. Just a diagram with today's date and 8:00 A.M. scribbled in the upper-right-hand corner.

At thirty-seven years old, I had no intention of ever leaving the Sunshine State. I'd wanted to live in Florida my entire life. I had a beautiful home on the water, a job I enjoyed, and every CD Jimmy Buffett ever released. Everything was fine until those planes hit the Twin Towers. Then everything changed.

Since September 11 I've proposed to my girlfriend, Cathy; married; sold her home; and moved her furniture into my place. Everything has happened so fast, my house—oops, *our* house—is not even on the market yet. Cathy continues to live in Florida while searching for a job in the Washington DC area.

I packed a U-Haul with enough furniture, linens, and clothes to get us started in an apartment and drove off *on her birthday* after only nine weeks of marriage. This drew a considerable amount of unwanted attention; family and friends besieged her.

"Is there a problem?"

"Do you need some money?"

"I know a great counselor, therapist, priest, pastor, or psychic that can help you with whatever it is."

Well-meaning people, but they were just getting on her already frazzled nerves. We weren't having problems and we weren't splitting up. We were making the first of many concessions for being an Agency family, adjusting to my one-year training program that will keep us apart even when we do manage to live under the same roof. There will be little downtime. Nights, weekends, and holidays are full for the next year. This is how things work inside the Directorate of Operations. The mission always comes first.

I enter on duty, or EOD, on Monday, July 15, 2002.

AFTER PARKING IN THE AREA highlighted on the nondescript map, I begin the long walk into the CIA's main building at Langley. I show my driver's license to the uniformed officers and am directed down a corridor into a meeting room. A large crowd of people is milling around and chatting, a mob of nervous faces trying to look poised and confident.

I pour myself a cup of coffee and find a seat. Our first day is indicative of what the next year is like. Every staff member who walks into the room goes wide-eyed. No one can believe how many people are here. Previous classes could meet in almost any standard-size classroom. We can't. We take up every chair and are sitting on every square inch of floor space. I barely settle into a chair when a woman steps up to the podium and asks us to settle down.

"Good morning, and welcome to the CIA. My name is Dottie. I am the Human Resources Manager for the Clandestine Service Training Program. Get used to seeing me—we will be spending a great deal of time together over the next year. I'd like to get everyone organized and take you on a quick tour. I need to show you the usual things like restrooms and what to do when you get lost, which, trust me, you will. I also will be taking you around the first floor of the building and showing you some of the neatest stuff you will ever see. We've got a few fun days to get through before your training begins, so let's make the most of it."

Our first stop is the Gallery of Directors—commissioned paintings of each Director of Central Intelligence since the Agency's creation in 1947. The gallery leads down one of two central hallways to the original front door of the CIA. We walk up to a bust of former President George H. W. Bush, where Dottie stops.

"This is, obviously, former President George Bush. Mr. Bush was also a former Director of the CIA. Though he was only with us for a year, he made an impression. People here genuinely liked him a lot. This facility is named after him, the George Bush Center for Intelligence."

She then leads us out of the security turnstiles and into the Agency's main lobby.

"This is what many of you have been waiting for."

We grin like maniacs.

Laid out on the floor is a sixteen-foot-wide carved granite rendition of the CIA seal. This famous logo is prominently featured on the covers of Robert Ludlum novels, in Tom Cruise movies, and on numerous popular television series, including *24, The Agency,* and *Alias.* Located directly inside the front door of the Original Headquarters Building, it is one of the most famous areas within the CIA. This is where presidents and dignitaries take pictures commemorating their visits. To stand here is to truly appreciate the exclusivity of our new jobs.

"There are three main parts to the seal," Dottie tells us. "The eagle, the shield, and the sixteen-point star. The eagle is our national bird and symbolizes strength and alertness. The shield symbolizes defense. The sixteen-point star symbolizes the gathering of information from around the world. Put them all together, and it stands for our mission of providing policy makers with the information necessary to defend the nation."

We jockey for position around the seal's edges, everyone taking a turn before moving to the rear of the large pack of bodies.

"I know this is the object you were most wanting to see," Dottie continues, "but I would prefer you walk away from here having seen *this*." She walks over to the wall. Five rows of stars are carved into the hard stone. Flanking the stars are the American and CIA flags.

"This is the Wall of Honor."

Across the top an inscription is engraved: IN HONOR OF THOSE MEMBERS OF THE CENTRAL INTELLIGENCE AGENCY WHO GAVE THEIR LIVES IN THE SERVICE OF THEIR COUNTRY.

Seventy-nine stars are carved into the cold granite, one for each Agency officer killed in the line of duty. Dottie points to a glass case below the stars.

"This is the Book of Honor. It lists forty-eight of the officers whose star appears on the wall. The remaining officers must remain anonymous. Their contributions to the United States are still classified."

Everyone is silent, struck by the realization that a star on this wall might someday represent one of us. It is a humbling tribute to the patriots who preceded us and a sad reminder that our work often comes at a terrible price.

"If some of you want to walk outside, there is a statue of Nathan Hale," Dottie continues. "He was the first American executed for espionage in the service of his country."

"I wonder if he got an honorary star," someone whispers.

OUR FIRST WEEK is an introduction to the CIA.

What we must first understand is we are not CIA *agents*. The FBI employs agents. The CIA employs *officers*. It's a small but significant distinction.

In the briefest of descriptions, agents are best thought of as representatives, and FBI agents are representatives of the Department of Justice. But FBI agents are also law-enforcement officers, which would seem a contradiction. As officers they are entrusted to take action on behalf of the Department of Justice to investigate and arrest criminals.

CIA officers are similarly entrusted to act in good faith on behalf of the U.S. government. The only difference is that we will clandestinely recruit and manage representatives (agents) of foreign governments to supply us with secret information. Our agents will be our lifeblood, the reason we take on the difficult work of being a Clandestine Service officer.

The CIA is comprised of four divisions known as directorates. The Directorate of Administration is responsible for things like Human Resources, Medical Affairs, security operations, and similar functions expected in a large government agency.

The Directorate of Science and Technology is the Toy Makers. From satellites that circle the globe to transmitters that fit on the head of a pin, the DS&T is legendary for a "no-such-thing-as-impossible" attitude. The DS&T's various offices conduct everything from remote monitoring of foreign nuclear devices to designing new disguise techniques. Their exploits are the subject of cable television documentaries and blockbuster movies.

The Directorate of Intelligence is the analytical cadre of the CIA. Without analysts there would be no way to turn raw information into actionable intelligence. They incorporate a wide range of information sources, including satellite imagery, foreign media articles, intercepted communications, and human-source reporting to divine an enemy's intentions, not just their capabilities. The DI is responsible for most of the Agency's briefing activities. From the White House to members of Congress to various officials within the government, DI analysts must interpret and communicate their insight effectively so that policy makers have the information necessary to make effective decisions.

The Directorate of Operations (DO) is the covert side, home to the Clandestine Service and, to most people's thinking, the *real* side of espionage. Without case officers in the field recruiting human sources to provide inside information, there is nothing for Directorate of Intelligence analysts to analyze. While previous administrations depended on technical espionage such as phone taps and satellite imagery, the September 11 attacks made it clear that technical prowess is no substitute for knowing what the enemy is *thinking*. This is where human intelligence operations, also known as HUMINT, is invaluable.

We are beginning the Clandestine Service's Training Program—the Directorate of Operations' primary means of training officers in the craft of

HUMINT operations. Over the next year we will learn to sneak, hide, conceal, lie, cheat, steal, and employ other subterfuge as needed. Our goal? Recruit foreign nationals who are willing to sell out their nation, leader, or religion for the benefit of the United States. Our mantra is "Recruit spies and steal secrets," a phrase repeated to us over and over again. It is the only reason we are here. Espionage is illegal in every country in the world. If we feel this is dishonorable, unethical, or against our basic moral fiber, now is the time to get out.

OUR SWEARING-IN CEREMONY IS conducted in the Agency's large auditorium. CIA Executive Director AB "Buzzy" Krongard conducts the formal procedure. It is an inspiring moment. Up till now we have been subjected to government paperwork and red tape. Our swearing in changes that.

Standing at full attention, our right hands raised, more than one hundred young Americans took the Oath of Office. But for us this was something far greater. It's a promise to those who perished on 9/11, individually affirming our pledge to the victims:

> *I do solemnly swear that I will support and defend the Constitution of the United States against all enemies foreign and domestic; that I will bear true faith and allegiance to the same; that I take this obligation freely, without any mental reservation or purpose of evasion; and that I will well and faithfully discharge the duties of the office on which I am about to enter. So help me God.*

No longer just private citizens, we are now sworn officers of the highest executive.

The class picture is taken from the back of the room, revealing only the backs of our heads as we stand in the auditorium. The photo is published the following day in the Agency's internal newsletter. Even among our colleagues, maintaining cover is a priority.

Every member of the class is undercover, our employment as spies veiled by a thin camouflage of deniability. There are two types of cover: official and nonofficial. Official cover means we are recognized as U.S. government employees. We will receive documents that support this facade of employment through several federal organizations.

Students under nonofficial cover, also known as commercial cover, work for imaginary companies created by the CIA. These firms, carefully researched and hidden from public view, do not exist, except on paper. Unlike government employees, these commercial entities can operate in areas of the world where a U.S. government presence either doesn't exist or is detrimental to recruiting foreign agents.

Regardless of which type of cover we have, all students have phone numbers and addresses that are monitored and maintained by a special team inside CIA headquarters. This office routes mail and phone calls from the outside world to our desks inside the Agency. To an outsider it appears no different from any other government office or private company. It's all a part of the complicated masquerade that allows us to work clandestinely.

I am under official U.S. government cover and spend a Wednesday afternoon getting an identification card from my cover agency's front office. Unfortunately, the people running the badge shops in these offices don't know who we are. We are quietly mingled in with legitimate new employees. Though this is very good operational security, it tends to make life challenging when you don't know your way around town. Fortunately, I was paired up with a student who was from the area.

Mel, a graduate of nearby Georgetown University, had been working in the private sector quite happily until September 11. He kicked around the idea of sending in an application to the CIA but couldn't really justify it. He had a new baby and a wife who depended on him being home at night. On September 11, their view of the Pentagon from their window changed her mind.

We made our way to the badge office. Nobody gave us a map of the building, so merely getting to the right entrance guaranteed we got our exercise for the day. Once inside, we had our pictures taken and immediately made for the cafeteria to link up with others who were also taking their first trips through the massive building.

In order to make our cover believable, we must speak intelligently about our cover agency's activities. While there will be numerous lectures by real and not-so-real cover agency officers, we were encouraged to kill a couple of hours inside the building. Learn our way around. Get a feel for it. Check out the library, the cafeteria, and other common areas. Be able to talk about the little things that make it obvious whether someone has or has not been in a certain place.

We meander around the building for about an hour, running into other students along the way. Someone remarks that there is a gift shop. A dozen students make a beeline for the store. T-shirts, jerseys, pens, coffee mugs, totes, and innumerable other items emblazoned with the agency's logo adorn the walls. I pick up a blue T-shirt and a coffee mug. Why not put some props in my apartment in case anyone comes by? Every little measure helps when it comes to maintaining cover. Visiting my office is certainly out of the question (I don't really work there, after all), so things like these lying around my apartment will sustain the illusion for family and friends.

While we are inside, the weather deteriorates and we have to run back to the Metro station in a driving rainstorm. We jog the first five blocks before realizing the futility of it. We take the train, run out to Mel's car, and make the return trip to Langley soaked to the skin. We pass through security to the snickers of the guards, park, and make the hike from the outer parking areas back into the main building and to our classroom. We are standing in soaking-wet suits when Director George Tenet walks in.

You remember certain parts of your professional life. Moments of glory where you make a spectacular move. You sell a major contract, save a child from a burning building, or create the next big thing that saves your company. You also remember when you were most humiliated. When you shredded the wrong document, or told an off-color joke about the boss's wife when he was standing behind you. This was one of those latter moments.

George Tenet walks in expecting to address the class. Deputy Director of Operations Jim Pavitt is with him. Pavitt is our boss. Tenet is his. These are the two top spies in the United States. The lone instructor tells him there has been a change to the schedule and that students are out getting cover badges. Tenet and Pavitt exchange mildly annoyed looks at having come downstairs for no reason. Unfortunately, they don't turn around and leave. Tenet sticks out his hand and offers it to me.

"George Tenet."

Pavitt is looking over Tenet's shoulder. I give Mel an "Oh, crap" look.

Wiping my wet hand on my dripping pants makes no sense whatsoever, but I do it anyway.

"Nice to meet you, sir," I offer, shaking his hand. "It's a pleasure. This is my colleague Mel."

I am not about to let Mel leave me swinging in the breeze by myself.

"Good afternoon, Mr. Director," says Mel. "You'll be wanting an umbrella when you leave, sir, just so you know."

Pavitt rolls his eyes. "Is that supposed to be information we can act on?"

Mel maintains his stoic appearance. "That's right, sir. It isn't intelligence if you can't use it."

Pavitt turns to Tenet. "Looks like the brainwashing is working."

Tenet laughs, amused by our soggy appearance. Leaving us to wring out our clothes, he exchanges a few pleasantries with the instructor before leaving. I beg the floor to swallow me up. So much for first impressions.

DOTTIE OUTLINES the program for the next year in our next morning briefing. We will spend six months in the Washington DC area, then six months at the DO's Special Training Center in Central Virginia, normally referred to as the Farm. Even when in Washington the hours will be long and the duty difficult for family and friends to understand. We are told to warn our spouses that free time will soon be a distant memory. Missed anniversaries, birthdays, piano recitals, and soccer games are commonplace. Due to the high stress and prolonged absences, the divorce rate in the

Clandestine Service is greater than 50 percent. Best to get the families prepared for it. Once more, she marvels at our class's large size, then leaves.

We learn the reason for our outsize number is due in part to a recent Agency decision to expand agent handling beyond the case officer cadre. For the first time, reports officers and desk officers will also be certified to handle foreign agents. To reflect this difference from prior programs, reports officers will now be known as Collection Management Officers, or CMOs.

They will be responsible for gathering information from case officers and getting it to decision makers in Washington. They will also act as liaisons between the headquarters staff in relaying information needs out to the field. Where necessary, CMOs will liaise with foreign intelligence services and conduct briefings for senior policy makers in Washington or in U.S. embassies abroad.

Desk officers, who have been moving into field positions more and more in recent years, are the unseen warriors of the DO. They receive the information at headquarters and ensure it is delivered to analysts or policy makers, then provide background relevant to the topic covered in the report. The position will now be called a Special Operations Officer, or SOO, to reflect that while they may be desk jockeys, when needed they can also mix it up in the field. Desk officers will serve as the case officer's right hand. Anything a case officer needs—an Internet search, box seats to a special event, or a car "abandoned" in a specific place—the desk officers will be their first points of contact. They are the wizards who make the magic happen.

Most importantly, when case officers are not available due to illness, travel, or simply caseload, a CMO or SOO will be able to meet with established agents. As a result, case officers will have more time to recruit, since CMOs and SOOs can collect from agents who are already on the books. It's quite a change from long-term Agency doctrine, when case officers met with agents and everyone else took second place.

ON THE THIRD WEEKEND, I fly home to see Cathy. I enjoyed my first few weeks in training, but as Dorothy from *The Wizard of Oz* so eloquently put it, "There's no place like home." I've spoken with Cathy every night, but it's better to be here in person. When we arrive home from the airport we waste no time getting reacquainted.

With the window blinds oriented a certain way we have privacy in our bedroom but are still able to see outside when the sun comes up in the morning. Saturday morning I roll over to witness a scene I had missed more than I expected: a spectacular sunrise reflecting off the water behind our home.

I slip out from under the covers without waking Cathy and go to the kitchen to start the coffee. Pulling on a pair of sweatpants I turn off the alarm system and retrieve the paper from the front yard. I open the sliding glass doors in the kitchen and walk out onto my back porch. I seriously question why I left this.

What kind of maniac leaves his new wife in a waterfront Florida home and moves to Washington DC? I throw the newspaper onto the deck table and walk across the back lawn to the water's edge.

A red-tailed hawk circles about fifty feet high over the water. Three box turtles balance on a tree limb that is sticking out of the water. About thirty feet out, a small alligator slowly swims parallel to the banks. It's an absolutely spectacular Florida morning.

A voice startles me from the tranquil scene. "So, do you miss me or the water?"

Cathy waits until I walk back to the house before applying a coy, come-hither tactic.

"I'm glad you came home," she whispers in my ear.

The coffee will have to wait.

When I get out of bed the second time, I turn on the radio and go into my office. Cathy has stacked my mail in a box, and it's overflowing onto the floor. The CIA may be the sexiest job in the world, but here at home, reality creeps back in. There are bills to pay and people to see while I'm in town. I take a stack of mail outside and sit down.

Cathy comes outside again and lies next to me on the two-person rocker my father built for us. She rests her head on my shoulder as I read. This was how we had spent almost every morning between returning from our honeymoon and my departure for Washington. I've missed it. Talking on the phone is fine, but it's no substitute for being together. The rocking motion is hypnotic. It's been three weeks since we spent any quiet time just hanging out together.

We fall back asleep with the hawk vigilantly circling overhead.

SITTING IN AN AUDITORIUM each day, stir-craziness takes hold. Side conversations between students start small and pick up in frequency and volume. Several times Dottie has to stop the lecture and stare until students stop talking. But with a roomful of type-A personalities, we can hardly be expected to just sit around like wallflowers.

We are here because our psychological profiles indicate that we are social, mostly extroverted (some to an extreme), and inquisitive. What do socially inquisitive extroverts do when sitting together? They engage in a bit of small talk to get to know one another. Given that the large class size makes assigned seating impractical, we are sitting next to someone new almost every day. We can't get to know them, can't bond with them, and can't forge a lifelong friendship unless we talk. So, talk we do.

One day I am sitting next to a young woman named Terry, who is a few years younger than me. We were getting an overview of how Agency families blend into the local environment of an overseas office. It was, well, boring. We engage in a bit of idle chitchat under our breaths.

Unlike most of the students, Terry has been an Agency officer for a few years. She was a Directorate of Intelligence analyst specializing in weapons of mass destruction.

When Dottie comments about overseas day care, Terry makes a face. Cathy and I don't have any kids, so I hadn't really been paying much attention to what was being said. I ask Terry if she has any children.

"Just one. A son," she says.

Being my socially inquisitive self, I ask if she has a picture of him. Of course she does. What mother doesn't? She digs into her purse and hands me a photo.

My jaw hits the floor.

Forget the Gerber Baby photo. No cutesy picture of a kid and Santa Claus. It isn't a toddler with dinner smeared all over his face, either. I'm looking at a fourteen-year-old on a motorbike! I don't hide my shock well.

"Wow!" I say, a bit too loudly.

Dottie points to me. "Was there a question?"

Terry's eyes widen. I'm still looking at her kid's picture as the whole class glances our way. Time to think fast.

"Yes. Do I understand you to mean we must sell our cars when we leave the country? Will they be replaced at fair market value by the government, or is that out of pocket?" I ask in as serious a tone as I can muster.

Dottie nods. "Good question. Actually, that is picked up by the government, and the reason is . . ." She continues on. I couldn't recall what she said if my very life depended on it.

Terry glances dubiously at Dottie, then back at me. "You pulled that one out of your ass," she mutters.

I am still holding the picture. "He's yours? He looks old enough to vote!"

I recognized too late this was not the most sensitive comment I could have made. Social. Inquisitive. Extroverted. But not always gracious.

She nods. "Yeah. I got pregnant kind of young."

She had been young, all right. Seventeen. Married at eighteen. Divorced and a single mom at nineteen. For a lot of young women that would have meant a life living just barely ahead of the bills. Terry wasn't willing to do that.

She got her life together and, with her now ex-husband's help, took turns babysitting while going back to school. Then she got a job. That job led to an analyst position with the CIA.

Once inside, she decided another degree would be invaluable, so she again worked out the logistics with her ex and went for a master's degree. As I said, her expertise is in weapons of mass destruction. Imagine spending your day studying death ratios, kill rates, and lingering trauma indices for weapons designed solely to kill Americans, then going home every night to fix dinner. It requires a certain emotional disconnect. She had gotten good at keeping that distance and conducting her analysis with cold dispassion. Then the planes hit the towers in New York. A few minutes later one slammed into the Pentagon, only a few miles away. This shattered her carefully constructed emotional detachment.

What if her son had been hurt? Or worse?

That was when she decided to send an application to "The Dark Side," as analysts call the Directorate of Operations. She wanted to be in the field, collecting the information firsthand. It was a long shot. The Agency has age limits on applicants to the Clandestine Service, and though she was several years under it, she knew it was going to count against her in the overall appraisal of her application. But she had a bigger problem. She had a child.

Though there isn't a written guideline, she was unable to find anyone who knew of a single mother who had been accepted into the program. It wasn't that they weren't welcome per se, people told her, it's just that the training program is so arduous and time consuming, there is barely time to take care of yourself. There is no time whatsoever to take care of a family. Fortunately, the Agency realized that a teenager staying with his father was not going to be an unusual burden on her. The transfer was approved.

The Dark Side had its first single mom.

THE AVERAGE CITIZEN cannot appreciate the sacrifices that people in the intelligence community have made and continue to make in the service of their country. This poor grasp of history is, in part, due to the nature of espionage: The successes must remain secret in order to remain successful. It is also because there are very few historical exhibits devoted to espionage subjects. The CIA recognized the hollowness of its history and took corrective action with a museum right here in the building.

As we wrap up our orientation to the Agency, we are given a tour of this museum, starting with an exhibit called the History of Espionage. It is located on the ground floor of the old headquarters building and features an unimaginable display of espionage artifacts from the Cold War. There is a full-time staff of curators, just as you would see at any federally funded museum. Toni Hiley is the CIA's curator in residence and Team Chief for the professional historians and restoration artisans who collect, refurbish, and maintain the Agency's extensive collection of spy paraphernalia.

What the Agency does not own outright it often borrows to be placed on public display within the compound: memorabilia from Gary Powers's ill-fated U-2 flight in 1960, the original 1963 satellite imagery of missiles in Cuba . . . But the museum is not restricted to only American hardware. There are foreign espionage items too, donated by defectors or captured during counterintelligence operations. Toni brings along a couple of items that weren't on permanent display for her lecture. One is a dead bug.

She holds up a common dragonfly. It is mounted on a block of wood in the style typically featured in biology classes throughout the nation. Not a particularly threatening insect, dead or alive. As she walks in front of the first row of students, however, a murmur ripples through the crowd.

The bug isn't real. Only when viewed directly overhead can we see small wires and microstitching on the wings. It's a remote-controlled drone, a life-size wing-beating replica of the real thing. A technician remotely operates the drone via a laser-beam control system that prevents electronic jamming. Toni makes the point that although it is a fake insect, from a certain perspective it's a "real" bug. The dragonfly is a listening device—a "bug" in spy jargon.

It was developed because the Agency needed a bug that could be deployed against two or more persons meeting in an open park area. A case officer could not deliver the device personally, because the targets would break up rather than risk being caught together. It had to be a transmitter delivered by an animal. Various scenarios were kicked around, and the consensus was against using a household pet.

Dogs or cats might scare the targets away, since the rightful owners often seek stray animals out. Anything that might startle the targets or force them to move the conversation elsewhere would be counterproductive. The device had to be delivered in an environment where it would not draw unnecessary attention or would be summarily dismissed if spotted. An insect was the only logical choice.

The Agency had first tried a bumblebee. Various prototypes were tried, but none worked out. With growing frustration, Agency personnel searched the Human Resources records and found that there was an entomologist—a bug scientist—on the CIA payroll. After being briefed on their needs and shown the poor results of the bumblebee, he was tasked with coming up with a better idea. He suggested a dragonfly.

It's a more stable platform, he explained. It can carry a larger payload (listening device), and will be easier to control from a greater distance. An outside contractor was hired to take the scientist's basic outline and create a prototype.

Carefully opening a box, Toni pulls out the engineer's original prototype for the dragonfly.

"Would anyone like to see a demonstration?" she asks.

Of course we would. Unfortunately, the real units are not flown anymore, lest they get damaged. Instead, she plays a videotape of dramatic test flights, both indoors and out. The dragonfly is completely silent and looks for all purposes to be absolutely real. It's impossible to tell the difference between it and a live bug flying around in the same scene.

Though the design was a success, the dragonfly was never used operationally. Winds above three miles per hour overwhelm the small drone's ability to react to remote control. Still, it's an impressive piece of engineering. Toni just smiles.

"The engineering isn't the impressive part," she says.

"It isn't?" a student asks. "What's the impressive part?"

Toni smirks. She's been setting us up from the start.

"The dragonflies are thirty-five years old!" she says.

Thirty-five! These so-called state-of-the-art drones are anything but. They are older than many of the students! A laser-controlled, jet-propelled robotic listening device available thirty-five years ago? Toni makes a round of the entire room to ensure everyone gets an up-close and personal view of the device. She then dismisses us for a quick break.

I couldn't help but notice something during her presentation, and my overly ambitious nature kicks in.

"Excuse me," I say. "I see the real bug's wing is broken. I know a biology professor who's got hundreds of these things lying around his lab. I'm sure he'd part with one."

Toni was delighted at the offer, and I made a quick call that night to a friend who could reach out to my old instructor. He didn't quite know what to make of the story about helping the CIA. But two days later I walked in with four professionally mounted dragonflies in a large display box. Toni was delighted and promised to send the instructor a note of thanks on Agency letterhead for his troubles.

She walks me around the limited storage space in the museum. There is a variety of spy toys and tools the museum simply doesn't have room to display. I play with several items before letting her return to her work. She senses my reluctance to leave.

"Relax," she says. "You'll see this kind of stuff soon enough. If the dragonflies are nearly forty years old, just imagine the cool toys available to you now!"

She's got a point. A wing-beating insect built on forty-year-old technology pales in comparison to what we will be using. These first thirty days have only whetted our appetites for more. I love the high-tech spy toys, but I also want to get down to the business of espionage. Al-Qaeda is as hard a target as any the United States has ever faced. How we will apply technologies such as these against it will require fresh new thinking and a willingness to take extraordinary risks.

On-the-Job Training
August 2002

TO PREPARE US for upcoming coursework, we begin thirty-day rotations in Agency offices, an on-the-job introduction to the Directorate of Operations. Each student is sent to an office to participate in the real work of espionage as viewed from headquarters. The positions run the gamut of Agency activity. While a few students go to area divisions (Europe, Africa, Asia, etc.), most of the class is assigned to offices within the Counter Terrorism Center, or CTC.

All counterterrorism reporting is managed by the Center. Any other "normal" espionage activity runs through the geographic divisions. Though the CTC was in place prior to the September 11 attacks, the nature of the adversary underscores the need for such a separation.

An enemy like al-Qaeda operates outside the typical Cold War doctrine the United States has historically followed. Though Osama Bin Laden managed to purchase the leadership of Afghanistan by opening his wallet, al-Qaeda is a worldwide operation. They use many of the same methods as national intelligence organizations.

They have false identities. They have cover jobs that justify where and how they move around the world. They create convincing travel documents and appear to be tourists, businessmen, or humanitarian aid workers. Their operational security—the means by which they control how much anyone can see into their operation from the outside—is outstanding. They use many of the techniques of the Special Forces community.

The United States has too often viewed Middle Eastern terrorists as illiterate cave dwellers, unworthy of real concern. September 11 proved that assumption wrong. Like our own Special Ops professionals, these men can improvise while in motion, alter operational plans around unforeseen problems, and adjust their timetables and plans. They can sneak into the United States, overpower flight crews, and fly commercial jets. So much for illiterate cavemen. Simply put, they're very capable and therefore very dangerous.

My assignment is in the Counter Terrorism Center's Office of Non Government Organizations, or NGOs. I will work directly with two DO officers, Elliot and Kim. Elliot is euphemistically known as the Mayor of Langley for his ability to assemble a pool of talented people on projects. He is my direct supervisor. Kim is a desk officer, irreplaceable to the team, and every bit the cool go-getter of Jennifer Garner's character Sydney Bristow from the hit television show *Alias*. Kim gives me the background on their work.

NGOs have become a growing problem for the United States in the past couple of years. It used to be that only foreign governments could wield sufficient political power as to require such oversight. Now there is a multitude of other players striving to alter or influence U.S. policies. So-called global corporations were the initial CTC concern as these corporations' financial positions became stronger and their annual sales reached the multibillions. Nonprofit organizations noticed this newfound political muscle and followed the same strategy.

"Osama Bin Laden is an effective user of NGOs," Kim tells me. "For Bin Laden and al-Qaeda, NGO offices around the world are used in the same way we use our overseas stations. They are a way of maintaining a presence in-country. It is a facility where your operatives know they can find help and assistance, a means for moving money around, and a collection point for information. It is also where any number of covert operations can be launched internally, reducing the risk of exposure in trying to control things worldwide from a single point."

NGOs typically use some charitable organizations as cover. As an example she explains the strategy employed by Hamas in Palestine. They operate the schools and hospitals, provide money and food to those who have none, and promote the general well-being of the Palestinian people. This becomes their focal point, their hook into legitimizing their presence and endearing them to the population. The Palestinian residents come to depend on the organization. It is so entwined with their daily lives that the recruitment of bombers for fanatical purposes is viewed as a normal, necessary evil to overcome horrible conditions.

With the success of this strategy, other groups follow the example. Organizations pop up daily in every corner of the Middle East, Latin America, and the South Pacific, promising assistance, education, and medical relief. Through such aid, these organizations are seen as the savior of the local populace, which feels left out and ignored by the United States and the West in general.

After the bleeding has been stopped and the bellies have been filled, when there is money stimulating the local economy, the hidden agenda of the NGO comes forward. Ever so slowly they reach out to the population. In addition to food and medicine, the NGO provides political education and assistance. Funding appears for newspapers to serve local citizens in ways not done before. What the population does not understand is that the news is directly controlled and manipulated by the NGO. Information that supports the NGO's political agenda is allowed through. Information that does not is deleted or the source is discredited. Images and commentary are often more inflammatory than the same stories reported by mainstream news organizations using international wire service feeds.

In Palestine it has become a self-sustaining recruitment machine. The more the Israelis shoot, bomb, or bulldoze, the more Hamas is able to rally the Palestinian population to its cause. The result is that more bombers volunteer for the deadly work. Israel has yet to find an effective counter-strategy for this fatal line of attack. Hamas's recruitment is so successful, it has expanded to include women and children as suicide bombers. The violence only escalates.

I AM READING some of the NGO offices' prior reports a couple of days later when Elliot taps on my cubicle wall.

"Want to go to the seventh floor with me?" he asks.

Seventh floor. A visit to George Tenet or one of his staff members. Either way, a big deal.

"You bet. Why, what's up?"

"KFOR grabbed a couple of guys yesterday claiming to be a part of some charity organization. General Campbell wants to hear what we know about them." KFOR is the UN-sanctioned security forces remaining in Kosovo.

"Why would we brief a general? Doesn't he have his own people?"

"Yeah, well, we are his people. Lieutenant General Campbell is assigned to the CIA as Director of the Office of Military Affairs. He's George Tenet's expert on anything military. Apparently, something's going on in Kosovo."

"I'd thought we won that fight already."

Elliot shakes his head. "No. It only looks that way."

"It's amazing what doesn't get reported on the news."

As we log out of our computers and put our loose documents away, Elliot tells me about the problem.

Kosovo is located in southern Serbia, which until 1989 enjoyed wide-ranging autonomy within the nation of Yugoslavia. Serbian leader Slobodan Milošević then revoked that autonomy and placed authority for it under his control in the capital city of Belgrade. Kosovar Albanians did not acquiesce to his wishes.

Military conflict between the Serbian military/police forces and Albanian forces killed 1,500 Kosovars and dislodged 400,000 refugees. Milošević ignored international and diplomatic pressures and continued his military campaign. On May 28, 1998, the North Atlantic Council met at the foreign minister level to set out NATO's objectives regarding the Kosovo crisis: achieve a peaceful resolution to hostilities, and promote stability and security in the two neighboring countries of Albania and Macedonia.

On June 12 of that year, as objectives had not been met, the Council moved up to the defense minister level, considering the various military options available. As the situation continued to deteriorate, NATO finally took action. On October 13, NATO authorized air strikes to force Milošević's forces from Kosovo. At the last moment Milošević backed down and air strikes were averted.

Despite numerous NATO measures to prevent it, the violence flared up again in early 1999. After much diplomatic wrangling U.S. Ambassador Richard Holbrooke flew to Belgrade and warned Milošević directly: Stop attacks on Kosovar Albanians, or face air strikes. Milošević refused, and on March 23 Operation Allied Force began.

After a seventy-seven-day air campaign, NATO Secretary General Javier Solana announced a suspension of air strikes. UN Security Council Resolution (UNSCR) 1244, passed the same day, called for the deployment of international civil and security forces in Kosovo under UN control. Elements of the transnational security forces—KFOR—entered Kosovo on June 12, 1999, synchronizing their takeover with the retreat of the Serbian military. By June 20 the Serbian withdrawal was complete, and KFOR was established in Kosovo according to NATO's security strategy known as Operation Joint Guardian.

Elliot looks at my loosened tie and unbuttoned collar. "Did you bring a jacket with you today?"

"Yes. Why?" I ask.

"You'll want it. He's a three-star general. The rest of the Agency is pretty casual, but OMA runs like a military operation."

I pull on my suit jacket and straighten my tie. We walk downstairs and cross the double-sided breezeway into the Original Headquarters Building.

From there we step into the elevator and Elliot pushes the button for the seventh floor.

"Welcome to the big time," he says.

Once upstairs we pass George Tenet's office and the office of Deputy Director of Central Intelligence John McLaughlin. Elliot continues to the end of the hall and turns a corner into the Office of Military Affairs (OMA). A young lieutenant is sitting behind a mahogany desk large enough to house a band of Bedouins.

"Can I help you?" she asks.

Elliot explains we are responding to a request. She presses a button on the desk and the general's private office door opens. His aide is a civilian CIA administrator, not a military officer, which I find surprising. He waves us inside.

"Good morning, gentlemen. This way, please. The general will be right in."

Elliot nods at a nearby wall. It is decorated with photos, medals, ribbons, and the many trappings one would expect of a career military officer. I am admiring the memorabilia when the general walks in.

"Good morning. I'm John Campbell," he says as he extends a hand.

Elliot explains he is there to answer questions about the KFOR detainees' charity, and that I was a CST student working in the NGO office.

"A student, huh?" Campbell replies. "Not the youngest person I've ever seen around here."

Ouch. Nothing like a good punch in the gut to start the day.

"What can I help you with, sir?" Elliot interrupts.

General Campbell explains that NATO forces had observed several men videotaping outside the American facility in Kosovo. They were arrested and detained. They claim to be part of an Islamic charity organization. What's the story on this group?

Elliot gives him a ten-minute overview of the organization the men claim to be members of. While it is a legitimate group, it had also been long associated with Islamic radicals and could be funneling money to them.

Elliot promises we'll look into the group's presence in Kosovo and get back to him in a day or two.

A FEW DAYS LATER, the *Washington Post* publishes a story outlining the CIA's attempts to recruit and hire a new breed of spy and how our class is the largest in history. The article outlines the variety of jobs we have in unusually specific detail. There is an age breakdown of the class, then a breakdown by gender, and how many of us are fluent in another language. This is not someone making guesses from the outside. They have good information or, to put it in the parlance of intelligence, "a source with good access." In other words, someone inside is feeding them information.

The article is not particularly kind, suggesting that we are too "American" to do the job effectively. But the article's stated position is at complete odds with what students assume would be the case. Sitting in the cafeteria at lunch that afternoon, we bat the issue around. There's a multitude of races and creeds in this class, but it is the students of Middle Eastern heritage who react loudest against the article.

"Being an American is not a liability to recruiting," insists Sarena. Her strong Pakistani features are offset by an equally strong Boston accent. "Does the *Washington Post* not understand the difference between race and citizenship? What era are they living in?" she asks.

"They're talking about Caucasians. That's the *Post*'s definition of an American," says Jordanian-born Ahmed.

"Don't think for a minute those highbrow snots consider us to be 'real' Americans. Funny how they question the CIA's diversity, yet clearly have a discriminatory streak of their own that's a mile wide." The voice belonged to another naturalized citizen, Faroud. He is on his second government job, having come to the CIA from the Department of Justice, where he was a translator.

"But it doesn't make sense culturally," Sarena continues. "You can't predict a foreigner's reaction based on appearances. It doesn't work that way.

A Bedouin tribal chief will avoid a stranger who looks like him. If he is receptive to a pitch, he's going to want the stereotypical American image. He wants the tall, clean-cut white boy, not someone who could be a neighbor out to kill him."

The other tall, clean-cut white boys around the table fidget in their chairs, just as I am doing. It isn't discrimination against me, nor is it bias toward me. It simply is. Americans tend to pigeonhole race relations as a black or white issue. In doing so, it reinforces the very mind-set we claim to be correcting. If modern America is a melting pot, we must acknowledge that the individual ingredients eventually become indistinguishable and the results considerably improved by the uncontrolled interaction of the constituents.

This is fairly deep philosophical ground to cover over a lunch break. But these brief respites have become increasingly more important. The cafeteria is our sanctuary, our means of escaping the prying and ever-judging eyes of the staff. What had begun as a few students sitting together has flourished. A few became a dozen, then two dozen.

Someone notices an upstairs landing over the cafeteria. It is for lunch meetings, allowing close access to the restaurant facilities but far enough away from the masses for a department meeting or to host an outside speaker. When it is not used for this purpose, it's simply spillover seating when the first-floor dining area is too full.

Around the second week of August we start eating upstairs. Some students assist in commandeering nearby tables and chairs. What was once thirty people continues to grow as word spreads.

Each new contact a student makes in the class is invited to join the group at lunch. Like a new railroad pushing back the frontier, the line of tables gets longer every couple of days. Soon it runs the entire length of the second-floor landing. So we do the only logical thing. We make a second row of tables immediately next to it.

By mid-month, close to 75 percent of the class sits together daily at two parallel rows of tables. Those whom I didn't meet in class I eventually meet while chatting over fast food or cafeteria lunches. Paula, for example, whose fiancé was killed in the World Trade Center, and Geri, who was a private chef for a wealthy family. I meet a New York City comedian, a Special Forces pilot, and a PhD biochemist. Regardless of what the *Washington Post* thinks, we are a cross section of the country. Every permutation of race, age, ethnicity, religion, or career path is represented in some way.

Every day these otherwise unrelated people meet upstairs for a generous helping of camaraderie. When some poor Agency employee unwittingly wanders up to look for a quiet lunch place, he is met with a hundred loud, boisterous, back-slapping students making as much noise as possible to scare the intruder away. It almost always works.

When it doesn't, the offending interloper sits at a nearby table and nervously watches the horde. It probably isn't wise that nearby tables can pick up bits and pieces of our conversation. Psychologists say that riots are started when a crowd of people is incited to lawlessness by an unintentional trigger from a single individual.

It's not unusual for Hal, who transferred in from another government post, to pepper his conversation with a variety of colorful expressions designed to scare off interlopers. Calls for belly dancers, beer bongs, and the respectful use of human sacrifice are oft-repeated topics. Far be it from him to sermonize alone. The banter usually escalates as more and more of the students' personalities emerge. It is very off-putting to the uninitiated. Intruders never invade our second-floor sanctuary more than once.

We jealously defend our territory. It is Class 11's refuge. Outsiders are welcome by invitation only.

TO ASSIST US in our temporary office duties several headquarters officers provide us an overview of the Collection Management Officer's (CMO) role in intelligence management.

CMOs are information junkies, thriving on the news of the day. I know I go through withdrawal if I don't have access to the national news at least every few days or so. I am on the Internet regularly to catch up on the latest world events. I prefer to know what's going on. CMOs are recruited for this trait. They like reading and writing. They must be comfortable in assimilating large amounts of data and sifting through it to see what is real and what is hyperbole. Only a wordsmith enjoys this type of work.

CMOs have an odd history with the Agency. Originally these report writers were either secretaries or the wives of case officers who couldn't type. Over the past few years, especially in the modern information age, these CMOs have taken on additional responsibilities and importance. CMOs are the first officers to read the reports turned in by case officers. It makes them first and foremost bullshit sniffers. Bovine excrement in the intelligence community comes in all shapes and sizes, from agents and case officers alike.

Because there is no emotional connection to the CMO (as there often is to the case officer who recruited him), an agent has less success using charm or charisma to skate by if his reporting is not up to snuff. The information is what it is: worthwhile or worthless. There is little gray area in between. CMOs examine information objectively and gauge its usefulness. Another role CMOs now work in is counterintelligence. The variety of software tools that are commercially available makes this job much easier than in the past. While the CMO is always critically evaluating the content of the reports they receive, they are also the first line of defense in detecting if a hostile intelligence service is running the agent against us. Simply put: Is he or she a double agent?

Double agents have been used successfully against the Agency over the years. We have come to learn that every Cuban agent we had over a twenty-year period was actually being run against us by the Cuban intelligence services. During the Cold War, the KGB, while feeding us morsels and tidbits of information to keep our interest but giving us nothing of any real substance, was similarly running every East German agent. It's a strategy that worked successfully because no one was confirming the information that was being reported.

CMOs eventually become subject matter experts. If an agent is reporting on the chemical warfare capability of a nation, the CMO will become familiar with the technology involved. The CMO is often charged with doing the necessary background work to ensure the story an agent is telling is true. Because case officers have only a limited amount of time, they tend to be more "jack-of-all-trades" rather than masters of any specialty. For CMOs it improves their ability to sniff out a lie. They become the quality control experts at validating information.

For instance, the CMO may know a particular model of centrifuge can't be used for biological agent manufacturing, or a reported metal alloy has too low a melting temperature for use in missile technology. The advantage of developing such expertise is obvious: The CMO's capability easily extends across geographic boundaries. Case officers are too busy out recruiting new assets, but a brand-new CMO can contact a colleague in a nearby country and ask questions. The result is a CMO well steeped in a particular subject matter. This advantage became apparent to me my second week at the NGO office when my office phone jolted me out of a report I was reading. I picked it up.

"Good afternoon. NGO office. Can I help you?" I ask.

"Hi, Tom. It's Annie. I'm working on something and have a question. You scuba dive, right?"

"Yeah, for longer than I care to remember. Why?"

"I'm looking at some reporting about a couple of guys in Europe. One of them is teaching scuba in a private fitness club at night. He doesn't allow anyone in the building when he's teaching and refuses to use the club during the day. Can you look this report over for me?"

"Sure. But what am I looking for?"

"I don't know. Anything unusual. I don't dive, so I don't know what I'm reading here."

"Sure. I'll take a look at it."

She forwarded the report to me electronically. A foreign national security service arrested a man who claimed to be a scuba instructor at a private gym. When investigators looked into the claim they found that the man did teach there, but only privately and only after hours when the rest of the facility was empty. A raid on his apartment turned up diving equipment along with materials on radical Islam and jihad against America and Israel. It did not, however, turn up a dive instructor's certificate.

There is a very small number of internationally recognized dive certification programs around the world. Two of the most popular in the United States are the National Association of Underwater Instructors (NAUI) and the Professional Association of Dive Instructors (PADI). Both of these groups equip students with the basics of diving instruction, the safety measures that must be taken, and the all-important *c-card*. The c-card, or certification card, is what proves a student is certified in scuba and allowed to rent the familiar cylinders that provide air. No c-card means no service. Annie's guy didn't have a c-card, much less an instructor's license to certify others.

Then there was the odd hour of instruction. Though there's nothing criminal about what he was doing, it was strange. Looking over my shoulder, Kim points out that certain Islamic sects forbid men to be unclothed around strangers or women. Perhaps that was the impetus for the late hour. It seems reasonable to me. Then I read the next section of the report. The men were training with Draeger rebreathers. I call Annie back.

"Hey. What do you know about the people who grabbed these guys? Can we get additional information on this?"

"I guess so. Why?" she asks.

"This equipment they're training on is . . . well, unusual."

"Is it illegal?"

"No, not illegal. It's just not what you normally learn to dive on."

"Why not?"

I hesitate a moment, trying to avoid a technical discussion of underwater physics and physiology.

"How old were you when you learned to drive?" I ask.

"What? I don't know. Fifteen? Sixteen?"

"Who taught you?"

"My father. What does this have to do with scuba gear?"

"Bear with me. Your father taught you. What did he teach you to drive in? What model of car?"

Silence on the other end. I'm not sure if she's irritated or trying to recall.

"It was a Buick LeSabre," she mutters.

"OK. A Buick. Brand-new? Trimmed out with all the extras? Turbocharged? Power everything?"

"Oh God, no. It was a family hand-me-down. It bounced around several people for years."

"So it was not state-of-the-art then?"

"Of course not. Why would you use something like that to teach someone to drive?" she demands.

That is my point. You don't.

"Well, that's what these guys are doing. Draeger is state-of-the-art. The best there is. The rebreathers referenced in the report don't exhaust the used air. They recirculate it so there are no bubbles."

"Why would you not want bubbles?" she asks.

"SEAL teams don't like them because they give away your position and they're noisy when you exhale. Rebreathers can also use a mixture of helium and oxygen to stay underwater for long periods of time and avoid nitrogen narcosis."

"Nitrogen? Helium? What are you talking about?" she demands.

Whoops. A bridge too far. I ended up talking physics anyway.

"Let me put it this way. These guys are learning to drive in a brand-new car. A high-end car with all the extras. A Porsche. A Ferrari."

"Oh. I've got you. Yeah, that's odd," she says.

"What's more, they can't use their new skills anywhere to rent tanks, because they don't have a certification card. They can only dive with this one instructor, and only using his equipment. All the great reefs around the Mediterranean, and they can't dive on them with anyone else."

Silence on the other end of the phone as she mulls it over. I am doing the same. This is starting to bother me. An odd circumstance here or there is human nature. Late hours. New equipment. No formal training program. Individually they mean nothing. Added together, though . . .

I hear paper rustling through the phone.

"Wasn't there something about terrorists learning to scuba dive re-ported a while back? Didn't the FBI warn oil tankers and cruise ships to be on the lookout?" she asks.

I vaguely remember something. I look at the reports again.

No c-card. No paper trail of student names. No surface bubbles or noise. Training only at night. Affiliated with known Islamic radicals.

"Annie, I think you may have something here."

ON AUGUST 18 several hundred thousand subscribers open their Sunday edition of the *Washington Post*. They shuffle through the advertisements; the kids read the comic pages, and the parents read the editorials. Many people also check out the *Parade* magazine insert. The cover story in *Parade* hit me right between the eyes.

The cover features a photograph of CIA paramilitary officer Mike Spann and his wife, Shannon. Under the masthead are the words THE FIRST U.S. CASUALTY. Mike was in the CIA's first wave of officers to land in Afghanistan a month after September 11. He was working from a forward base in Northern Afghanistan when a prison rebellion occurred near Mazar-e-Sharif. Mike was shot and killed Thanksgiving weekend. His body was returned to the United States and buried with full military honors be-fitting his prior Marine Corps service. In late spring he was honored in a separate ceremony with the placement of the seventy-ninth star on the CIA's Memorial Wall of Honor, a wall I had stood in front of only a few weeks earlier.

Mike and Shannon had met in the Clandestine Service Program I am enrolled in. I knew Cathy was not going to be happy when she read the story.

Cathy has had no previous exposure to the military. No close family or friends have served in uniform, so the *Parade* magazine pictures of Mike Spann walking around with an assault rifle and charging Taliban positions on horseback doesn't go over well. She calls and wastes no time getting to her point.

"Have you read the paper?" she asks.

"Yes, I have."

"Did you see the *Parade* piece on the CIA officer that was killed?"

"Yes, Cathy. He died last year, remember? A lot has happened since then. Things are calmer there now." I know. I'm lying like a dog. What else am I to do? She's a thousand miles away.

"I didn't know the CIA has its own army."

"Yes, baby, they do. They have their own navy and air force, too," I tell her. That was a mistake.

"You aren't thinking about working for them, are you?"

The tone of her voice makes it clear that the correct answer is no. Unfortunately, I'm not very mindful in the early hours of a lazy Sunday morning.

"Actually, I was talking to someone in their maritime Special Operations group the other day. He was interested in talking with me when I finished training."

I had invited one of the Special Activities Division's Marine Special Operations people to participate in my group's discussion of suspicious dive equipment. Rebreathers are not something that recreational divers use, so I deferred to the higher authority. He was a nice enough fellow, and we chatted after the meeting. One thing led to another, and soon we were talking about where I might want to work when I finish training. I enjoyed the conversation immensely, but I didn't realize how bad an idea it was until this talk with Cathy.

"You would actually do it?" Cathy inquires. Tone and volume are up. She's pissed off.

"Baby, we are a long way from deciding anything about where I'm going to be working. I've barely even started training, much less finished it."

Too late. She has a full head of steam.

"I can't believe you would go hopscotching around the world for six months or more without telling me about it. Is this how it's going to be? Am I going to be living in Washington, where I know no one, while you are shooting it up with your friends?"

It volleys back and forth for half an hour. I assure her that I have not accepted an assignment with maritime Special Ops. For one thing, nobody has offered me a job. Secondly, I am not prior military, which all of the Special Operations people are. One individual officer made a side remark how *maybe* they might talk to me when I finish training. Way too much has to happen over the next year for that thread to be picked back up. I shouldn't have even told Cathy about it.

By the time we hang up I'm pretty pissed off too. I hadn't planned an argument this morning. We aren't even two months into this mess and we are arguing on the phone about an assignment that doesn't exist.

Not the way to start a week.

ON A WEDNESDAY MORNING we are briefed on the Agency's Special Operations Training Course, or SOTC. This is arguably the most fun anyone can have with his or her clothes on. SOTC has changed over the years but still reflects the Agency's ancestral roots in the World War II–era Office of Strategic Services, or OSS.

During the war, the United States had to ramp up its intelligence capability from virtually nothing. It needed to get qualified officers into forward areas as quickly as possible. Once there, they had to be able to survive without being caught. So officers were given something of a crash course in military operations. The program is every schoolboy's dream.

There's a weapons course. Students are introduced to a wide variety of Western- and NATO-used weapons and are subsequently qualified for concealed carry of a Glock pistol (on official U.S. government business only). We also practice with assault rifles.

The "Crash and Bang Course," as it is known, is a high-speed demolition derby designed to teach us how to avoid or break through a roadblock and avoid a vehicular kidnapping. Students are required to crash, wreck, and otherwise destroy their cars so if faced with a real incident on the street, they can react with proper skill, timing, and experience.

A land navigation course is conducted in various places throughout the country where space and privacy allow. Land navigation is designed to train students how to escape on foot when no other means of leaving a region is available. This is not the preferred method, but in a world where hiding has become ever more difficult, it is useful to have the skills for eluding authorities as opposed to facing capture and imprisonment.

Rounding it out is a marine and helicopter assault course, using high-speed boats for infiltration (getting people into) and exfiltration (getting people out of) of various coastline topographies. We are required to swim, snorkel, and generally tread water for a few hours. Not only will we need to be proficient in escape for our own purposes, we must also assist other personnel in the event of an emergency. Once we finish the helicopter exercises, we will jump out of airplanes.

Jump school is the final part of SOTC. Learning how parachutes work, why they work, and what to do when they don't. Then a series of hands-on exercises, conducting five to eight jumps during the week, depending on weather. Who wouldn't love such an opportunity?

Over the course of the past fifty years, the SOTC program evolved as needed, but it's not an automatic in for everyone. The course runs separately from the basic field training course at the Farm, so we must qualify through an additional physical examination. Not a medical screen, a fitness test: running, push-ups, and sit-ups. We are urged to begin training for this test. An instructor outlines the physical requirements and hands out a multi-page briefing packet that contains all the details.

There are several pages of tables that show how many repetitions of each exercise must be completed in the allotted time. We are required to complete 70 percent of the normal Army requirement in order to attend the SOTC course. The numbers of repetitions are adjusted for gender and age in a series of long tables of numbers. I am pretty accustomed to Excel spreadsheets but can't make heads or tails of these tables. Fortunately another student walks me through it.

As everyone is going through the material, I can't find anyone with the same numbers as mine. I introduce myself to several people I'd not yet met, hoping to find someone in the same boat. I finally find two guys with the same numbers.

One is Tim. He is married, has a couple of kids, and has experience living overseas in Africa. The other is Rick, who left investment banking to enter the Agency. They also noticed that no one else has as small a number set as we do. We gawk at one another, uncertain if the question on each of our minds should be asked aloud. Rick caves first, pulling out his wallet.

"OK. Let's see your licenses," he says.

Tim and I reach for our wallets. My relief in finding people with similar numbers is short-lived when we compare birth dates.

I am the oldest person in the class.

OUR ASSIGNMENTS from General Campbell get more interesting each day. While Elliot looks into the charities' less-than-charitable activity, I read up on Kosovo. U.S. military personnel operate under the scope of Task Force Falcon. Unfortunately, it doesn't include any intelligence officers.

What we need is someone inside the command structure. We need someone to recruit one of the detainees and agree to work for us. We need a case officer on the ground in-country.

"Who do we have in the area?" Elliot asks.

"No one," I answer. "I've contacted every station within five hundred miles. Nobody has a case officer who speaks Arabic and is available. We've got to fly someone in from the outside to talk with them."

"First thing we have to do is get permission," Elliot informs me. "These guys aren't in U.S. hands. Send a request to Camp Bondsteel, and ask them to secure permission to speak with the prisoners. One-on-one, not as a group. We need more background on them to work up a dossier."

"Right. I'll get it out today. Anything else?"

"Yes," Kim says. "You're probably going to have to fly someone in anyway. KFOR is under French control. Anyone we send is going to be burned by the DGSE."

DGSE stands for Direction Générale de la Sécurité Extérieure, or

General Directorate for External Security, France's equivalent of the CIA. It is their military, electronic, and strategic intelligence arm for all external espionage. Cooperation between the two agencies is limited at best. If we send a case officer out, the DGSE will be all over him. We can get the officer an alias, but it won't last long. The French will ensure they record the officer's photograph, along with a fingerprint and DNA sample if they can get it. They are extremely aggressive and quite good.

"Nobody wants to burn a linguist," Elliot says. "That's why we're having trouble finding an Arabic speaker. If the French compromise them, they can't work the majority of counterterrorism targets we're chasing right now. Can't say I blame them. I wouldn't want to be responsible for that either."

He hangs his head, for the first time considering that this may not work out at all. The French will want to be a part of any interrogation, demanding to know what we're after and why. Elliot and I exchange glances.

"Let's see what happens when we ask," he says hopefully.

True to her skills, Kim was right. The KFOR commander, French Lt. General Marcel Valentin, denies our request for access to the prisoners. He is unwilling to consider it without knowing why. He is planning on freeing them.

"Miserable Frenchies," Elliot retorts. "Why didn't we let the Germans keep them?"

HOW INTELLIGENCE IS MOVED through the CIA has gone through considerable upheaval since 9/11. Understanding how this is carried out is an evolving process that continues to change.

It is obviously important to share information across the various agencies, since there will always be a certain amount of overlap in their responsibilities. At the same time, operational intelligence such as case officers' reports triggers analysts to review the information and make inferences from it. Combined with other products (satellite imagery, intercepted communications, HUMINT reporting from other areas of the world), analysts must make sense of what is being reported. They put the information into context so decision makers can act on it. This is easier said than done.

Before a finished intelligence report is published, it must be coordinated through the other agencies that may be affected by it, a process called "chopping off." It means relevant subject-matter experts have reviewed the information and have no objection to its publication. For instance, an analyst writing about currency fluctuations in Argentina will have to get his report chopped off by the Argentina country team, the South American Division office, and the international economics offices of a number of agencies including the CIA, DIA, and NSA. The information then can be published either in various reports to the intelligence community, or to the White House. We are, in essence, investigative reporters for the most expensive newspaper in the world: The President's Daily Brief.

The "PDB," as it is called, is the intelligence community's most sacred product. The secrecy and protection around this document rivals the most secure missile silo. The president receives the leather-bound file every morning, even when he is traveling around the world or on vacation. Supplementing the hard copy is a special DVD player, which can supply additional background information, augmented with high-quality photographs, video, and audio files should the president request them. He doesn't simply read the PDB over his morning coffee, though.

A team of analysts works with the president and any senior staff members he deems worthy to receive identical copies of his brief. Under President Clinton, the PDB was shared across a wide range of administration staff members. With President Bush, only the Cabinet and other select senior officials are allowed copies. Analysts present the brief, answer any immediate questions, and relay taskings for gathering additional information back down the chain of command to case officers, where the process begins all over again.

The president has several briefers who rotate the duty of sitting down with him to review the day's brief. Actions and travel being undertaken by the leaders of other nations are chronicled for the coming week. There is follow-up to questions from a previous PDB article. There are detailed charts, graphs, and tables to supplement the text. Typically numbering fewer than twelve pages, it is an overview of world events, succinctly tailored to each president's preferences.

A retired printer in the PDB publications center gives us the history of this unusual document. In his day, he printed it but was not allowed to read it. This, he said, tended to make correcting errors much more difficult. Now, with electronic publishing systems, it is much easier to proof and print the final document in time for the next morning's briefing. Since its inception in 1964, the PDB has never been delivered late—nearly forty years of uninterrupted service to the highest executive, a special point of pride for the Agency.

The president can be a demanding customer. He wants to know who, what, when, where, and why. But unlike mainstream reporters, we are less interested with the *what* and more concerned with the *why*. Newspapers merely report the news for the edification of their readers. The president reads his daily paper to know how to effect policy on behalf of the United States. Knowing *what* will happen is only useful in the context of *why*. Why does a foreign leader or group want to take a position, change a policy, or attack an enemy? What do they hope to gain? What will they risk? This is what we are paid to learn before the rest of the world knows.

I AM STILL BOTHERED by my argument with Cathy. Though we've spoken several times since, it is a strained effort. Our conversations are clipped and short.

I guess I haven't considered how difficult all of this is for her. Nine weeks into a marriage, and the groom picks up and moves a thousand miles away. She is stuck with unpacking the wedding gifts, sorting through her household effects piled in the garage, and getting our house ready to sell. Then there's the whole relocation issue: finding a new job, making new friends, and acclimating to the Washington DC area. I probably wouldn't be too happy if the situation were reversed.

In any event, I realize I need to make up. This can't be the token flowers or candy to say "I'm sorry." That's only for a standard, garden-variety screwup. This is much bigger. I need to come up with something truly meaningful to bridge the gap of a long-distance physical separation. Not an easy task.

I ask a few people in the class what they recommend. What am I thinking? Single people are absolutely worthless on this kind of thing, and the other married students have their spouses here already. No one else has been separated over such a time and distance, and no one is a newlywed. I am in uncharted territory.

Still trying to come up with something a few days later, I am sitting in my apartment reading news off the Internet. A story leaps off the screen. It is one of the most disturbing and heartwrenching things I've read since the 9/11 attacks, and it will be my olive branch to Cathy.

A tribal court in Pakistan recently ordered the gang rape of an eighteen-year-old girl because her eleven-year-old brother had been seen walking around the village with a girl from another tribe who was of higher class than he. Four men carried out this "punishment to her family" on June 22 in the southern Punjab village of Meerwala while hundreds of tribesmen stood outside laughing and cheering. Where to even begin with such a story?

Rape used as a punishment is despicable on its own. That a tribal court ordered it is unthinkable, especially since another person committed the offending "crime." The story sparks outrage around the world. In the United States there is much hand wringing about how our Pakistani allies are not as advanced as we want to believe. Perhaps they are no better than the cruel, inhuman Taliban in nearby Afghanistan.

I instantly know this is the means I will use to make up with Cathy. The argument was stupid and unnecessary. It was also mainly my fault, not hers. I should have realized how upset she'd be about long-term absences as a rule rather than the exception. Our prolonged separation simply aggravated a contentious issue. I e-mail her the story along with the following note:

Years from now, when we are old and gray, someone will ask you how I ever talked you into moving out of Florida and relocating to the cold and crowded area around Washington DC. Please keep this news clipping to show them. These, our partners in the war on terrorism, have gang raped a girl simply because she had the misfortune of being someone's sister. Their righteous indignation over an errant US bomb injuring civilians rings a bit hollow when they are raping their own children in the name of Islam. It's no wonder they are so easily manipulated into becoming suicide bombers. If your own children mean nothing to you, someone else's children mean even less. It is my hope, my goal, to make sure men like this never reach our shores.

She calls a couple of hours later.

The story has her in tears. But it is the reason I am here. The reason all of us are here. Anything worth having is worth protecting. It's also part of what makes us Americans. We don't tolerate crimes like this. We protect our own. We hunt down those who do our family harm. Exactly what *kind* of family is irrelevant. Family linked by blood is obvious. But there are other types of families too. Family linked by uniform, or team, or payroll.

Or family linked by murder on a commercial jet.

WITH SO MANY of us working in the Counter Terrorism Center, it seems logical to learn more about extremists. This turns out to be more difficult than we thought. Our overture to Dottie requesting additional training (not something she has ever been asked for before) results in a stunning response. We can't receive such a lecture from the Agency. Singling out Islam is discriminatory!

I am floored by her knee-jerk reaction. Who the hell does she think flew the planes into the Trade Center? Catholic nuns? Buddhist monks? We cannot believe the U.S. government is so politically correct that it could not provide training on our current, and some would argue most lethal, enemy because somebody might think it was discriminatory.

Instead, several dozen students attend a lecture by Dr. Gerald Post, a former Agency political psychologist, now a George Washington University Middle East scholar. We learn that Islamic extremists don't exclusively kill

Jews and Christians. Extremists have no concerns over killing other Muslims when they believe it necessary to further the cause. He outlines other extremists, overseas and domestic, and what they mean to our national security.

The profile of extremist behavior is outlined in graphic detail. What strikes me as most interesting is a comparison between the bombers in Israel and the terrorists who attacked on 9/11. In Israel, bombers tend to be young, uneducated, and unemployed. Once a part of the terrorist group they are emotionally unable to leave it.

With the 9/11 hijackers there was a completely different profile. These men were older, middle-class, three of them with master's degrees. They had been in the West, out of direct control, for up to seven years. Their individual identities were subordinate to the group at large. It is a fascinating briefing, one that has direct impact on the work we are doing right now.

As we wrap up our thirty-day assignments, I am forced to concentrate more on my evaluation and hand off projects that, only a few days prior, made me feel like a real intelligence officer. It is difficult to let go, especially when the two main projects are handled in such different ways.

Annie's scuba aficionados generated some concern and are being pursued by an impromptu group of officers from across the Agency. Representatives from CTC (terrorism), European Division (responsible for Kosovo), and SAD/Marine Branch (diving experts) are meeting regularly to chase down what could be a change in terrorism tactics away from civilian aircraft to the less-secure maritime targets.

The scuba divers, who pose no immediate threat to U.S. national security, are attended to by an ongoing cadre of officers. There is no team infighting. There are no formal lines of communication or chains of command. They meet regularly but informally. Yet they are on top of these men and everything they do.

In contrast is the situation with the detainees at Camp Bondsteel in Kosovo. Five men are caught videotaping a U.S. military compound. We know Islamic radicals threaten U.S. lives and interests in the region. Yet there is little interest or support in learning more about who they are and what they are doing. The dissimilarity between the two issues can't be starker. The decision to not pursue the detainees is a shortsighted one and, according to several longtime CTC officers, eerily similar to the pre–September 11 pursuit (or lack thereof) of Osama Bin Laden.

I hope we don't regret it later.

As I finish my last day in the NGO office, we learn that Lt. General Valentin has released two of the captive videographers. We are unable to get a case officer to them in time. Every time we make progress in one area, another problem emerges.

We need an Arabic linguist. We need someone willing to take the project on. We need a neutral country (away from the French) to work in. We have to arrange for a security detail to escort the case officer. After a week of assembling the proper team, thinking we have it all accomplished, the entire process falls apart again. In the end, bureaucracy does us in.

Our case officer is moved to another place, his time and language skills needed elsewhere. Kosovo is not considered a top-level priority. Plus there is the little matter of history. KFOR is under the command of French military officers. Given France's long history in Algeria, they have little interest in holding Algerian citizens unless there's a compelling reason. Lt. General Valentin prefers to cut them loose and get back to running his base.

Once again I follow Elliot to General Campbell's office. It's our fourth trip up in a week. If this keeps up he can claim us as tax deductions.

"Good morning, General," Elliot calls after the lieutenant waves us through.

"I don't have good news," General Campbell answers. "KFOR refuses to allow access. No way at all. Unless they are running the interrogation—which they will only do after knowing what we are after—we cannot even access their part of the base."

He tried commanding subordinates, cajoling old comrades, and even appealing to the United Nations. Nothing worked. There is no way to see these men while they are in NATO hands. Lt. General Valentin has us over a barrel.

"The question for you now is, can you grab them on the street?" he asks.

"A rendition? We hadn't planned that. We want to run them, not imprison them," Elliot replies.

"Well, find other options. I've done what I can. The rest is up to you." The general returns to a stack of papers on his desk.

"Until they're released, there's nothing to be done," his aide tells us on the way out. "The general pulled every string we had. This is the way things are at this level. We can't bang the drum too hard against the French. We might need them later for something more important."

My frown fits my attitude.

"What's the old joke?" the aide asks. "I'd rather have a German platoon in front of me than a French one behind me?"

"Yeah, I've heard that," Elliot said. "But I still thought of them as our allies."

"It's important to keep them in the proper context," the aide replies.

"What's that?" I ask.

"France is an ally. It doesn't mean she's a friend."

There's no resolution to the problem. But the time for my involvement is over. Elliot and Kim will have to run with this on their own. For Class 11 our quick look into the Directorate of Operations' everyday routine at headquarters is concluded. But one instructor cautions us to not become too keen on these surroundings. He eloquently states, "When it comes to headquarters, you want a taste, not a meal." We are field officers, not headquarters-based cubicle dwellers. We're supposed to get our hands dirty, hence the training program at the Farm. But before that can happen we have to master the tools that are used to develop and nurture spies.

That bit of cultivation occurs in a hidden little garden a short distance away.

Training Daze
September 2002

MY BIRTHDAY FALLS ON LABOR DAY most years, which means I get a long holiday weekend to celebrate. Cathy decides this is the perfect time for a trip to Washington. The weather is spectacular. Fall colors hit the area like a kaleidoscope, the entire region awash in hues of red, orange, and yellow. It's beautiful. Coming from a single-season state, she is blown away.

We go out for dinner and take a stroll through Old Town Alexandria before returning to the apartment. Slinging her suitcase onto the bed, she goes into a frenzy of digging out her clothes. I am thinking lingerie, or some leftover item from our honeymoon. I am thinking wrong.

I am a longtime fan of the Tommy Bahama brand of clothes. Shorts, golf shirts, deck shoes—I like everything they make. Living in Florida it's such a perfect conceptual fit that I can't help being drawn to them. Tropical clothes for a beach lifestyle. I fell for the whole marketing strategy.

Cathy bought me a Tommy Bahama camp shirt, but not one I even knew existed. It is a limited-edition design created in response to the 9/11 attacks. A short-sleeved silk shirt, wooden buttons down the front, and a pocket on the left side. On the back, a flagpole skewers the olive in a martini glass, with Old Glory flapping in an imagined tropic breeze. The caption underneath reads SHAKEN, BUT UNDETERRED.

She heard about it from a friend and thought what better gift for me than a James Bond reference that memorializes September 11? I hold it aloft like a newborn baby. I don't want to drop it, hurt it, or breathe on it wrong. I am stunned, which gives her a delighted case of the giggles. Turning the shirt around again, I take another look at the back: The James Bond–inspired martini. The flag. I'm speechless.

WHEN THE HOLIDAY WEEKEND ENDS, we move from our interim assignments to a special facility across town. In the Directorate of Intelligence (DI), analysts are schooled in the diagnostic arts at the Sherman Kent School of Analysis. The Directorate of Operations (DO) has a similar training facility in Washington. Similar, but still different.

On Tuesday morning, Dottie provides us with directions to the school with the caveat that it is an undercover facility. It's in a typical suburban Washington office complex with a host of real companies around it. Nobody in the building or in the complex knows it's a CIA facility. They especially don't know it's a training facility for spies. That is how it must remain. We have to take every precaution to protect the site's secret. Cover for the site comes first—for ourselves, second. To dismantle the facility and move it elsewhere would cost millions of dollars. A great deal of planning and effort went into designing a site that could blend into its surroundings. The training conducted here is limited to things that can be done reasonably in a business atmosphere. Anything "cheeky" or unusual has to wait until we go to the Farm.

One by one we arrive at the appointed office complex and park in the garage. Taking the elevator up to the appropriate floor we step into the corridor. An unmarked door is open, revealing a receptionist and desk, but little else. The receptionist raises an eyebrow at us. "Can I help you?"

We identify ourselves with our driver's licenses. She has a long list of names in alphabetical order. Once she confirms our identities, she waves us individually through a second door, a buzzing sound indicating she is unlocking it for each and every student one at a time.

"Someone will meet you inside and show you the main meeting room."

Once inside, we make small talk with one another as the class size swells to the room's capacity and beyond. I doubt the fire marshall gets in here very often.

At two o'clock a man about my age walks up to the front of the room and introduces himself as Steve. Steve is the course chairman for our training in the Washington area. We will be spending the next ninety days in his special facility, so he wants to go over the entire story of what's here, what we are doing, and how we are going to do it.

"This is a covert facility. Can anyone define that?"

Several people try, but no one gives him the answer he wants.

"There is a difference between clandestine and covert. This is lesson one. This site is covert. It appears to be one thing when in actuality it is another. We are not hiding the fact we are here; we are only hiding what we are here for. We are in the Clandestine Service. Clandestine means hiding our existence completely. We do not want to be seen or heard in any operational context. We do not disguise our operational activities; we completely hide them from view. Everything you do from this building will be covert; it will appear to be something else. There will always be some plausible explanation that does not give our neighbors any reason to think we are anything more than what we claim to be. Got it?"

Everyone nods.

"Good. This is a training facility. It is not open to the public. If anyone asks you about renting it out, please direct him or her to my secretary. She will quote them a price so outrageous, it will make the national debt pale in comparison. She will explain to the inquiring party that we mainly do government leadership training. If one point doesn't scare them off the other usually does."

Laughter ripples through the crowd.

"You will be assigned into two groups due to the size of the class, designated East and West. There is no difference between them; it's just a method for managing the instructor scheduling. You will be assigned offices and officemates today. In each office there will be a packet with your name on it and an inventory of equipment that should already be in the office. If something is missing, please let one of us know."

Steve hands out the office assignment lists.

"While you are looking these over and finding out who your officemate is, let me tell you about this facility. There is a snack area with vending machines down the main hallway. There is an office-supply storage closet with anything you might need. Please help yourself. There are two main classrooms, two computer laboratories, and several break-out meeting rooms. You are free to use these rooms unless an instructor needs them. Otherwise, this floor is all yours except for the instructors' team room. You can't miss it. There's a large picture of a lion on the door."

We file out of the room and make our way down the hallways. It is not a large complex, and we are constantly bumping into one another while moving from room to room. True to Steve's word, I turn a corner to find a door with a huge lion's head taped to it. Signs on either side of the door indicate that students are to keep out. A placard above the door reads LION'S DEN. Cute. Walking back down the hallway and turning down a different corridor I find my assigned office and step inside.

It is a big corner unit with large windows on two walls and desks in opposite corners of the room, facing away from each other. There is a credenza between the desks and two file-storage cabinets. Two cork bulletin boards grace the walls above the desks. Unlike many of the other offices, the corner orientation gives it an enormous amount of floor space. This is a good thing, considering who my officemate is.

Daryll played football for several years in the NFL. Everyone knows him. Even if they didn't know his name, they know who he is. He's about six feet seven inches tall and tops 275 pounds. Fortunately, his personality is every bit as oversize as his body. His smile is large, and he laughs loud and frequently. You expect a jock to be jocular, but he has some brains in his head too.

Daryll spins around in the chair.

"What's up, slacker?" is out of his mouth as soon as his feet crash into the credenza. Our professional athlete is a klutz.

He left a lucrative corporate position to enter the Agency. He was single and enjoying the Agency's well-earned reputation for being the world's most expensive dating service. His former job had him traveling so much that he rarely had time to meet anyone and even less time to date. Perhaps things would change now. We spent the afternoon getting the office set up.

The following morning we are introduced to a special cadre of instructors. Just the way many of us volunteered for duty after September 11, so did a large number of the Agency's retirees. These men and women won the Cold War, intending to spend their golden years basking in the memories of a job well done. Instead, they reacted to the attacks on America with the same sense of loyalty and duty they had previously shown. They were under contract for one purpose: to show us the ground truth of espionage. While the staff would teach us theory in the classrooms, these independent contractors work as role-players, putting what we learned to the test.

The exercises are to be conducted inside our secret facility and on the streets of Washington DC. We will practice hotel and restaurant meetings right out in the open, having innocuous conversations alongside congressional aides, lobbyists, and every variety of private-sector vendor who prowls the swirling maelstrom of the capital city. Hiding out in plain sight, our activities in public must not raise the interest of any casual observer, our conversation designed to minimize what we reveal about ourselves.

We not only have to conduct the meetings themselves, we also have to perform the work behind the scenes. Meeting sites will be cased well in advance. We have to know the location of security cameras, guards, operating hours, traffic flow, and areas to avoid because of too much activity. After each exercise, the instructors will write a critique of our performance, identify weak areas, and offer hints for improvement. Course completion is not automatic. We have to earn our way through each section before continuing.

WE SPEND A WEDNESDAY working on fake and alias credentials to use while undercover. We need *alias* documents for use in the field training course down at the Farm. We need *fake* documents for training purposes here in Washington. Confused? So are we. It takes a couple of explanations to iron it all out.

The alias documents are real U.S. government–issued identifications (for official use only), when we are undercover. We will test-drive these alias materials in the real world only after endless hours of practice with fake documents. It's like teaching a child how to handle money by using Monopoly currency. You wouldn't give them real greenbacks to make mistakes with. You use fake money and keep it "inside the house," so to speak. That's what our fake documents are for.

The fakes are for our onsite business parties, border crossings, and to practice in the challenge of light scrutiny. Each student is given a new name and is responsible for developing a cover he or she can remember and defend.

My cover name is Jim Essentson. For no particular reason, I decide my last name is of Scottish origin. Essentson. Sounds Scottish to me. I am a Scot. I work up a family history going back two generations and chart it out in a family tree that I commit to memory.

We cannot put anything real into our fake family histories. An analyst from one of the Agency's technology offices comes in and does a demonstration to make it clear how easy it is for anyone with a computer and Internet access to break a cover built on a real family.

The staff keeps a previous student's cover story on hand as an example and, with just a few keystrokes, the analyst pulls it apart. The student had intermingled his real parents' and siblings' names and birth dates, thinking this was an easy mix to remember. From Dad down to little brother, he moved everyone's middle name over one position, then did the same with their birthdays. Dad's name was now split between him and Mom. His birthday was now hers. Mom's was the brother's birthday, whose middle name was now the sister's name, and so on.

It takes less than ninety seconds for the analyst to figure out that the student was lying and provide the interrogator with enough background to tear the story apart. At one time, only the United States had access to such technological prowess. With the Internet any banana republic can do it from virtually anywhere on the globe.

I decide to base my alias family on old friends from college. Freud would probably have me in therapy for the rest of my life, but using old fraternity buddies was the easiest way to remember my artificial life. They and the women they married became parents, grandparents, brothers, and sisters. We spend two days working up passports, company letterhead, financial documents, marketing strategies, business cards, and the usual assortment of corporate propaganda an employee is likely to have on his or her person while traveling on business. The staff collects this material and grills us on the details. Do area codes match office addresses? Does the etymology of our names match our stories? Do I know anything about the city I allegedly grew up in?

Where students trip up the most is questions that are impossible to check out and therefore not well developed. It starts off innocently, but we quickly learn that we are not prepared with adequate peripheral materials.

"How big is your firm? How many employees? What are annual sales? What is your profit margin?"

These are pretty straightforward. But then it gets personal.

"What is your boss's name? What is his phone number? What is his supervisor's name? What color is your office? Who is your closest colleague at the office? What is his or her phone number? Where do you go to lunch? Can you give me the driving directions? What is the name of the shopping complex or plaza the restaurant is located in? If you can't name the plaza, what are the two streets that intersect there?"

This is nothing. It's just misdirection, the setup for the rough questions.

"Do you have a secretary? What is her name? Have you slept with her?

Who have you slept with at the office? Would you be fired if your boss knew you had slept with your secretary? Have you slept with your boss's secretary? Have you slept with your boss? Aren't you a little young to have such a position? How did you get it if you didn't sleep with the boss?"

This forces students to step outside the carefully crafted story, which is where everything falls apart. A typical exchange looks like this:

Interrogator: You didn't sleep with your boss to get your job?

Student: No, of course not. I got it based on my talent.

Interrogator: What is your talent?

Student: I am in marketing. I increase sales.

Interrogator: How good are you?

Student: I increased sales by thirty percent last quarter.

Interrogator: Thirty percent? Wow! That's great. What were your previous quarter sales?

[*Long pause.*]

Student: What?

Interrogator: What were your sales the previous quarter? You said a moment ago your firm did $118 million in sales over the last year, that you were responsible for twenty percent of sales, and you increased sales by thirty percent last quarter. What were your previous quarter sales?

Imagine a two-legged deer staring into headlights.

Real corporate managers know those numbers better than their children's names. It's how they keep those high-dollar expense accounts. But most students just break out in a big smile and stall for time. They couldn't do that math with a pad of paper, a calculator, and complete silence in college. They sure as hell can't do it in their heads while being stared down by two interrogators and a camcorder. They've just been nailed. Welcome to indefinite detention or worse, depending on which country they're arrested in.

Cover is hard. Cover is expensive. Cover is something that must be maintained, massaged, and managed by a full-time office in headquarters to make it believable and defendable. Making up some clever name or quirky company was easier before the technology revolution, but those days are over. Now it has to be as real as possible. Otherwise, it's just too easy to pick apart. That's why our alias identities are, in every respect, completely real.

AN AGENCY PSYCHOLOGIST comes in to help us prepare for surveillance work by improving our visual acuity. From the podium she shows us different types of cars. We don't understand until she makes a point of saying that in other countries we will see cars that aren't common on the streets of the United States.

There are makes, models, and even entire brands of automobiles that are not sold in this country. Either they are unsafe and cannot meet our standards, or they simply don't make economic sense in a country where there are already more car choices than people can effectively choose from. So, how do we identify surveillance? We won't know many of these models or the years they were produced. We must identify them some other way. The only worldwide commonality for distinction is the license plate.

We begin an exercise to test our short-term memory. Without using pen and paper, can we spot license plates that are flashed on the overhead screen more than once? The instructor starts up a presentation showing the backsides of vehicles, most of which are completely unfamiliar to us, and only shows each of them for one second.

MEW1975
071365-CEM
RHW-38394
CB-22914
Ql-32143
1967-RCW
OE-93196
RHW-38394

It goes on for ten minutes. There are three repeated plates. Because one is shown once at night and once in daylight, it is often overlooked. The same is true with another plate seen on an older Mercedes two-door, then again on a Citroën sedan. We must be able to look past the extraneous details and only recall the license-plate information. We practice this drill three more times before taking a break. Then we do it some more with one minor change: The license plates are backwards.

This is how license plates appear in a rearview mirror. Backwards. Now we must not only read the plates, we must also transpose them without repositioning the numbers or letters. It is an unimaginably frustrating exercise. Even when we can use pen and paper, the mistakes pile up.

RHW-38394 becomes WHR-38394 or RHW-49383. It's impossible to transpose the letters in our heads in the time given. The plates flash across the screen for a moment, approximating the time we have to see the plate, memorize the numbers, jot them down (if we are able), and continue driving normally without signaling our real activity.

She provides photos taken by surveillance teams of prior classes working this exercise. There are students turned all the way around in the driver's seat in traffic. Students pull down the vanity mirror on the passenger's side as a "second-chance glance." Students crane their necks out the windows to see through outside mirrors. Others try to feign hand gestures at cars as an excuse to stare outside. None of these work. When the surveillance teams see this, it's an automatic ding on the student's record. Those are the lucky ones.

Her next series of photos are of cars wrecked during this training. Mainly fender benders, with the rear-end collision being the most common. Students are looking into the rearview mirror as the car behind them makes its final approach, not considering they are closing in on the car in front of them at an equal rate. They drift into the backs of minivans, executive sedans, taxis, and even tractor trailers. It is an equal-opportunity incident. What we have to do, she insists, is simply pay attention.

As we file out of the classroom Daryll notices a small crowd in the next room. A guy on the wide-screen television is talking about climbing over a prison wall. It catches our attention.

If they don't want us to see the video, they should watch it in the Lion's Den. That's their area. The office supply/mail/conference room is for students. It just happens to be the room with a large-screen television and a DVD player. Several contractors are watching a video briefing of what happened to Mike Spann.

A debriefing is de facto when an intelligence officer is captured, kidnapped, or killed in the line of duty: What happened, why did it happen, and how can we prevent it from happening again in the future? It's very similar to the debriefing done by military personnel after a raid.

When the prison in Afghanistan was overrun, Mike was shot. The other CIA officer escaped over a wall. But he had seen Mike get hit. He knew Mike was down. While the rest of the world was digesting that someone was missing, this officer was reporting through the Agency's chain of command that Mike had been killed. This video was something beyond the basic debrief. I'll call this officer Stuart (I don't know his real name). An instructor tells us that Stuart felt it was important to offer an explanation to a larger audience. The video was made to describe what happened and why he escaped when Mike didn't.

Blinking into the camera, Stuart stands next to a whiteboard diagram of the prison facility. It shows where the various players were when the uprising began and how the principal people involved (Mike, Stuart, and a detainee) were oriented when the shooting started. The poor guy is trying to give a dispassionate briefing, but the anguish on his face is unmistakable.

With the diagram of the prison facility mounted to the wall behind him, he indicates key areas. Here is where Mike fell. Here is where he (Stuart) went over the wall. Here is where the released prisoners came running in. The video cuts back and forth to other footage taken during the military response to the uprising and the first U.S. personnel to return in the aftermath. The pictures aren't pretty.

This poor guy has probably relived this incident a hundred times in briefings and another thousand in his nightmares. Mike Spann was his friend, not just a colleague. We had heard scuttlebutt that some officers faulted Stuart for not staying with Mike. But the finding from the follow-up investigation concluded that doing so would have only resulted in two dead officers and no way for the world to know what had happened inside the prison.

One of the retiree contractors shakes his head at the screen before noticing a few of us standing in the doorway. He points a gnarled finger our way.

"Did you learn anything from that?" he asks.

Not having a good answer, we keep quiet.

"It's all fun and games until your buddy gets killed," he continues. "Funny, he doesn't mention all the guys that were there to protect him. Did he?"

Again, we trade glances but don't speak.

"A special Army security detail was there for no other purpose than to protect those guys while they were inside the prison. What do they do? They go off and interrogate a prisoner without their security detail."

He slaps aside a chair and sits down in disgust. He's genuinely angry.

"Now the man's dead and his family is alone. How's it feel now? You don't take unnecessary risks. You don't work alone. This is not Hollywood; it's the real deal. There was a goddamn security detail *right there* for no other reason than to protect those two during interrogations, and instead they slip away to work alone. That's what being a maverick will get you. Killed! 'We don't need the military, we don't need a security detail, we can do it ourselves. Just leave us alone.' I'll bet old Stuart there didn't enjoy being alone when he went over the wall."

The retiree looks back at the screen to see someone is replaying a segment of rocket fire hitting the prison.

"That must have been one helluva dark moment. His friend is dead. His position is overrun. He knows there are a dozen heavily armed men nearby to deal with the problem. Had they followed proper procedure, he would have been quickly and safely moved out, or the uprising would have stopped as soon as it started. But, oh, no. We couldn't do that. The CIA admit we need help? Never."

He looks back at the screen again.

Another instructor suggests we get back to whatever we are doing. Daryll and I start back down the hallway in silence, but the old man wasn't finished yet. Still talking to the television, his final indictment haunts the hallway behind us.

"You stupid shit egomaniac! You should have been the one to break it to Mike Spann's family!"

OUR FIRST DIPLOMATIC PARTY. This is starting off on an easy note. Minimal dress up, located onsite in the oversize conference room, and only basic finger foods. This could be any type of social gathering, the object of which is to find a specific person. The instructors call it culling from the crowd.

We are to cull out our target individual and move him off on our own in order to have as lengthy a conversation as possible. This is an ungraded exercise, but that just means the grade isn't written down anywhere. In actuality, every exercise is graded—every interaction with staff and instructors is evaluated and reviewed. It's just part of the program.

We enter the party on a timed schedule based on our office number. Daryll and I walk in together and immediately split up. We both learn which contractors are playing our targets and make a beeline for those people as soon as the exercise begins.

I am chatting with a Swedish economic officer. We engage in a bit of small talk before ramping up to more serious topics about politics, economics, the war on terrorism, and how much he misses home.

I have several Swedish friends and know the geography of the country reasonably well. Apparently, this contractor doesn't, so I change the subject to something else. The back-and-forth exchange of probing goes on for about an hour. I learn he is divorced, has no kids, and is German, not Swedish. How a German national is a Swedish diplomat I'm not sure, but I note the fact for my report. He likes sailing and chess. He is an avid model-airplane builder, but finds the hobby too expensive to enjoy here. I make another mental note to include that in my report too.

This is the learning point for the exercise. Whatever the target likes, we have to like. Our aim is to build a connection with this complete stranger in a short period of time, but only in a social context. We don't know that we want or need him as a spy, but we want the option of recruiting him if need be.

We have to share their passion for whatever interest they have, be it fine wine, creative writing, or fifteenth-century Peruvian goat roping—regardless of how unlikely it is that we have the same interest. What are the odds? Small world, huh? In this case, it's model airplanes. From everything I can tell, the meeting went fine. I go back to the office, write up my report, and submit it around 11:00 p.m. The instructors will come in tomorrow morning while we are in class and evaluate our performance after lunch.

Daryll's laugh can be heard for miles. It shakes the walls and rattles the floor of the hallway. You stop for a moment and question if someone has just told God a really good knock-knock joke; the laughter spills out of the hereafter and ricochets across the earth. Whatever he found funny must have been a doozy.

When I walk into the office that morning, he moves from laughter to hysterics. His eyes are shut, he's pointing, and his knees are up to his chest. That can only mean one thing: He's laughing at my expense.

Milton is sitting in my office chair. He is our assigned mentor, a retired Agency officer now working as a contract role-player and mentor. The contractors role-play against one half of the class and mentor the other half. That way they never have to role-play against their own students or any of our immediate officemates, a weird sort of separation of church and state. Milton is in midsentence when I walk in.

"Ah, there he is," Milton says. Daryll is still laughing.

"Hello, Milton. Why do I suspect we will be having a chat?"

"A chat we will have, Tom. Here, sit down. Tell me about dumpy dwarfs."

Daryll doubles over, bordering on hyperventilation. Milton suggests he should speak to me privately. Daryll closes the door behind him, and we listen to the laughter drop off down the hallway.

I turn back to Milton. "Somehow I don't think I will find this nearly as amusing as he did."

"No, probably not, and I probably shouldn't have said anything, but it's just such a bizarre episode that I had to ask him if he overheard any of it," Milton replies.

"Episode? What episode? Are you referring to last night? I thought it went quite well," I said.

"Really? How so?" Milton asks. There is a healthy measure of sarcasm in his voice that I don't appreciate.

"We chatted, found some common ground, and I wrote it all up in the report. What's the problem?"

"There were a couple of problems, Tom. Let's start with the second one first. On the physical description here, you called him a 'dumpy dwarf.' "

My eyebrows leap. "I said no such thing!"

He holds up my report. There is so much red ink along the margins, it appears to have bled to death.

"You wrote 'subject is about five feet two inches tall and weighs around two hundred and fifty pounds.' "

I nod. "Yes, that's what I wrote."

"Well, Tom, that's calling him a dumpy dwarf. He's at least five-seven, and closer to two-twenty."

"For Christ's sake! I gave a general description of his appearance. Height, weight, hair and eye colors, general body style, just as we were told to do. I've never estimated a man's height and weight before. He was shorter than me and heavier than me. I'm not working some circus act where I guess his weight for a prize."

Milton looks over his glasses at me. I've always been annoyed by that, and I was already irritated with this conversation to begin with.

"No, but you were certainly a clown last night. What the hell are you doing making up some bullshit about being a marine biologist?"

"Excuse me?" I ask.

"The whole marine science nonsense. You were a fisheries biologist? Who would believe that?"

"What do you mean 'Who would believe that?'" I say.

"That's such a lame attempt at making small talk. I can't believe you came up with something so idiotic."

"Idiotic?"

"Yes. Suppose he had a science background? You would have fumbled around like a retarded Jacques Cousteau. What the hell were you thinking?" he asks.

I'd built a full head of steam now.

"Well, Milton, I was thinking that your instructor pal should stick to his assigned role of being a Swedish diplomat, per the exercise outline." I hand him back the report. "Furthermore, I would expect him to be a little less insulting and a little more focused on the task at hand. For your information, I *was* a fisheries biologist, and anytime that asshole wants to discuss the economics of commercial fishing, I'd be happy to accommodate him."

Milton gets out of his chair.

"You were not a biologist," he said.

I move closer to him but remain seated. Standing up could be misconstrued as a physical threat, though I'm not far from it.

"What would you like to see? Press clippings? Pictures from the field? How about my tax returns? Which appetizer would be best for the crow I'm going to serve you?"

He shakes his head. "Tom, we have your bio. You were a consultant before you came into the Agency."

"Milton, I'm thirty-seven years old! My marine science job isn't on my bio because it was my first job out of college fifteen years ago."

It takes a moment, but reality filters down through the first layers of crap he calls brains.

"What?" is all he managed.

"My bachelor's degree is in biology. My first job was as a contract fisheries biologist for a federal agency. I worked in the water-quality section. My area of interest was closed-circuit aquaculture for finfish and shrimp. Unfortunately, your Third Reich diplomat's knowledge of marine science is limited to ordering at Red Lobster."

Milton stands there dumbfounded. "We discussed this at some length this morning. Everyone was sure you were just a consultant."

My ears perk. "Everyone? So basically he has told other instructors I am a bold-faced liar. Is that correct?" I ask.

He nods.

"He was pretty certain you made it all up. The economics of farming shrimp, the declining catch in commercial shrimping, and that whole issue. He made up the German ancestry to throw you off topic, give you a chance to start over without having to make anything up."

"Well, if you would be so kind as to take that report back and have him un-ink it, I would be most grateful," I retort.

Milton stares at me for a moment before speaking, assessing me. Once a case officer, always a case officer. "You aren't going to forgive and forget this, are you?" he asks.

I turn in my chair and flip on my computer before answering. "No more than that dumpy dwarf will."

THE NEXT DAY, Milton says he spoke with the role-player and told him I had the background I claimed. Just to ensure that there was no backside ambiguity on the issue, I put pictures and press clippings from that job on the bulletin board over my desk. They aren't as impressive as Daryll's NFL team and player photos, but I know the right people will stop by for a look when I'm not around.

Daryll takes me out for a few beers on Saturday, but I am still pretty annoyed by the entire episode. I am outlining my conversation with Milton when, like a lot of people are prone to do, I think of something I wished I had said during the argument: I'm a real-life Doc Ford.

Ford is the central character in a series of mystery novels by Florida writer Randy Wayne White. White is a professional fishing guide who has a very successful sideline as a mystery writer. Or perhaps it's the other way around. In any event, his central characters are Dr. Marion Ford—an ex-CIA officer—and Tomlinson, a long-haired spiritual-guru hippie. Ford is a marine biologist. In the popular series of books, Ford left the Agency to return to his beloved aquatic pursuits. Though he now runs a marine research company in Florida, his espionage expertise always seems to come into play through fate, circumstance, or the foolishness of others.

I have enjoyed White's books for several years. Cathy found the similarity between his fiction and my reality amusing. But if I am playing Doc Ford in this out-of-the-ordinary world, then Daryll is the largest, most conservative, clean-cut Tomlinson that Randy Wayne White could ever imagine.

As Daryll and I drink our way through my recollection, several other students join us. We hear about other problems during the exercise. Mistaken identity. Role-players forgetting their names. Foul language used on a female student. It creates an air of tension as we kick off the new week.

The staff is getting along great with students, but many of the independent contractors have erred badly. Something must be done to clear the air. Since the contract staff only conducts role-playing exercises with students in the opposing half of the program, we are still getting along well with the contractors who are mentoring us. Someone makes the decision to solidify this close tie and ensure that it doesn't get unraveled as it had with the role-players. If students can bond over beers on Friday night, students and their mentors should be able to bond over beers on a Wednesday night.

Ahmed, Hal, and Sean go on a beer run midafternoon. With this many students, staff, and mentors, they are buying a lot of beer. Putting the multitude of twelve-packs away is no easy feat. They end up using plastic mail totes for coolers and icing down the beer for the remainder of the afternoon.

Steve had said he is leaving promptly at five and anything that occurs after that time happens without his knowledge.

At five fifteen the mail-coolers appear in the break room. On the East side, about a dozen students crowd around a cluster of tables and prop our feet up. Eight mentors come in and pop a cold one. After a few ounces of seminervous small talk Sean asks Harold, a legendary Agency officer, to tell us his best spy story.

Harold had shut down his lucrative consulting practice to return to the Agency as an independent contractor. He was one of the Cold War's best operatives, with nearly fifty years on the front lines of America's espionage program. He doesn't have a best story. He has dozens of progressively better ones as the night goes on (all still classified, I regret). Having set the example, other mentors join in. Some are good spy stories. Others are good escape stories. Still others are just funny stories. Disguises screwed up. Adversaries screwed over. Chiefs screwing around. The longer we talk, the looser we get and the closer we become.

Harold, the master spy, makes the most significant remark of the evening. "What you guys have to understand is that espionage is salesmanship. It's the ultimate sales job. Forget about guys who sell yachts or Gulfstream jets. You want to really sell? Get into the spy business," he says.

That creates a stir with some of the former salesmen in the room.

Harold holds up a hand. "Now, now, now—it's not that selling those high-end toys isn't important. They don't sell themselves. But keep in mind what you are here to study. If you learned nothing else on September 11, at least know this: Satellites, telephone intercepts, and hidden microphones are all well and good, but they're no substitute for knowing what someone is thinking, what they are planning in their heads. All the billions we've spent on advanced technology, and nobody knew about September 11. Salesmanship, my little spies. That's what intelligence work is."

Ahmed holds up a hand. "So what is the product? What are we selling?" he asks.

Harold's eyes close.

"You have to sell someone, often someone of considerable authority, that betraying their country is an intelligent thing to do."

Every mentor nods, but remains silent. Each is staring into the open mouth of his beer bottle. Harold continues.

"Intelligence is the ultimate people business. You have to convince someone that the only way to reach their goals is to sell out their country to you. You have to convince them that you can run them as an agent even though many of them face execution if caught. They have to believe you are, hands down, the smartest American son of a bitch that ever walked in the door. You have to convince them this Agency is the only way for them to escape whatever circumstance they are in. Believe me, guys, it's not an easy sell."

Another mentor pipes up. "And it will get a lot harder by the time you folks are out there."

"That's right," Harold agrees. "It's all about relationships. Being a case officer is about *managing* relationships. What begins as a relationship between the recruiting case officer and his agent must be turned over into a relationship between the agent and the U.S. government. That then becomes a relationship between the information and the president. But the whole process begins with selling that person, making him or her believe that working with an intelligence officer is in their best interests. For many of them it may be the only real opportunity they ever have. Selling communists was easy compared to the radical fundamentalists you guys are going to be chasing. You have to make them *believe*."

And with that, his sermon is over. We had listened to their stories for five hours. The beer had run out long before, but nobody went home. What had started as a measure to fix ruffled feathers and hurt feelings morphed into something more. The contractors don't get any input into the training curriculum. They are here to role-play, not offer advice or counsel. But something happened among the attendees to this impromptu social gathering.

We understand better what the exercises are supposed to accomplish.

The contractors understand that we aren't complete idiots without our own international experiences. What began with animosity had morphed into a collegial exchange of ideas, philosophies, and professional advice.

It was a sincere passing of the torch from one generation of spies to the next.

Surveillance Detection
October 2002

WE QUICKLY SETTLE into our new training facility. It's not the same as passing through the massive gates into the CIA's headquarters building, but there's a certain esprit de corps about working and training in a covert facility. We're not on edge, but we're never really completely comfortable, either. It's like being at someone else's house. It's their responsibility to make you feel at home, and your responsibility to remember that you aren't.

Just the same, most students bring in some personal effects to tone down the stark white walls. Pictures of family, posters of their favorite college team, or kitschy items from their hometowns. This place is going to be home for a couple of months; we may as well be comfortable in it. I put some items on my desk to differentiate it from any other random student's. There was some Florida stuff of course—a Tampa Bay Buccaneers logo, a Tommy Bahama sign I got somewhere, and some paraphernalia from last year's Clearwater Jazz Festival. I also had Cathy's picture. That turns out to be quite the conversation piece.

Daryll has still not met Cathy, though she has now been up to visit several times. We typically keep to ourselves for the brief period she's in town.

We have less than forty-eight hours together, so I tend to be stingy with her time. I assure Daryll that at some point they will meet. He likes the idea. He tells other students that he and Cathy are "starting to get serious now." It's not often a colleague talks about dating your wife. I don't need to see his psychological profile to know Daryll is all extrovert. Once I react to a comment, he pours it on even more hard and heavy.

He asks, "Do you mind picking up my keys from your dresser? We want to go away for a weekend, so would it be OK if she didn't see you at all the next time she is up here?" When other students hear it for the first time they are shocked, but I ignore him. I keep hoping he'll start dating someone steady and take his attention elsewhere.

One morning I come into the office and he is on the phone. By the way he is acting, I can tell he's talking with a girl.

"So, when I can I see you?" he asks, giving me a wink. "Cool. Sounds good. I can hardly wait."

Nice to hear he has a lady friend. I busy myself by logging in to my computer and checking e-mail.

"What do you want to do while you're here?" he says into the phone. "Uh-huh. Gotcha. We can do that. Sure, sure, that sounds like a blast." He is gyrating at his desk.

I'm going to have to hose him off if this keeps up.

"So what are you wearing? Nothing? Whoa baby! Now we're talking! Where are the video phones when I need one?" He's yelling now. Nicole, a fellow student, sticks her head into the office from next door and asks who he's speaking to.

"I don't know. She sounds nice, though," I offer innocently.

Daryll cups his hand over the mouthpiece. "I'm talking with Tom's wife."

Nicole has heard so many variations on this theme that she automatically ignores it like I do.

"Ah," she says, "give her my best."

Daryll removes his hand. "Nicole says hi."

There's a pause as he listens.

"Cathy says hi back. She enjoyed meeting you at the Irish pub, and could you please tell Betsy that Cathy lost her e-mail address, so would she e-mail Cathy instead?"

Nicole gives me a look. I wave it off. He could have overheard us talking about her and Betsy meeting Cathy. "He's full of it. Ignore him, and maybe he'll go away."

Daryll listens some more before speaking again. "Cathy says Kevin had a last-minute change on his Vegas trip, and she can come in next week on an earlier flight."

I almost soil my armor. I spin around in my chair to face him. Daryll's face is beet red and still speaking into the phone.

"Yes, I think he's got it. He's thinking it might actually be you. Sure. What do you want me to say?"

I look at Nicole, but she appears to be an innocent bystander in this.

"Right. OK," Daryll says into the receiver before turning to me. "Cathy had dinner with Pat and Karen last night, Eric and Inika want to see you when you come down next month, and Woody says he can get your ladder from Chris."

Shit! He *is* talking to Cathy.

Daryll turns back to his call. "Yeah, I think we got his attention with that one. Anything else? Do you really want to? OK. Yeah, you're probably right. It's only fair. After all, it's his phone."

Nicole shakes her head and leaves, saying she didn't want to see how this was going to end. I take the phone from Daryll.

"Hi, baby," I say into the receiver. "I guess it's good I'm not the jealous type, or does that just mean I'm a dumbass and too stupid to see you cheating with my officemate?"

"He sounds like a handful," she says, "but he's really nice."

I'm glaring at Daryll. "Well, don't defend him too much. He was humping the desk while talking with you."

After finally getting to the purpose for her call, we chat for a moment and hang up. Daryll and I walk down the hall to class. He wonders aloud, "I wonder, what will our children look like?"

It's going to be a long three months.

TODAY IS OUR FIRST SESSION on detecting surveillance. The projection screen in front of us lights up to reveal actor Al Pacino riding in a car.

I love *The Godfather*. This is a good scene. Michael, Al Pacino's character, is riding in a car driven by an archrival. The rival wants to be sure that none of the Corleone clan is following them, so he executes a 180-degree turn on a bridge between New York and New Jersey. When nobody attempts the same crazy turn, the driver is sure they are alone. From the clip it's hard to tell if they wanted to detect or elude anyone who may be following them. The instructor turns to the class with an admonition.

First rule: Never, ever, try to lose surveillance. All the Hollywood films of high-speed car chases through traffic, bumping objects into the road to block a pursuer, are just that: Hollywood. In the real world, our goal is to bore them to death. Be the most boring human in the world, and tomorrow they will follow someone else and let you get on about your work. If you are doing something sneaky, suspicious, or just plain interesting, the five people following you today will be ten people following you tomorrow. The skill is not in losing them, but rather just knowing they are there. Watching. Waiting. We cannot do any spy-related activity unless we are absolutely certain that no one is surveilling us.

When we are overseas, we will conduct something called a Surveillance Detection Route, or SDR, to ensure no one is following us. An SDR precedes every operational act we ever do. Every agent meeting, dead drop, or secret photography—anytime we do anything even remotely spy oriented. If we have any suspicion that we aren't alone, we must abort our plans and do something else. Wait for another time when we are confident in being alone—or "black," as it is called—then conduct our operational act. As

Steve had said at the beginning of the course, we want to be clandestine, not covert. That means being alone.

Each SDR leaves from a designated public area representing a CIA office overseas. After leaving this kickoff point we drive around, making various stops for personal errands, eventually going to our final destination, where we conduct our operational act (signal, dead drop, agent meeting, etc.). Each SDR must have a series of cover stops that justify the direction taken and give the officer an opportunity to spot surveillance. Who averts their eyes? Who pulls into a parking lot but doesn't exit the car? Who quietly maneuvers in your direction when you return to your vehicle?

If terrorists or a foreign intelligence service believe you are aborting your plans because you detect their presence, they will just follow you around again tomorrow. And again the next day. And the day after that. The result? You can't get any work done. You've got too many people following you around expecting you to do something nefarious. Bore them to death and they will seek amusement elsewhere.

Daryll and I share a surveillance instructor named Herman. He will meet us at our kickoff point for each run and mill around the area, listening to the radio traffic of the surveillance teams. Each team is composed of CIA and off-duty law-enforcement officers who will follow us around town and report on our movements without being seen.

To help everyone get a flavor for what this will be like, we do the first run together. Daryll and I listen to the surveillance team's radio chatter as Herman drives. Daryll monitors the radio and I diagram our movements on a map. Kicking off from a supermarket parking lot Herman radios the "Rabbit" is loose. Rather than calling us a target or some other quasi-military reference, the instructors have chosen the innocuous reference of Rabbit.

We are the rabbit because we are being chased. Whoever has eyes on the rabbit is known as "the eye." We are extremely careful about what gets said over the unencrypted radio. The other surveillance vehicles are not called anything suspicious like "prowler," "terminator," or "chase-4"; they are simply known as individual numbers.

Herman pulls the car out of the parking lot. The radio bursts to life: "This is One. I have the eye. Rabbit is making a right onto Democracy Boulevard."

"Roger that. One has the eye. Rabbit turning right on Democracy."

"Two, pull up behind One and take over the eye. One, take a left at Divine Boulevard and parallel on Collins."

"This is Two. Pull up behind One and take the eye. Roger that."

"This is One. We are left on Divine."

"This is Two. We have the eye."

"Roger that. Two has the eye. Rabbit is left on Collins heading south. Rabbit is passing intersection of Collins and Darby. Continuing south."

"Rabbit is left on Collins passing Darby. Four, move parallel south on Pickens and stand by if Rabbit moves your way. Three, hole up in the country club parking lot in case Rabbit takes the service road."

"This is Three. Stand by in country club. Copy."

"This is Four. Parallel to Pickens and hold. Roger that."

The back-and-forth chatter continues for twenty minutes. Then we arrive at our first stop. Herman parks the car and turns toward us.

"Either of you yahoos smoke cigars?" he asks.

I nod. "I enjoy the occasional. Why?"

"What brand?"

"Don Tomas, but just for special occasions."

"OK. That's not a celebrity brand, so I'll assume you know something about them. Go into that smoke shop over there and tell me if someone follows you in. But don't buy anything unless you're paying for it. The Agency doesn't pay for tobacco or liquor on cover stops."

I step out of the car and walk toward the smoke shop. As I walk in, the proprietor calls out to me.

"Good morning, sir. Can I help you with something?"

"No, thanks. I'm just looking around," I offer. I worm my way around the windows of the shop, but there is so much clutter that I can't see out.

"Humidor's in the back. You sure I can't point you somewhere?" the man asks.

Doesn't this guy have anything else to do?

The door to the shop swings open, and in walks a guy in his midforties. Tan jacket, salt-and-pepper hair, mustache, blue jeans, and a white button-down shirt. He looks quickly around the shop and walks up to the counter.

"Can I help you, sir?" the overly helpful clerk asks.

"Yes, can I get five of the special-edition Macanudos please?"

"Certainly, sir. What else can I get for you?"

"That'll do it, thanks," he replies.

I'm watching from behind a rack of cigar shirts. The man isn't in a rush, nor is he shielding his face in any way. He points at a couple of items in a display case. He knows cigars but is not known in the store. That puts him in the same boat as me. Paying for the items in cash, he departs with a quick wave to the clerk.

I linger around another five minutes and make an excuse to leave the store. I walk briskly across the parking lot and get into the backseat of Herman's car.

"Well?" he asks.

"Yeah, a guy walked in. Salt-and-pepper hair, mustache, tan jacket. You guys must have seen him."

"Yeah, we saw him all right. So did the surveillance team. They figured you'd mistake him for one of them and be right out. None of them got out of their cars," Herman says.

I look at Daryll sheepishly. He shrugs his shoulders.

"Sorry, dude."

"You have just called a ghost," Herman tells me, "reporting a surveillant when in actuality there was none. What you have to understand is that people are weird. They act weird. They talk weird. When you are actively searching to see if someone is following you, it makes you ten times more aware of your surroundings. Their weirdness is magnified. A single sighting, weird or otherwise, is not indicative of surveillance."

We pull out of the parking lot and Herman starts to speak, but Daryll cuts him short.

"Dude, if you think you had it bad inside, look at my hand. I nearly wrote my fingers off. How freaking long were you planning to be in there? Were you growing the tobacco?" He has three pages of notes in his lap.

"Daryll had the same problem you did. Everyone looked suspicious. That's human nature," Herman said. "What you have to do next is decide if you see any of them more than once."

The radio crackles again.

"This is One. I have the eye. Rabbit is Romeo on Wilson Boulevard."

"Roger. One has the eye. Rabbit is Romeo on Wilson heading west."

We continue the exercise for another half an hour, listening as the surveillance team follows our every move, every turn, and every stop. Just before our time is up, Herman announces he is going to intentionally lose them so we can see what happens.

He makes a series of turns through a neighborhood that backs up to a strip mall. Rounding a corner, he makes an immediate hairpin turn into a two-story parking garage and drives up the ramp. We hustle out of the vehicle and move to a nearby wall overlooking the area. Herman points down the street.

"One of you watch each direction and listen to the radio chatter."

Car Four had lost us in the neighborhood. When they do not immediately pick us back up, the controller calls in the other cars and tightens the ranks between them. This is known as shrinking the bubble. Surveillant cars act as a bubble around the Rabbit, moving with him turn by turn, stop by stop. When the Rabbit is moving fast or in a desolate area, the bubble can be quite large—miles in diameter. When there are multiple ways out of a neighborhood or when the eye has lost the Rabbit, everyone pulls in tight. The control van is the first car we spot.

"This is control. We are at the intersection of Culvert and Madison. One, take Madison south. Two, take Culvert west. Three and Four, parallel Madison for two miles and initiate the grid. Everyone report in five minutes."

All cars signal that they heard the instruction and fan out. Herman turns away from the street back to us.

"This is a standard search-and-rescue setup," Herman explains. "No different than if you were a lost little boy in the woods or a ship missing at sea. Control will set up a command point and have the vehicles fan out in a collapsing grid. When they find you, they will reset the bubble and start all over. Most times this is an accident. But keep in mind they can decide to do more than just tail you. A person can be cased as easily as a building. They grabbed Buckley right off the streets of Beirut. Terrorists don't play by the same rules. Remember that."

This is a chilling reference. Islamic radicals kidnapped CIA Beirut Station Chief William Buckley in April 1984. Press reporting indicates that he was transported to Iran and extensively tortured during his interrogation. Radicals announced his execution in October 1985. It was not until 1991 that his badly decomposed corpse was callously dumped in southern Beirut. Nearly eight years after his abduction, Buckley's remains finally returned to the United States.

Herman points to a surveillance car pulling into the parking garage and heading for the ramp. Apparently Herman is not the only intelligence officer seeking a high vantage point.

"If they think you did something on purpose, if you lose them to conduct some funny business, there will be more people on you tomorrow than there are today. Don't lose them! You know what they say . . ." He pauses for us to finish the line.

Daryll pipes up first. "Keep your friends close and your enemies closer."

WE SPEND SEVERAL DAYS driving around looking for places to make stops for our SDR routes. Retail and convenience stores, tourist shops, specialty boutiques—anything that can justify getting out of the car, walking across a parking lot, and observing the behavior of those around us. But there are some stops that the teams have simply gotten bored with.

Forget going into a strip club, we are told. It's passé and been done by a thousand other students. Ladies should forget trying to go into lingerie stores or obstetrics offices. That, too, is discouraged. They wouldn't go somewhere overseas and take their clothes off if they thought they were being followed.

Don't do it here, either. But this week the concern has gone from someone taking a peek to someone taking a shot.

Washington has a sniper on the loose.

The murder rate in Washington DC is extremely high for the capital city of a Western nation, and those who have time to watch television only give the story a moment's attention. However, when six area residents are shot and killed and one critically injured within the forty-eight-hour period of October second and third, the emerging threat becomes all too real.

What begins with a random drive-by shooting at a Michael's craft store Wednesday night ends with the murder of James Martin, age fifty-five. This is followed on Thursday with the murder of James "Sonny" Buchanan at 7:45 a.m. Then taxi driver Prem Kumar Walekar at 8:15 a.m. Sarah Ramos at 8:45 a.m. Lori-Ann Lewis Rivera at 10:00 a.m. The day's rampage mercifully ends with seventy-two-year-old Pascal Charlot's death as he stands on a street corner at 9:20 p.m. On Friday the carnage continues when forty-three-year-old Caroline Seawell is shot outside another Michael's craft store, this one in Fredericksburg, Virginia. Seawell survives the assault.

Authorities have a growing body of forensic evidence linking the victims in the Maryland area. Law enforcement comes to a stunning conclusion: They have a serial killer on their hands, one with a gift for killing people at a distance rather than the more common up-close-and-personal methods typically used by psychopaths. This guy is different. He's not honing a new skill. He's practicing one he already has. The threat is much more grave than initially thought.

Ten students have been assigned southern Maryland as their SDR training area, including Daryll and me. After a weekend of hysteria in the Washington area, our instructors pack us into a classroom on Monday and brief us on the situation. Steve takes the podium.

"OK, everyone. By now you are aware we have a sniper in the metro area. We are in touch with law enforcement, and they are aware that this is a large class and you are on the street conducting casing and surveillance exercises. This is good and bad. It's good because if you learn to work under highly aggressive conditions like this, you should be able to work anywhere. It's bad because law enforcement and every person on the street is going to be watching for anything out of the ordinary. That includes people driving around with maps and timing sheets."

Steve holds his hands up to quiet the murmur rippling through the crowd. The SDR instructors line the back of the room. Daryll points out that a number of them are scowling, arms folded, and whispering quietly amongst themselves. Perhaps there is disagreement about whether or not to continue training.

"Some of you will be detained by the police. I can't imagine how we will conduct this training without some of you being reported by anxious citizens. There are simply too many students operating in too small an area to escape notice under these circumstances. So, until otherwise instructed, here is what you will do. If you are pulled over and you have compromising material in your car, explain that you are a U.S. government employee on a training exercise. Do *not* reveal what agency you are with. They are not in a position to have that information. I'll be honest with you guys. That will piss the officer off. Many of you will feel handcuffs and/or the backseat of a patrol car. We want to avoid this as much as possible."

The head of the SDR training group takes the front of the class. Ted is a retired case officer with a hearty laugh, typically aimed at the students' frequent mishaps during SDRs. He's not laughing today, however.

"Listen up!" Ted shouts. "We are keeping you on the streets now because at the moment it doesn't appear you are in imminent danger. If things change over the next few days, we will change the schedule as needed. If you are detained by law enforcement, you are to call me. No one else. Not Steve, not your SDR instructor, not your attorney, and not your mommy. You call me. I have the contacts to get you off the hook. But I don't need a zoo on my hands. If the press starts buzzing around, explain to the officer that you are undercover and would appreciate being detained out of the camera's eye. These guys have operated in the area for years and, like I said, they know you're out there. You won't have a gun in your car, so it's an easy issue to simply wait until the proper higher-ups have confirmed you are to be released. Everyone clear?"

We nod, but one student has a question.

"I realize this is a long shot—pardon the pun—but what do we do if we see the sniper?" he asks.

Steve and Ted exchange glances before Steve answers.

"Officially, while you are out on the streets," Steve says, "keep your eyes open, but stay out of it. I realize that's asking a lot. But if you see something, such as a guy that doesn't look like law enforcement drawing down on someone, keep in mind you are just as much a target as anyone else."

Ted pipes up at this point, supported by several staff officers along the wall. "Folks, at the moment, nobody is calling this an act of terrorism. We simply don't know what's happening. If they are terrorists, it's certainly a new methodology. There've been no anonymous claims—none I'm aware of anyway—and shooting victims one by one instead of blowing up a crowd is not a normal MO. That said, if we are dealing with al-Qaeda, or any other fundamentalist radicals, killing an Agency officer in training will win them terrorism's Nobel Prize."

"So, what do we do if we see someone?" the student repeats.

"Shit happens," an instructor behind us snaps.

"I beg your pardon?" The student turns around.

"Shit happens," the instructor repeats.

Steve is about to say something when the other instructor cuts him off. "If you see someone pointing a gun at an innocent person standing on the street, don't feel bad about losing control of your car. You froze. It could happen to anyone. Accidents. They are the bane of the traffic conditions in Washington. Shit happens!"

Steve tries to break in when a staff officer runs into the room. She waves at him.

"I hate to interrupt, but there's been another shooting. This morning. It's a kid."

She reaches up and turns on the television that is mounted to the wall.

The scene is chaos at Benjamin Tasker Middle School in Bowie, Maryland. Thirteen-year-old Iran Brown is still alive, says the voiceover, but in very critical condition. Police do not have a suspect or an eyewitness. Once again the sniper has simply vanished.

Everyone looks around, waiting for someone to say something. Ted doesn't remove his gaze from the television, but simply turns and calls back over his shoulder: "Just make sure you don't miss the son of a bitch."

WE MAKE A ROUTINE of getting together on Friday nights when there aren't exercises to conduct. We try out a number of different watering holes around the city. One of our favorites is Carpool in the Clarendon area. It's big enough for a crowd of our size, good music blares overhead, and there are plenty of munchies for hungry spies.

I meet the usual suspects there on Friday afternoon: Daryll, Nicole, Betsy, Sara, Sean, Mike, Hal, and a host of others I'm just getting to know. We socialize for an hour or so. I only have one beer and keep minding my watch. Cathy's flight is at 7:00 p.m.

Around six fifteen, I excuse myself from the crowd and drive out to Reagan National Airport to pick her up. She is full of questions about the sniper and well-wishes from friends and family. She knows we are heading back to Carpool before going home, and she ducks into the ladies' room to freshen up after the flight. When we arrive, I make the introductions. She's met a few students on previous visits, but the group tonight is unusually large. Speaking of unusually large, she finally meets Daryll.

He is very gracious, very polite, expressing how glad he is to meet her. Having not eaten yet, she declines his offer of a tequila shot, but he makes sure everyone comes over to meet her. We order food and have a wonderful time. Around nine thirty, Cathy and I start making the rounds to say good-bye—no small feat in a crowd this size. We are waving good-bye to Hal when Daryll cuts loose.

He looks at his watch. "Dude, it's only nine forty. You can't leave yet. The night is still young."

"But *we* aren't," I tell him. "The big house calleth."

"Seriously, man, don't go. We're going dancing," he roars.

"Well, have fun, Fred Astaire. We're out of here."

Cathy interjects. "We haven't seen each other in a while. We kind of want to be alone. You know what I mean?"

It takes him a second, but then the show starts: "Yeah baby!! I know where you're going." He wiggles his hips and pantomimes leaning over the ropes of an imaginary wrestling ring. He extends one hand to me. "Make the tag, make the tag!" he bellows.

God love her, Cathy doesn't let an opportunity for fun go by.

"I don't think you could handle me," she coos.

"Nice!" he replies. "Do you kiss your mother with that mouth?"

Cathy grabs my hand and leads me away. "Not tonight I won't, no!"

The crowd screams its approval.

When we get outside, Cathy pulls me close. "There's another reason I wanted to leave early tonight," she whispers.

"Yeah?" I ask. "What's that?"

She smiles as tears stream down her face. "I'm pregnant."

Wednesday, October 9. Fifty-three-year-old Dean Myers is shot while pumping gas in Manassas, Virginia. Word spreads among the students via our cell phones before local radio stations report it. Who knows what's really happening with the sniper? Snipers? Could there be more than one? That would explain the difficulty in catching them. A terrorist cell spread out across the area would be more difficult to find than a lone gunman criss-crossing the region. We watch the news and get regular updates in our morning briefings, but the situation continues to deteriorate.

Friday, October 11. Kenneth Bridges, fifty-three, is shot when the killer returns to Fredericksburg, Virginia. Like Dean Myers's murder two days ago, Bridges is pumping gas when he is shot. Again the sniper is able to elude law enforcement and disappear. Concern gives way to panic.

Gas stations erect large black tarps around the pumps to protect patrons from sniper fire from nearby hiding points. Full-service stations are popular among single women and parents with children who are afraid to get out of their cars in public. Movies, concerts, and sporting events see dramatic decreases in sales. Despite all of this, we continue training.

Now that SDRs are becoming second nature, we practice conducting car meetings with a foreign agent. Car meetings are convenient for several reasons. Though the space is small, it is easily controlled, and seeing two people in a car is not particularly suspicious to any random passersby.

Car meetings have long been a preferred method for getting together with agents in many parts of the world. It's fast, it's simple, and it can be customized around the often busy schedules of high-ranking officials. This point was made clear to me during one of my early interviews before joining the Agency. The case officer had asked me what I would do if I were debriefing a French diplomat when he suddenly has a heart attack in the car. I said I would drop him off at a hospital claiming I had nearly run over him when he stumbled into traffic. It was a good answer. Most potential students just dump the poor bastard out the door and leave.

This is one of a hundred scenarios we train on during the next few weeks. Every possible variation the instructors can come up with is tested. We are graded on the type of pickup point we choose, the time of day, location, security considerations, and the cover stories we craft for our agents. Cover stories are what typically get agents into trouble. How does a French third secretary justify to an inquisitive police officer why he is standing behind a Dumpster at 1:00 a.m.? It has to be a credible but not a complicated story.

Car meetings may be the most preferable, but they also create problems for the case officer. After picking the agent up, we must still navigate traffic. We cannot have an agent who is violent, or we risk a traffic accident. If the agent is giving us complex information, we need to take notes. If we take notes and drive, we risk a traffic accident. So picking the agent up is only half the problem. But before we pick him up, we must make sure he is the correct person. I learned this lesson with an instructor named Paul.

I was picking Paul up, but I didn't know what he looked like beyond a basic description. This is common when case officers have to substitute for each other. Each agent is given code phrases, called oral bona fides, to use when being picked up by car. But the code phrases can't be cryptic passages that a random passerby would find odd.

Things like "What's the difference between a duck?" answered by "Nothing, goldfish don't have feet" make no sense and are distinctive to anyone standing nearby. That will make the person look at you and your agent. They may remember you and your agent. They could remember what time of day it was, where they were standing, and what color and make of car you were driving. They might later think this was something worth sharing with the security services.

Code phrases give the agent and the case officer every chance to walk away from the encounter and not be associated with each other in the event there is a problem. The phrases have to be innocuous and believable. "Charlie sends his regards" followed by "Gracie said to tell him hello" is not going to raise anyone's interest. The random public will never know the code words of Charlie and Gracie have been successfully used right in front of them. I was expecting the exercise to test my preparedness, but there was an added wrinkle I hadn't anticipated.

Everything had gone well so far. My ninety-minute SDR was flawless, and I did not have surveillance. I go around the corner from the pickup site and hunker down. There is excellent natural screening to conceal my instructor/agent from the road without him appearing to hide. He has a cover story in case anyone asks why he is there. I roll down the passenger-side window in advance so I can speak to him and unlock the door to speed his entry into the vehicle. Textbook preparation. At the appointed time I whisk around the corner to the pickup site and realize I have a problem: There are two people standing there, not one.

Now what?

Both are men. Both are in their midfifties. Both are reading a newspaper. Neither has a duffle bag or briefcase with him. They are eyeing each other and me as I drive up.

A screech of tires explodes behind me. My heart races. I sweat profusely. Leaning over the console between the front seats I see both men's heads turn quickly toward the car behind me. What is going on? I lean back to look in my rearview mirror.

It's a black Ford Taurus. No rack of blue lights, no siren. No officers on foot surrounding us. What gives?

One of the men leans into my car.

"Are . . . are . . . are you Archie's uncle?" I stammer.

He looks at me, shakes his head, and withdraws from the car. He walks back to the Taurus. The second man leans in. He's trying to not laugh.

I realize I'm probably zapped, but I refuse to go down without a fight. My car is clean—no compromising material—and I have an even better cover story than my agent.

"Are you Archie's uncle?" I repeat.

"No, he is on vacation," the man replies, opening the car door.

"Archie" and "vacation" were our code words. Here is my agent. The other man is still bent over the Taurus's passenger-side door as I punch the accelerator. It's only after the exercise finishes that I learn what happened: Another student had the same pickup point at the same time.

It's something that happens occasionally. There are some very good pickup points around the Washington area, and students tend to gravitate to them. The instructors normally de-conflict the pickup sites and times. But this class is excessively large. There are new instructors who don't know the area well, and they are role-playing against two students each day. There is not enough time to check out each student's plans before the exercises begin.

The pickup may not have been perfect, but it was good enough. As long as the agent gets into the right car and I don't drive off with someone else's agent, the instructor is happy. The other instructor felt the same way. If the site is so good that two students are unknowingly using it at the same time, it must be OK.

Monday, October 14. I am casing a small shopping center outside Bethesda, Maryland, when the radio announcer interrupts a song with a breaking news story. There has been another sniper attack. The victim was coming out of a Home Depot with her husband in Falls Church, Virginia. By the next morning, the victim's full identity is revealed. FBI intelligence analyst Lynda Franklin is the eleventh victim and ninth fatality of the sniper.

At the Tuesday morning briefing Steve and Ted remind everyone that there is no evidence to suggest that Franklin was targeted because she is a federal officer. At the moment it appears to be simply another random victim in the wrong place at the wrong time. Still, there is considerable debate about whether to continue with our street training. In the end, the decision is made to not allow terrorists to interfere. Everything runs fine all week with no additional shootings. The region finally begins to relax.

Saturday, October 19. A thirty-seven-year-old man is shot outside of Ashland, Virginia, eighty-five miles south of Washington. A three-page note to police is found near the victim.

Despite huge outcries from the community for information, police refuse to share the contents of the note. Rumors are rampant in the media, speculating the note's potential demands for money or threats of additional violence in the area. Police put out a request for the public's help in finding a white panel van that may be involved in the shootings. White vans are pulled over by law enforcement the entire weekend.

We continue to case the area of northern Virginia and southern Maryland. While we have always been aware of our surroundings, our guard is up even more. The class is noticeably less amicable. The media onslaught, the cautious tones of the instructors, and the growing apprehension of our families is compounding the pressures of the program.

Monday, October 21. This is our first day of first-aid and CPR training. Case officers must often work for extended periods alone. Given that the streets of Washington DC are increasingly painted with the blood of innocent gunshot victims, the idea of training us in basic first aid seems especially relevant. Today we are receiving a quick-and-dirty course in cardiopulmonary resuscitation, or CPR.

Someone notes that CPR is designed for helping others, not for patching up oneself. This catches Steve and the other instructors off guard, and it becomes immediately apparent that today's training is only intended to give us some time away from Washington's mean streets. We oblige the gesture, glad to be stationary and temporarily out of harm's way. The class even had its humorous points.

Watching a class full of type-A students kiss plastic mannequins is fairly entertaining all by itself. Watching someone of Daryll's size practice on a child-size mannequin is absolutely hysterical. He fumbles with the doll, holds it by the head, and when he bends over to give it the "breath of life," it looks like he's going to swallow it whole. The jokes run fast and furious. Good-natured as he is, Daryll quickly gets frustrated. Our comedic distraction is short-lived when an instructor once again runs into the room to turn on the television.

Police have pulled two Hispanic men from a white van. A media circus surrounds the scene in minutes. Rumors and speculation create a firestorm, but what began with a citizen's tip results only in the arrest of two illegal immigrants. They have no connection to the sniper. He remains as elusive as ever, and police appear no closer to apprehending him.

Tuesday, October 22. Bus driver Conrad Johnson is shot at 6:00 a.m., barely half a mile from where the killing rampage originated nearly three weeks ago. Later in the afternoon police, reacting to the near-riot condition of the public, release part of the three-page letter that was left for authorities in Ashland. The sniper wrote "Even the children are not safe" and that he would only quit killing if authorities paid a $10,000,000 ransom. Hysteria reaches a feverish pitch.

Working again from a citizen's tip, police quietly surround a car with two men sleeping inside. One of them has a rifle. John Allen Mohammad and Lee Boyd Malvo are arrested and arraigned on a number of federal and local charges. Police profiles are completely wrong. Instead of a lone white male in a van, it's two black men in a blue Caprice Classic. After twenty-two days of terror, the nation's capital can finally relax.

Friday, October 25. The phone rings at 5:15 a.m. Nobody calls that early with good news. After taking a moment to clear the fog away, I pick up the receiver and grunt a hello. I can hear someone on the other end of the line, but sobbing obliterates any voice recognition.

"Hello? Who's there?" I ask.

More sobbing followed by a throat clearing. It's a woman's voice.

"It's me."

"Cathy?"

"I think I've miscarried." More sobbing.

"Oh, baby . . ."

I spend forty-five minutes on the phone, calming her enough to understand what is happening. She had awakened bleeding and was certain she could no longer be pregnant. Her doctor's office had a physician on call, and she was on her way to see him. I promised I would call in a couple of hours.

I take a quick shower. I get dressed and drive to the training facility with only a single thought: How fast can I get to Florida?

When I arrive, Daryll is not in yet. I put my briefcase down and walk up the stairs to Steve's office.

"I need to be excused," I said.

"Why? What's going on?" he asks.

I explain the phone call, the pregnancy we had only learned of a few weeks ago, and Cathy's likely miscarriage. I ask if I can slip out around lunch, after my 9:00 a.m. exercise, and quietly disappear for the weekend. He gives me his blessing.

We are practicing walk-in exercises—how to handle people who walk into our overseas offices and volunteer information. Walk-ins have been incredibly effective in the war on terrorism, but they must be properly scrutinized. Today's exercise lets us practice "vetting" a walk-in—questioning the veracity of his or her information and properly documenting and communicating it back to headquarters in a series of reports. I have to do all of this knowing of my wife's shattered emotional state a thousand miles away.

I return to my office and prepare for the exercise. When one student is using the office, the other must find somewhere else to go—the break room, the library, or the computer lab. We then reverse positions until the second student's exercise is finished, then write our reports. We often ask each other for help, proofreading on format and content. Fortunately, I was doing my exercise first.

As I work up my preparations my mind wanders: What is Cathy going through? Where is she right now? Is anyone with her, or is she facing this alone? Will she go to work after the doctor's appointment? Juggling the multitude of questions in the back of my mind, I somehow conduct my walk-in meeting on autopilot. When I walk my illicit informant out and thank him on behalf of the U.S. government, Steve is standing outside my door. He comes in and quickly gets down to business.

"OK. There are nine flights leaving Washington for Tampa today. Three from Reagan, two from Dulles, and four from BWI. Your best bet is the two o'clock from Reagan, but another one at three leaves from Dulles."

He has been on the telephone finding flights from all three airports. He has airlines, flight numbers, times, and costs written out on a legal pad.

"Either way, you're going to have to hurry," he continues. "Call this number and ask for Sheryl. But don't call from here. You can't use your credit card from these phones. Order a ticket on your cell phone once you get onto the highway. Don't worry about writing up your reports until you get back, and don't come in Sunday night. Wait and write it up Monday night. I'll tell the role-player there's been a problem. Get out of here."

I can't believe he has found all the flight options for me. Not only has he given me permission to leave, he's done all the necessary homework to find the best way to do so. I owe him big-time.

I square away my office and stick my head in the break room to tell Daryll that the office is all his. I'm halfway to Reagan National Airport when I dial the number and buy a US Airways ticket to Tampa. I arrive with barely fifteen minutes to spare for the two o'clock flight. I have no clothes, no toothbrush, and no transportation when I arrive. But I am on my way.

Once on the plane, I am alone with my thoughts: What am I going to do when I get home?

Cathy doesn't know I'm coming, and I don't want to startle or upset her by calling. Somehow I've got to catch her between the office and home.

When I arrive, I call her office to make sure she's there, but hang up before the operator can connect us. Then I grab a taxi to take me there. I've been casing office complexes for weeks now and apply these techniques to her building. Carefully navigating around security cameras, contract guards, and her office windows, I find her car on the third floor of the garage. I make several trips up and down while deciding a strategy.

I will go up one floor to an overhead perch where I can see her exit the building. I will follow her to the car and make sure she gets in and is not picked up by someone else she may have called. Walking up behind her will scare her, so I need to let her see me from a distance without getting onto the street. I will move down one level to the ramp. She will be driving slowly to negotiate the curve, and it's a perfect place to intercept her before she exits to the street.

It's warm, the birds are singing, and I can see a school of dolphins in the bay. It's a beautiful afternoon, but I know Cathy is probably barely able to hold herself together. I hope she can make it to five o'clock. I buy a news-paper from a nearby machine and take my position on the fourth floor of the garage. My cell phone rests nearby, and I craft a defendable cover should a security guard challenge me. Now all I have to do is wait.

At five fifteen she emerges.

Some of her officemates are walking her out. The day has taken a toll on her. She's walking slowly, head down, shoulders slumped. She's not smiling, not looking forward to a stereotypical Florida weekend. From behind the sports section I watch her enter the garage and part from the others. I pick up my phone and quietly slip down the stairs to the ramp.

As she drives around the traffic circle I step out from behind a column. Her first look is surprise, then disbelief, and finally release. Crying, tears pouring uncontrollably, she pulls the parking brake, jumps out of the car into my arms. She can't speak. That's all right. I know what she's saying. She's no longer carrying the burden alone.

I'm home.

Crossing Borders
November 2002

I CAN TELL he's pissed off just looking at him. Jean-Paul is not a guy we normally see mad. He's pretty laid-back. Almost quiet. To see him jumping-up-and-down mad is really quite a spectacle.

When he joined Daryll and me for beers a few weeks back, I had only been partially aware of the conversation. I was still pretty irritated at the role-player who had called me a liar. I was marginally aware that Jean-Paul had told a similar story of woe, but his has continued on now for weeks.

Jean-Paul worked the diplomatic reception last month just as the rest of us had. He also had a bio on file that the contractors could look at, so they knew a bit about him. He had an overview of his target and the two made contact. For the most part, this worked out quite well. They both played their parts and engaged in the requisite small talk. The problem came not from the cover story he had been given, but from Jean-Paul's real collegiate background.

Jean-Paul was a Phi Beta Kappa, an exclusive coed fraternity reserved for only the highest academic achievers. It is quite an honor to be accepted. The few students who know about it agree that of the people who might have been bestowed with such an honor, Jean-Paul would likely be one.

In college I majored in fraternity with a minor in partying, which was more than reflected in my parking tickets and abysmally bad attendance. I am impressed that Jean-Paul accomplished such a lofty achievement, seeming to have gotten not only a well-rounded education but also to have become a well-rounded guy. Nothing about him causes me to second-guess his intelligence, sincerity, or principles. I guess that's why he got so mad when one of the instructors questioned his ethics. Like me, an independent contractor/role-player called him a bold-faced liar.

At this point we consider the possibility that the role-players are simply messing with us. Pouring on a certain mental abuse could be somewhat akin to the physical abuse endured in the Marine Corps' infamous boot camp. It's a possibility, but not one that held up to even a quick analysis.

Some of the students know recent graduates of the CST program, and a quick phone call to those officers proves this is not a normal tactic. It could be something new, but students with professional backgrounds in psychology suggest that such an approach will do more harm to group dynamics than it will benefit individuals. They don't think it's a part of any exercise or evaluation. It's just a few indies inflating their egos, making us jump through hoops, earn our spurs, that sort of thing. Since my problem has been dealt with, it leaves Jean-Paul out on his own. That isn't going so well.

His contract role-player has taken issue with Jean-Paul's bio, which states he is Phi Beta Kappa. He challenged Jean-Paul on it, saying he didn't believe he actually received the award and generally didn't think much of Jean-Paul. At first, Jean-Paul thinks it's some tangent on the exercise, a diversion away from the real objective. So he plays it off as a joke. But the guy isn't joking.

Every meeting Jean-Paul had with him since over the past four weeks, the indie has found a way to bring the issue up. Jean-Paul is methodically planning his meetings and working the case like we are expected to do, but the indie only wants to talk about Phi Beta Kappa. When that isn't getting on Jean-Paul's nerves enough, the guy starts recruiting help from the Lion's Den.

Jean-Paul's next two role-players, who are in completely unrelated exercises, also bring up the Phi Beta Kappa question. At this point Jean-Paul has brought in pictures, official documentation, and even the ubiquitous gold key indicative of membership in the organization. He says it took him forever to find it because he hasn't touched any of this material in years. Still the harassment continues. Today, he's had enough.

Jean-Paul marches up to Steve's office, taking with him the box of Phi Beta Kappa materials. Dropping it on the desk, he gives an ultimatum: Get this lunatic off his back and squash the conspiracy floating through the Lion's Den, or Jean-Paul is marching directly over to Langley and lodging a formal complaint with the Inspector General's office.

By the end of the day Jean-Paul has satisfaction.

He receives a written letter of apology from the indie (who was given no choice in the matter). His exercise with every instructor is reviewed by Steve personally as well as by a cadre of other senior staff officers. Anything an indie cannot directly recall as being pertinent to the exercise is expunged from the record. All the indies receive a warning that similar shenanigans will not be tolerated, or their contracts would be immediately terminated.

The fact that former Agency personnel would become so loose and free with accusations they could not prove is troubling. Everyone in the class knows about it. Even students who have no issues with the indies now keep them at arm's length. There's not as much chumminess in the hallways as there has been. It is not so much an "us versus them" mentality as it is a "let's just get this behind us" one. It's not what the Agency envisioned when the independent contractors were brought on, and the implication is many of them will not see their contracts renewed. That was fine with us.

Especially Jean-Paul.

AS COOLER TEMPERATURES TAKE HOLD of the Washington area we prepare for a chilling new exercise. When traveling across the world, case officers are undercover. This often means they are under an assumed name, a false one used specifically to get between different parts of the world without the local intelligence and law-enforcement services knowing they are there. In order to do this, they must be able to get into a country legitimately, crossing the border like any other visitor.

In his book *The Master of Disguise,* retired CIA disguise chief Tony Mendez speaks eloquently about the border crossings he endured as a field officer. Mendez points out that a disguise is only a tool; it is *deception* that must be mastered. The necessity of such a skill makes this an important exercise.

We take a bus out to a warehouse that has been mocked up exactly like a foreign Immigration office. The holding pen, offices, and support areas appear genuine in every respect. While they don't have wings, the buses' interiors are transformed into airliners arriving from overseas, complete with stewardesses, Immigration paperwork, and a "pilot" speaking to us over the PA system. Once we disembark, suspending disbelief becomes obligatory.

We claim our bags from the luggage carriers and are herded into a holding area. The exercise is complicated by the addition of "sleepers." Masked as tourists entering the country, these are Agency staff officers intermingled with us to keep us from concentrating. It's hard to remember your fake name and address when someone is singing Madonna's "Like a Virgin" at the top of her lungs right next to you.

Overhead, hidden speakers blast the background noise one would expect in a third-world airport. Our instructions are delivered by a thickly accented voice over this system and made even more complicated by repeated feedback and static, further legitimizing the scene. It's going to be a long morning. But it is not without its pleasant diversions.

I am standing in line with Caroline, one of the more attractive young ladies in the class. She and I are at the end of a line of students, filling out our paperwork to enter the Immigration area. A security guard is barking orders and "assisting" us in filling out our forms. This is where Caroline makes a crucial mistake. She asks for help.

"Excuse me," she says to a guard, "what do we write down if we don't know the address of where we are staying? My hotel was arranged by my corporate travel office."

"Stupid American girl!" he shouts at her. "What do you want?"

Caroline takes an involuntary step back but recovers very well. She repeats the request.

"You don't know where you are going?" he screams.

She again explains that a travel agent arranged her trip, that she was a new employee and was just now arriving.

If she was expecting the welcome wagon, she's in for a disappointment.

"How stupid are you Americans?" the guard roars. He walks around her, taking his time to look her up and down. Though she is dressed conservatively, it is obvious that she is an attractive young woman. This would be a typical bit of harassment in any number of countries. I think she handles it quite well. Apparently she is used to being stared at.

After completing a circle around her he stops, pointing toward a desk. "Show me your papers!" he demands.

Another man in a guard's uniform walks over, picks up her bag, then exits with it through a nearby door.

"I must see your papers!" the first guard yells again.

Caroline empties her wallet and pulls out her identification. He asks her a few questions. Where is she going? What is the address of her company? What will she be doing? What is the name of her supervisor? Is there a phone number where he can be reached?

She gives him a contact number, and he makes a production of walking off and discussing it with yet another uniformed man who has walked over after hearing the commotion. The two confer for a moment then split up. Guard One returns to Caroline. Guard Two motions me to come over. I walk over to him and let go of the handle on my hanging bag. I have a good idea of what's happening.

She and I are the last people in line. There are no other witnesses. When Guard Two asks about my travel arrangements, I slowly and imperceptibly shift my weight to my right foot. Then I lift up my left foot and roll the heel to the left until I feel resistance from the hanging bag. I then slowly lower it down onto the corner and shift my weight back to normal so that I am standing on the bag. I didn't bump it and I never took my eyes off Guard Two, but I accomplish my goal. Nobody was stealing *my* bag.

I answer Guard Two's questions while listening to Guard One fluster Caroline. My suspicions are confirmed when he finally lets her go.

"Excuse me, miss," he calls as she hurries off. "How is it you are coming into my country for a new job, but you don't have any bags?"

"I do have bags," Caroline answers. "The other inspector has them."

There is no one else in the room but the four of us. She is zapped, and I can't help. I can't act like I even know her. On a real assignment, we would pass through Immigration as strangers, not colleagues.

"What other guard? You mean him?" pointing at Guard Two, who promptly waves me through to the holding area.

"No, there was another gentleman that walked up while we were talking. I saw him take my bag and go through that door."

She still doesn't understand that it's a setup. She's about to learn an expensive lesson.

"Are you accusing me of stealing your luggage?"

The inquisition is just starting when I pass through the double doors into the holding area.

If crowded public transportation is referred to as "cattle cars," then this must be the barn. The place is swarming with students, sleepers, Immigration officials, and enough luggage for a Cirque du Soleil performance. Everywhere there are people in starched-white uniforms, issuing orders. Whatever we are doing, it is wrong. We are given corrective advice by a guard screaming at the top of his lungs.

"Are you talking to him? Do you two know each other? No? Then shut up!"

"You, put that newspaper down!"

"You, take those headphones off! This isn't a concert!"

"What the hell are you looking at, you American capitalist pig?!"

Meanwhile, the sleepers are waking up. One is a young Asian woman I recognize from the Agency's security office. She is prancing around the room, talking to the male students. She is not shy.

"Wow, you're cute," she says to Jay.

"You have a wonderful tan," she coos to Brandon. "Did you come from the Bahamas?"

But she really takes a shine to Eric. Poor bastard.

Eric is a fine young gentleman from South Carolina whose Southern charm and genteel ways earned him the nickname of The Colonel. It's an appropriate title, because this girl is trying to get him fried. She starts feeling his muscles.

"Do you work out?" she asks.

He shakes his head no when no one is looking, but doesn't speak.

She plays with his hair, twirling it around on her finger in a suggestive way. The guards come over and mercilessly hassle Eric for the way she is fawning over him. They don't believe that he isn't somehow related to this woman. Otherwise, why would she be so gaga over him? Who does he think he is, Brad Pitt?

The Colonel would normally appreciate such contact from an attractive young lady. But right now, she's just marked him for interrogation.

When Tony Mendez discusses the exfiltration of six American diplomats during the 1979 takeover of the U.S. embassy in Tehran, he relates how he watched from a distance as their airport screening unfolded. He was not directly participating in their interrogation, but he was no less stressed by it. Close enough to witness, but far enough away that he could not directly help. I have a minuscule understanding of what that perspective must have been like, having seen what has been happening to my colleagues in this exercise.

I'm at a good vantage point to watch the ongoing saga. Everyone around me is trying to ignore what is going on, but we are all equally unable to appease the guards. Eating, reading, talking—all the normal activities that one does to kill time are forbidden. It's an effort to get us to think too much, forget our rehearsed lines, and make us nervous. It's working on everyone.

Except Scott.

We meet unique individuals such as Scott at key points in our lives. I don't know him well, but every interaction I have had with him thus far has been memorable. He is not the typical Agency recruit. He has a unique air about him. He has an unusual fashion sense, but it's a style that works for him. He is extremely intelligent, very well read, and has seen a good bit of the world. Scott had made a powerful first impression during the first week of class, but not for the best of reasons.

He has a tendency to nod off.

I had noticed Jed and Daryll snickering through a lecture one day. Hal was also watching, barely containing his laughter. Scott was not just sleeping. He was snoring. Ever so slowly the effects of gravity had their way with him. He leaned to the side and nearly fell out of the chair. It wasn't narcolepsy; the guy just wasn't getting enough sleep to keep him awake during some of the more attention-numbing parts of the curriculum. To fall asleep in the holding area during the border-crossing exercise, however, was quite another story.

Yet he managed to do it. Chin tucked firmly into his chest, he takes a deep breath and lets it out. One by one students give one another quizzical looks before staring. How we admire him. If you can't escape in body, then by all means escape in mind. Unfortunately, it is still his body they want. Specifically his ass.

"What the hell do you think this is? The Hilton? Are you too tired to stay awake there, pretty boy?" a guard roars.

Scott jumps to life and makes the mistake of speaking. "What? Oh, sorry, I was just passing the time . . ."

"Time? Time is your problem? Well, I can fix that for you," the guard yells. "Walk over to that clock." He points at the wall.

Scott walks over to the clock.

"What time is it?" the guard yells again.

"It's six fifteen," Scott replies.

"Well, since you're so damned concerned about wasting your time, why don't you stand there and watch that clock until I tell you to sit down?"

Every time Scott tries to look away, he gets caught. When he locks his knees and starts to sway, the guard yells at him again, shocking him awake. I never get to see how his episode ends, because I am called up into the line. I present my papers, remembering my name, address, and even the name of the conference I am attending. I get sent to a secondary interrogation anyway.

Yeah. I'm not too surprised either.

I've seen a couple of students simply breeze through, but it appears that the deciding factor is the availability of a secondary interrogation room. If they are full, students pass right on through. If a room opens up, the next student through primary is flagged and sent in.

Secondary for me is a room about ten feet square with a standard government-issue desk and credenza. Two chairs are positioned in front of the desk. I am instructed to sit in one and place my hanging bag in the other. A table fills up the far wall, where a guard promptly dumps the contents of my bag. In one corner is a camera on a tripod. The entire discussion is being videotaped.

For cover I had devised my own company and am using names of old friends as employees. It's not hard to remember someone's name when you were the best man at his wedding. You just have to notice if your interrogator switches your alias name with your real one to try to trip you up. Fortunately I catch that. I also catch him when he substitutes a different area code for my firm. Had I not taken the time to look up the proper area and zip codes for my made-up firm, I would have gotten caught right here. When he asks about my company's product, I immediately launch into a sales pitch.

When he finishes, the inspector tells me how well I did. My bags are in perfect order and I know my cover story inside and out. I am given the videotape and encouraged to review it when I get back to the training center. He tells me to put the clothes back in my hanging bag and "enter the country." That's where the doughnuts are.

The backside of the Immigration office is a large break room, where fresh coffee and a variety of pastries are available. About seventy-five students are there when I walk in and, like everyone else, I receive a hearty round of applause for leaving interrogation safely. We watch a large television monitor wired to the video camera out front where the last few students are leaving the holding area on their way to interrogation. But not all of us leave it the same way.

Ahmed has a brilliant cover story that many of us will likely copy in various forms during real operations. It's just that elegant. Unfortunately, Ahmed hasn't traveled much in recent years. He doesn't own a big piece of luggage to support his story of extended travel, so he borrowed one from an aunt. Unfortunately, it still has his aunt's name on the tag.

Zap!

The secondary inspector makes a big production of finding the tag and pulling it off. He asks Ahmed who this person is. Ahmed explains that it is his aunt, that he borrowed the bag for his trip. No problem, the guard said, calling Ahmed's bluff.

The guard then calls Ahmed's aunt.

In the Iranian exfiltration Tony Mendez had supplied special phone numbers for the escaping diplomats to use if Immigration authorities wanted to confirm their hastily crafted stories. An Agency officer well versed in the case staffed the bogus numbers. Ahmed's aunt, however, is not an Agency staff officer.

She doesn't know anyone with the alias name he is traveling under. No, she told the inspector, she's never had any luggage stolen. She doesn't really travel much in her old age. She can't remember the last trip she took. In fact, she loaned her only piece of luggage to her wonderful nephew Ahmed, who is going on a business trip. He works for the government, you know. When the Immigration officer hangs up, he tells Ahmed to turn around and place his hands behind his back. He's under arrest.

A couple of other students also wear the stainless steel bracelets and take a considerable amount of ribbing from the rest of us. Even after coming into the break area nobody takes their handcuffs off. The learning point remains for the duration that they are on the exercise.

The head of the Immigration office calls the exercise officially over and herds us back into the main holding area where it's more comfortable. He goes around the room, introducing us to his staff and other Customs/INS officers who have come in from other cities to assist in the exercise. We give them a round of applause.

He outlines what went well and what didn't go so well. He explains that catching spies is not what the entrance process into a country is designed for. They are trying to catch drug dealers, contraband, and counterfeit documents. Then he talks about the September 11 hijackers.

"They all came through Immigration into the United States. They came in right under our noses. I think we do this job pretty well. We've got people that can sniff out a lie. Now, you guys are learning how to lie, how to sneak, how to create a cover that can stand a fair amount of scrutiny. Most of you did very, very well. But be aware that technology is catching up with you. With some of the biometrics and even the commercial databases out there, it's going to be damn difficult for you to slip in and out of countries like your predecessors did. We are working with the Agency and keeping tabs on what other countries use for detecting passport and identification fraud, but just be aware that you can't do it on the fly."

Caroline raises her hand. "What do you know about problems women have going through certain countries? Is there anything we can do if things get, you know, out of hand?" she asks.

He smiles and nods. "Yeah, we get that question every time we run this course. Short answer is, yes, it happens. If an inspector wants to go through your bags and pull out your garters and leather whips, I suggest you let him do it."

Ahmed, still in handcuffs, looks over at Caroline. "Maybe we should work together?" he says playfully.

The inspector ignores the snickers and continues. "The problem comes when they want to inspect your person, a strip search. I'm sorry, ladies, but it's out there. If you are pulled into secondary, it is a very real possibility they will ask you to strip. It's not common, but it does happen."

"What can we do?" another student asks.

The inspector defers to Steve, who steps in from a side door.

"You can refuse, but be professional. Be indignant. If you are under offi-cial cover, demand a supervisor and the embassy be notified. If push comes to shove, tell them you don't want to enter their miserable country. Get on the next plane out, regardless of where it's going. We can arrange for some-one else to take your place if necessary."

The Immigration chief speaks again. "On behalf of my team, I want to thank all of you for coming into the Agency. Your instructors have been talking you up all over town. Everyone knows you are the 9/11 class. We ap-preciate the sacrifices you made to come into this program, and we wish you the best of luck. The hijackers came right through the exact type of setup you just passed through. It's not perfect. We can't always detect them in the ninety or so seconds we have them in front of the desk. We depend on folks like you to chase them down before they get here. So if there's ever anything we can do to help you on the job, please don't hesitate to ask."

STEVE CALLS the morning briefing to order. "Grab a chair, guys. I've got instructions for you from Langley."

He waits for the chatter to calm and reads from a red folder stamped URGENT.

" 'All employees are warned to be on especially high alert. There is an el-evated possibility of violence in the area that might specifically target CIA employees. If you see anything out of the ordinary, take no action on your own but immediately contact the Office of Security.' "

He puts the paper down. "Quite simply, folks, we're about to execute someone. It could get pretty dicey around here."

Controversy is swirling as the execution date for Mir Aimal Kasi grows closer. The thirty-eight-year-old Pakistani opened fire with an AK-47 as-sault rifle on a line of traffic waiting to enter CIA headquarters on January 25, 1993. Agency officers Frank Darling and Lansing Bennett were killed in the attack. In addition, two other Agency personnel and a telephone company contract employee were wounded.

"Some of you have seen the memorial to Darling and Bennett out in front of headquarters," Steve said. "It was just dedicated a few months ago in May. I urge the rest of you to go by and see it."

The memorial is on VA Road 123, the geographic front entrance to the CIA, and is accessible to the public. A simple but poignant granite memorial embossed with the CIA logo marks the men's service to the nation. A bench flanks each side of the memorial, one dedicated to the memory of each officer.

Kasi fled to Pakistan the day after the shooting. He was arrested there by the FBI and returned to the United States for trial. He admitted to the crime and was convicted in 1997. Four Americans were killed in Pakistan after Kasi's conviction. The government is taking no chances on similar violence occurring when he is executed. All CIA facilities worldwide are put on heightened states of alert, as are all U.S. embassies and consulates. Virginia Governor Mark Warner refuses a clemency request from the Pakistani government.

Mir Aimal Kasi is put to death by lethal injection at the Greenville Correctional Center in southeast Virginia on November 14.

Though Kasi had fled to Pakistan, he actually spent most of his time hiding in Kandahar, Afghanistan. The Taliban's radical control of the country offered him the necessary protection and shelter. He said he wanted to punish the United States for its bombing of Iraq, its treatment of Muslims in Palestine, and because the CIA had become too involved in the affairs of the Middle East. It took the FBI four years to find him.

Steve reminds us that the first bombing of the World Trade Center occurred one month after Kasi's attack. Terrorists had hoped to topple one tower into the next and kill the thirty-five thousand people inside with a combination of destruction and cyanide. Instead, the gas was consumed by the bomb's explosive fireball—a lucky break for the people of New York.

Only six people died and a thousand were injured, a ghostly trial run for what happened eight years later.

Frank Darling, Kasi's younger victim, was an undercover Operations officer, just like us. Only twenty-eight years old, his wife was seated next to him at the time of his murder. DO officers assigned to the Middle East Division took Darling's death especially hard. Many Beltway insiders whispered that if Agency field officers found Kasi before the FBI did, he would not live long enough to enjoy the privilege of a trial. With the Bureau making an arrest it kept the unremorseful Kasi in the hands of the Department of Justice, away from Agency personnel who might want to circumvent the rule of law.

Steve alters the schedule of classes to take advantage of this point. Kasi was given a fair and impartial trial, and he admitted to his crime. He appealed his conviction multiple times, which was his right. Everything was by the book. Steve makes it clear that the only reason the prosecution worked at all was because the Agency had no part in it.

There has been animosity between the Agency and the FBI that harks all the way back to the CIA's formation. At the end of World War II the Office of Strategic Services, or OSS, the precursor of the CIA, handled all foreign espionage. The OSS was run by the legendary spymaster William "Wild Bill" Donovan. FBI Director J. Edgar Hoover hated Donovan passionately. When the war ended, Hoover convinced President Truman to fire Donovan and dismantle the OSS. Hoover wanted the FBI to handle all domestic and foreign espionage activity. After several Communist spy rings were discovered operating in Washington in 1945, the CIA was formally chartered two years later and tasked with foreign espionage collection.

It's better that the two distinct needs are assigned to separate entities. The FBI is not designed for intelligence work. The field offices around the country were established to support the local district attorneys' offices. The Bureau was created to prosecute felony interstate crimes such as bank robbery, kidnapping, fraud, and organized crime. It is not an agency that pushes information into the field.

Then there is the Bureau's archaic electronic infrastructure. Agents are woefully unprepared for the information technology revolution. If CIA information technology is considered old by modern corporate standards, FBI systems are downright ancient.

Numerous books have been written about the nearly six decades of rivalry between the two organizations. Thus far, it doesn't appear that the events of 9/11 have changed it much. The Agency is now training Bureau agents in the skills of intelligence analysis at the FBI Academy in Quantico, Virginia. The CIA is also placing domestic officers at FBI field offices throughout the nation to maximize each organization's strength.

Will the Bureau's admirable handling of the Kasi case help improve the links between the utterly opposite organizations? That's hard to say. But it's a good start. Hopefully, we can all learn to get along. As 9/11 proved, we have more than enough enemies to keep both organizations busy for decades to come.

WE ARE SPENDING so much time on vehicle surveillance, many of us are actually dreaming about it during the small amount of time we have available for sleep. I have. Repeatedly. I've awakened several times in the night after dreaming about the route I am running later in the day. Sometimes I come up with an entirely new route for a future exercise. This doesn't bother me, because I can use the additional search time.

I live in Alexandria, Virginia, but my operational areas are all in Maryland. I can't use my personal car for SDR work, so I have to drive all the way out to the training center, park my car, pick up my government rental, and drive up to Bethesda to practice my SDR or case new sites. Each night I finish by reversing the procedure, my rental car returns to the garage, my car is picked up, and I return home. I'm burning a couple of hours a day just getting to and from my operational areas. It's time I don't have to waste.

On the positive side, I haven't misidentified surveillance even once. Not that it has always been difficult to detect. We are getting so accustomed to watching our surroundings, we even notice one another's vehicles during

SDR runs. We also see one another's surveillance teams. As if noticing our own shadows isn't nerve-racking enough, we start seeing other people's teams. It really begins to wear on our nerves. Sharon, in particular, is having trouble.

She's a quiet student and doesn't socialize much. I can't recall her ever being at one of the Friday night social events, which is too bad. She's a very intense person. Perhaps too intense. A few students tried getting her to socialize over the past few weeks but with no success. The SDR work requires her undivided attention. She can't be distracted, she told a few students. Instructors are giving her additional work that no one else seems to have.

Odd, but not impossible.

She says that the surveillance teams are following her home. When she drives to the training center in the morning, they are always there too. They follow her on weekends. They followed her when she went to visit her parents. They just won't leave her alone. She is really getting tired of it. How much longer will she have to put up with this?

Finally, someone takes an instructor aside.

"Um, it's none of my business, and I don't want to get anyone in trouble, but have you had a conversation with Sharon recently?" the student asks.

"No, I haven't. Why?" the instructor replies.

"Maybe you should have lunch together," the helpful student says. "Take her somewhere and just ask her how training is going."

"Is there a problem?" the instructor asks, clearly not interested in random lunches with students.

"I'll let you decide," is all the student will say.

The instructor stops by Sharon's office and has a quick chat. He rides along on her next SDR run. They talk some more. He then stops in to see Steve. Sharon is removed from the program the following day.

She has some mental-health issues that preclude her from participating any further. Speculation runs wild about what must have happened with the instructor, but no one has any real information. Finally, the issue is addressed in the classroom.

Several female students had become close friends with Sharon, but that must now end. We are to have no further contact with her for any reason. For the record, if she calls us, we are to report it immediately.

Off the record we learn that Sharon does indeed have some psychological troubles—the type that should have come up during her entrance examinations but for some reason did not. The problem now is her commercial cover. That entity will now be shut down; the cover is "blown." Every student who is also using this firm must be reassigned to a new cover company.

Of course, the companies only exist on paper. No real firm is being dismantled. But the logistics and expense of shutting down a commercial cover firm are enormous. The name must be put on a disavowed list to ensure the Agency never uses it again or publicly acknowledges it. The other students must tell friends and family that ABC Consulting went through a management change, lost its funding, or some other manufactured excuse and they have taken a new job with DEF Incorporated. The telephone operators in the cover office's call center must be briefed on what has happened and what they are to say if someone calls for Sharon or any other student who had been using the same cover firm. Even after the fact, cover must be preserved. Otherwise the illusion simply falls apart.

For the students who have lost fictional jobs in their fictional company, they will have a nearly identical job in the new firm. It's expensive and difficult to destroy a company, even if it doesn't really exist. But that's only part of the problem. We can make the company disappear, but what about the students whom Sharon knows? They are very real and pretty happy with the names given to them at birth. Fortunately, the Agency has learned from past mistakes.

In previous years, someone like Sharon might simply be shown the door. Several high-profile incidents taught the Agency that it's better to take care of people rather than abandon them. We are informed that Sharon's security clearance has been canceled. She is no longer a CIA employee. That can't be helped. But she has been given a job in another government agency and seems to like it. She will receive two years of counseling with an outside psychotherapist, courtesy of the U.S. government. She will be fine. She will be a productive member of government, serving the war on terrorism—just as she wanted.

But she will never be a spy.

Hoofing It
December 2002

I N THE CLASSROOM Steve calls us to attention with the announcement that he has good news and bad news. The good news is that we no longer have to worry about driving around on SDRs. The bad news is that we are now conducting SDRs on foot. We practice walking surveillance during the coldest weather the area has seen in nearly thirty years.

The sleet, snow, and incredibly cold temperatures make even a quick exercise unbearable. The temperatures dip into the teens, the wind chills dropping it into single digits. At night it drops even more. Cover stops are less an opportunity to spot surveillance than an opportunity to warm up before returning to the cold. But our vulnerabilities aren't limited to the weather.

Vehicle surveillance offers a certain amount of protection from prying eyes. People are so accustomed to seeing fellow commuters talk on cell phones, shave, apply makeup, or read the newspaper, everyone allows a reasonable amount of privacy when in a car. For us this is a crutch. Maps and timing sheets are easy to pull out for reference and immediately stash under doors, seats, or a dashboard. These tasks are not so easy when on foot and bundled up to beat the elements.

Foot surveillance is also tough on the surveillance teams. In this post-9/11 world, the average Washington DC citizen is on guard, especially after the recent sniper attacks. A few citizens, noticing a student being followed or surveillance teams wearing earpieces, have interfered with a few of our exercises. More and more of the Washington region is designated a denied area to prevent students (and instructors) from being detained.

Once again Daryll and I are assigned to the same geographic area. This time we will be walking around in Bethesda, Maryland, which is across the Potomac River from Washington DC. Joining us on our frosty excursions are Mary and Big Mike. Mary doesn't seem to mind the cold. She's from out West, where frigid temperatures are common. Big Mike is more like me, raised in the South and accustomed to temperate climates. If it's less than sixty degrees, I'm freezing.

Cathy flies up from Tampa for the weekend. Unfortunately I have a veritable mountain of work to do and can't waste away the hours in the apartment with her. I explain this to her on the phone, but she can't be deterred. She is coming up, bad weather or not, weekend work or not; at least we will be together.

I pick Cathy up at the airport, but she is no longer my wife. She is a ten-year-old little girl fascinated by the white stuff outside the airport windows. Walking through the terminal to baggage claim, she keeps bumping into me. She is staring outside the window at the snow, which starts coming down again at sunset. There's eight or nine inches of snow on the ground when we walk outside. After slowly crawling through Alexandria traffic to our apartment, I sling her bag over my arm and walk toward the warm light of the building. Cathy suddenly sidesteps the sidewalk and yells, "Catch!"

I scramble to catch her purse before it hits the ground.

Cathy holds out both arms, falls backward onto the ground, and is immediately swallowed up by a foot of loosely packed snow. I can't believe my wife is making snow angels.

I let her get the full experience while standing there laughing at the passersby who give her odd looks. Mothers hurry their children along the sidewalk away from us. They smile nervously, especially after I explain that this is her first Virginia snow. I'm glad she's enjoying it. Snow is a rare treat for Florida natives. I hope the positive disposition lasts when she's around the stuff for longer than a weekend.

We were told it was OK for our spouses to join us on practice runs and foot casing, but not our graded exercises. So, bright and early the next morning, Cathy joins me for the full experience of conducting a foot surveillance drill. We leave the apartment for the long ride out to the training center. Once there, we switch cars to my government-issued rental. I drive us across the bridge into Maryland and park downtown. From now on, it's all on foot.

Bethesda is laid out perfectly for foot surveillance. There are long sight-lines for spotting people and lots of kitschy stores to justify ducking into if you need to check behind you. Right now, we are looking into any and every store that simply has heat.

It doesn't take long for Cathy to lose her love of the snow. What was an amusing entertainment the night before is now an irritating drain on energy and mood. After three hours we are cold, and the wind whips snow around us wherever we walk. I paced out a route yesterday I want to try, so we run to the Metro stop in Bethesda to get started.

The snow, now coming down as sleet, interferes with our timing from the start. It slows us down and makes traffic impossible to anticipate when crossing the street. We are required to follow posted street signs and traffic signals at all times. With cars moving as slowly as they are, traffic lights run longer, people ignore them, and pedestrians are simply moving targets.

Because we are not entering any of the stores I had cased, we are absolutely frigid. I don't want to enter the store today with a story and risk running into the same clerk on Monday when a surveillance officer might potentially follow me in. Better to walk in with fresh conversation than have a shopkeeper yell, "Hey, buddy, good to see you again!" That's called "heating up the area." We don't like areas to be hot in the figurative sense, though in the physical sense that would be welcome right now.

So we walk and walk and walk. The sleet turns back into snow and falls much harder now. It's not the light, fluffy snow featured on television

Christmas specials. This is wet and sticks like glue. We are soaked, cold, and irritable. If we are this miserable, everyone else must be as well. I pull out my cell phone and call Daryll. Yep. He's out here and more than ready for a break. I call Mary. Count her in too. Mary calls Big Mike, who can't wait to get out of this mess. We decide to meet at what we euphemistically call our local field office.

La Madeleine is a French bakery and coffee-shop chain with a number of stores in the area. Daryll and I have used it several times as a cover stop. We have also tried about everything on the menu, since the shops are open extended hours when we are casing for early morning and late evening SDR runs. We use it to dry out our maps, to recalculate our timing for cover stops, and to have a place to just sit down and rest.

Daryll arrives first and sets up in a semiprivate room toward the back. Most important, he gets a room with a fireplace. Cathy and I come in. Cathy gives him a quick peck on the cheek hello and sits directly on the hearth. We down our first cup of coffee before Big Mike and Mary arrive, accompanied by Mary's husband, Duane.

After a small amount of socializing we get down to work. Spreading our maps out, we compare the neighborhoods that each person has covered. Mary has a good cut-through that forces surveillance to move in close, making them easier to spot. Daryll found a back entrance to the Metro stop that will force surveillance to scramble and catch up. I know a great choke point at the top of a staircase to a retail office building that gives me a great view from an elevated position. We are working quietly for about an hour, making notes and comparing routes. It doesn't take long for Cathy and Duane to become bored.

They stand behind us socializing and discussing the downfalls of being a spouse in the Agency. Suddenly a young woman walks over and asks if we are new to the area.

"Why do you think we are new?" Duane asks.

"Because you are poring over those maps. They look pretty marked up. Are you looking for apartments in this weather too?"

"No," Daryll replies, standing up to block her view of the table. "Are you looking for a place around here?"

She sizes him up. She's apparently attracted to dopey jocks with dimples. Go figure.

"Yes, I'm moving here for a new job. I can't decide whether to get a big apartment in Bethesda away from everything or get a smaller place over in Dupont Circle. It seems that's where all the action is," she says.

Mary moves around the table to shift the young woman's line of sight away from our materials. I flip the maps over so she can't see them. Routes are in yellow, cover stops have a big red X, abort stops (if we detect surveillance) are marked in blue, timing numbers are listed on the margins, and our meeting areas are highlighted in green. Not exactly apartment-hunting guides. There are no Agency logos anywhere, and we have not put any spook-specific markings on them, but to any random observer they would look odd.

Her name is Abby. She is a newly graduated PhD and has taken a job with the FDA. Cathy gives her some sisterly advice about a single woman living alone in a big city. Mary throws in her two cents' worth too. When they start talking about the quality of the young men in the area, Duane considers walking back out into the cold.

Abby takes a real shine to Daryll. We cannot turn our maps back over and get back to work while she is here, nor can we divvy everything up and go back out into the snow without being obvious. Cathy keeps pulling her away to give the four of us privacy, but it's only a temporary effect. She keeps coming back under the pretense of asking another question about the area—such as "Does Daryll have a girlfriend?"

"If you guys aren't new to the area, what's with all the maps?" she asks.

Cathy looks over her shoulder at us and explains it was a corporate team-building exercise. The company had not expected the weather to be so bad, but the winning team gets a nice trip to a Florida resort as grand prize.

"Wow! That's great," Abby said. "Who do you think Daryll would take if they win?"

* * *

DESPITE THE "FUN" of our foot-surveillance training, we are required to attend a briefing in a nice warm classroom the following week. A makeup artist from the Agency's disguise office conducts the briefing. We will be fitted for disguises to use at the Farm in the next phase of training. Now *this* feels like the CIA!

With the help of a PowerPoint presentation she explains what disguise craft is used for, what it can do, and what it cannot. Many students in the class have read the book on Agency disguise craft by former chief of the disguise bureau Tony Mendez. She shows us side-by-side examples of what the disguise artists can do given enough time, money, and access to the face they need to alter. The range and depth of their skills is extraordinary. Every student is assigned a day and time to be fitted for his or her disguise.

We are fitted for basic wigs and glasses. Men also get stick-on facial hair. That's it. It is one hell of a letdown. We try on our "disguises" and can't believe how outrageous we look. It's embarrassing. But the disguise equipment is outrageous for a reason. There is a method to this madness.

A successful disguise lets you become someone else. You can no longer be yourself; therefore you are comfortable being the new character you are playing. But the instructors don't want us comfortable yet. Our disguises are outrageous to remind us that we are in character, to make us uncomfortable, to remind us we are not this other person. We have to remember that we are professional intelligence officers trying to manipulate someone into giving away secrets. They don't want us to be able to blend in with the crowd. It's a successful tactic.

We look like the cast of the musical *Hair*.

Our reprieve from footwork is short-lived. Before the end of the week we are back out in the snow and slush, trying to look innocent as we watch behind us. But we also learn that we aren't the only people being followed.

For example, Nicole was walking on an SDR through Old Town Alexandria, only a few blocks away from my apartment, earlier this week. She needs a double-back—a place she can walk into then double back on anyone following her without being obvious. It can't look like a trap, or the instructors will not accept it. Double-backs are the coup de grâce of surveillance tradecraft. If we find one, it should be jealously guarded like the family jewels.

Nicole chose a cut-through in the Torpedo Factory along the waterfront. Now used by artisans as studio space, it no longer produces munitions. Instead, there is a variety of paintings, sculptures, and other artists' products for sale. There's a great deal of foot traffic and multiple entrances along several levels. For surveillance to follow, they are going to have to be close by or risk losing her in the crowd.

She enters the factory and sees a man in his midtwenties. Blond, medium build, slight mustache and goatee, wearing a blue foul-weather jacket and jeans. He has the telltale signal of a curled wire running up his neck to an earpiece. He's wired for private radio communications. He gives her a look and keeps going. She sees him again inside the building, looking at paintings.

She sees him more than once, which would normally be enough to call him a surveillant, but there is not enough distance between the two sightings. He might be legitimately shopping and listening to music on a Walkman radio. To find out for sure what his status is, she decides to use her special double-back. She is walking toward the exit when the shouting starts.

A black man in an expensive suit stops just inside the doorway next to a jewelry shop. Facing him is an older white man with sunglasses and a Green Bay Packers jacket. Both men are in each other's faces. Both have their hands dug into their pockets. Both have a wire sticking out of their ears.

Nicole stops a few feet away, realizing too late there is no other way out of the factory without turning around to Mr. Goatee. She can't move forward because the two men are in the doorway, still shouting at each other.

"Who the hell are you?"

"Who the hell are *you*?"

"Show me some identification."

"Show me *your* identification."

There are gestures and name-calling, but each keeps his hand in his pocket. That's when it dawns on her. Those aren't mittens in there. These guys are armed.

A dark gray sedan skids to a stop on the street behind them. Two more men jump out. Nicole backs away a few steps, no longer concerned with getting dinged by surveillance for an illegitimate double-back. She'll risk taking the hit on paper rather than getting hit by one of these yahoos. That's when Mr. Goatee runs past her and confronts them all.

"What the hell is going on here?" he asks.

Both men turn toward him.

Nicole sees a young woman across the room. Like Nicole, she is startled, wanting to leave through the door but anxious about interrupting a potentially violent altercation. She stands frozen, watching the three men challenge one another as a crowd gathers. Finally, Mr. Goatee pulls out his identification.

Then the black gentleman in the suit does the same. Followed by the guy in the Packers jacket. All three are carrying U.S. government credentials.

Nicole *was* under surveillance. But the young Mr. Goatee was not following her. He was following someone else, and not someone in our class. Nicole had unknowingly stumbled across a surveillance exercise by the Department of Defense in the same area. At the same time, the Secret Service was providing security for an unidentified family Christmas shopping in the Torpedo Factory. The three surveillance bubbles collided on the Old Town waterfront.

The CIA isn't the only agency adding to its ranks in the post-9/11 world.

DURING ANOTHER WELL-DESERVED BREAK from the outside temperatures a psychologist briefs us on how to assess someone for manipulation purposes. Assessments are a hot topic right now. Everyone and their sister is interested in forensic psychology. Crime-scene shows are among the top-rated dramas on television. Audiences love the bizarre and complicated themes that are so easily tied together in a sixty-minute episode. In the real world, however, things rarely work this way. The sniper case in October is a prime example.

How far off had the profile been? Law-enforcement officials were searching for a white van when the suspects were actually driving a blue Chevy Caprice. Police were looking for a white male, twenty-five to thirty-five years old—a loner with a longtime knowledge of the Washington DC area. Instead, the culprits were two black men from Washington State, one of whom was acting as mentor and surrogate father to the other. How could the profile have been so misguided? Some of it was random chance, some faulty analysis, and some was bad adjudication of the available evidence. It's indicative of how astray assessments can be when outside influences interfere with tradecraft.

What authorities did not have in October and still do not have now is the shooters' motives. What was the motivation to kill innocent people pumping gas, standing on street corners, or walking out of stores? When assessing a target for recruitment, we must be able to answer questions about their motivation.

There are two ways to recruit someone, whether it's for espionage, college basketball, or a Fortune 500 firm. You can play to a person's *vulnerabilities* or to their *motivations*. Your success will be largely dependent on which one you pick.

The psychologist advises us that if we go with vulnerabilities, we'd better hope the person recruited is never in a position to get even. Recruiting through vulnerabilities typically leads to the target digging into a defensive position. You are attacking his or her weak spot, an area where he may be exposed to criticism or even open attack. This is hardly going to put them in a positive frame of mind for our purposes. If they can't trust you, why would they work for you? This is why blackmail is never used as a recruiting method, despite its oft-repeated use in Hollywood spy features.

Recruiting with motivation is more successful. You are playing to a person's natural tendency to talk himself into something if it appears to be a positive move for him. Playing to his sense of accomplishment, his sense of purpose, or to a cause he feels strongly about. Get the ball started, and the recruitee will often take over the recruitment process on his own.

Every person has ambitions, some unmet goals or aspirations. Get the recruit talking about them and play to those ambitions. People have an established picture of themselves. But if they do something inconsistent with their prescribed character, if they break a law or engage in morally reprehensible behavior, they can often rationalize it internally. It's how pedophiles, rapists, and Washington-area snipers sleep at night. Rationalizing their behavior either puts the blame on someone else (parents, boss, society in general) or allows the person to believe that this behavior, despite its obvious deviance in the short term, is in their best interest down the road.

"Motivations change over time," the psychologist says. "Look at yourselves. You guys have almost nothing in common except you were all motivated by the attacks on 9/11. That's why you are here. Be aware, motivations change over time. We grabbed you while we could. If we waited a year or two before bringing you into the Agency, many of you would not be here at all."

She's got a point. I can see a good third of the class not being here if given a longer time line.

"You must understand an agent's motivations in the context of their values and beliefs. Do you think it's easy for Afghan fighters to volunteer to speak with us? Trust me, it isn't. You have to appreciate the complexities of their world. Forget your own motivations. You can't put yourself in their shoes, so don't try. People outside the U.S. live such a completely different life, you can't begin to project yourself into it. You must let them *tell* you about it."

She walks to the chalkboard; VALUES + BELIEFS = BEHAVIOR.

"This is what you want to keep in mind. Know your target's motivations in the context of their values and beliefs. Values govern behavior as motivation for our actions. Beliefs are how we express our values to ourselves and others, how we operate them. When you can understand this concept, how all of these things work together, you will understand human behavior better than ninety percent of the world's population."

Her brief is impressive. The motivators that had brought Class 11 together—patriotism, ideology, security, revenge, or intrigue—are how the Agency coaxed us into accepting the strange lifestyle we now lead. Our behaviors are radically different from those we had only a few months ago. We must connect to the core values and beliefs an agent possesses if we are to make them work for us. We must understand the agent's history, the background fundamentals of how they became who they are in order to understand their motivations.

We practice our new profiling and assessment knowledge in an exercise that re-creates a common enough problem: refugees. We will interview people who are seeking asylum in the United States.

Our office takes on the role of overseas government facility. My would-be refugee comes into the conference room and explains his situation. He is a Kurd, and living in Iraq is too dangerous for him. He helped America during the Gulf War and is now persecuted. He's afraid that if he doesn't leave the country, he and his family will be in danger.

I take down his name and relevant contact information. I make some notes outlining the U.S. Army units he allegedly worked with ten years ago, other Americans he knows and can describe, and his travel habits in the area. I note that he is a biochemist and his wife's father is a Ba'ath Party official. Throughout the interview I am polite, quiet, and unassuming. I sit with my shoes flat on the floor, hands folded in my lap unless I am jotting down notes. I don't interrupt and only ask questions when I see an obvious break in the conversation. At the end of our time I promise him that the U.S. government will consider his request, and I will contact him again sometime in the next week. I usher him out the front door.

Later in the afternoon the instructor comes back.

"Hi, Tom," he says through my door. "Have you got a minute?"

"Sure," I reply. "Come in."

He comes in and closes the door. My evaluation is in his hand.

"Tom, I want to chat about the exercise. How did you think it went?"

"I thought it was OK. You made a legitimate case for your claim. I think I asked all the relevant questions. I wrote it all up. Why? Did I leave something out?"

"No, not at all," he said as he pulls Daryll's chair around to face me. "Your write-up was dead on the money. Everything documented, clearly differentiating what I said from what was your commentary on it. Good questions, good follow-up on obvious areas of interest, and a plan to re-contact later. The write-up was textbook."

I nod. "So why are you here?"

"Well, Tom, to be honest, I couldn't figure out *your* motivation."

I frown. "Come again?"

"What were you thinking when you were interviewing me?"

"I was thinking I was a diplomat. I've never met one, but that's my impression of what they are like. Pretty staid, serious people. Joe Friday in a wrinkled suit. I thought that's what they would be like."

"It's exactly what they're like. It was really annoying," he said.

"What? Why? Wasn't that the point?"

"No! We are not diplomats. We don't sit back with our feet firmly planted and take notes. We jump into the fire. You were sitting there like a bump on a log. Everything in your report"—he's shaking it at me—"is dead on, but your bedside manner was terrible."

"Bedside manner?" I ask.

"Recruitment is a seduction. You've got to play the game in that context. Think of it that way. I would never want to come back to talk to you. I'm trying to avoid being killed by coming to the CIA. Instead, I'm bored to death by the conversation."

"So, I need to be more aggressive?" I ask.

"You need to be more *you*," he says sharply. "I've seen you the past few months with other instructors. I've seen you in class. You're no wallflower. I walked by the other day, and you were wrestling Daryll, for God's sake. Who does that? He could crush either one of us with a single hand. But there you both were, putting on a show for the hallway. That's what you need to do when you interview someone."

"Put on a show?" I ask.

"Yes! Put on a show. You're an American. Maybe the only American that refugee will see for a while. He or she will walk into the office with a pre-conceived notion about what Americans are like. Back-slapping, bar-fighting, girl-chasing, beer-drinking, and every other stereotype out there. Find out what his perception is and play to it. This guy wants asylum. He wants someone to listen to him, and he may have information he's not even aware is valuable. People want an American to listen to them. Their own governments are either in shambles or so corrupt, the suffering of the masses is irrelevant. Americans can do anything in the eyes of the world—the only remaining superpower. Play to that."

"No more quiet, laid-back government official, huh?" I ask, smiling.

"Keep in mind, every bureaucrat thinks the government will shut down without his constant supervision. When have you ever met a 'minor' government official? They all believe they're Don Rumsfeld or John Ashcroft. A lot of people overseas think the same way. They think every American government employee is sitting on the right hand of the president. If they walk in with the wrong idea of who you are and what you can do for them, it's in your best interest to stretch this notion out until you know if he will remain in-country and may be of some use to us."

He makes perfect sense. I misplayed the role. I learned his motivations but didn't come up with an appropriate way to exploit them.

"Gotcha," I said. "Bag the Clark Kent persona."

"Exactly!" he said. "We need every Superman we can get."

STEVE CALLS the morning brief to order. He's a pretty levelheaded guy, not someone who gets worked up easily. Today something has him energized.

"Is there anything one of you would like to tell the rest of you?" he asks.

A hush falls over the class as everyone stops slurping coffee and exchanges glances. This can only mean one thing. Somebody's in hot water.

"Nobody? Nobody at all?" he asks again, walking toward my table. "I had a call from Sears. Anybody been to Sears recently? Maybe a little Christmas shopping during an SDR run?" His voice is loud, but he's not angry. Then again, we've not done anything to make Steve angry. Not before now anyway.

He turns toward the front of the class and returns to his lectern.

"Daryll! Why don't you tell everyone what you bought at Sears?"

Daryll's head disappears under his hands. I take a full three seconds before whispering, "Oh shit. What happened?"

Daryll's head turns. He's caught off guard. He's shocked. He's . . . smiling?

"Dude! I'm so busted," he whispers back.

"Ladies and gentlemen, we have a bona fide hero in our midst. Allow me to play a message I received on voice mail."

Steve produces a small tape recorder and presses Play. The class hangs on every word coming from the tape recorder.

Daryll's mumbling is unintelligible next to me. He finally pulls his head up but his eyes are shut. Then the inevitable happens.

He receives a standing ovation.

The message Steve got was from a store manager at a nearby shopping mall. Daryll was standing in line combining a little Christmas shopping with his SDR—something we have all done. A strange gasp behind him catches his attention, so he glances over his shoulder while paying for his purchases. A young mother is shaking a baby at arm's length.

The child is purple.

"What's wrong?! What's wrong?!" she shrieks, bursting into tears.

Daryll grabs the baby with one hand and with the other sweeps away everything on the cash register counter. His purchases and store Christmas decorations go crashing onto the floor. The shocked clerk jumps back. Everyone in the area stops and stares.

Daryll flips the child over and slaps him gently on the back. He then lays the little boy on the counter and tries to give him two quick breaths. When that doesn't work, he puts the child back over his arm and slaps him on the back a little harder. A piece of hard candy rockets out of the child's mouth, shattering on the countertop.

The baby takes one look at the huge stranger and his screams immediately ascend to one hundred decibels. Daryll hands the shrieking child back to his mother.

"They made me learn it at work," he stammers to the clerk, slipping away as a crowd gathers around the mother and child.

Store security soon catches him in the mall. Daryll gives the officers his cover company information for their report. He declines an offer to return to the store, where the manager is waiting to thank him personally. He begs off, claiming a pending appointment, but in actuality doesn't want the undue attention such a formal procedure will bring.

He doesn't anticipate the store manager calling the "company" to report what a fine employee they have. The store is making a donation to promote child and infant CPR training for all employees at the mall. This was the message left for Steve, the only real manager we have, that he played for a wretchedly embarrassed Daryll. This is my officemate. No flash, no grandstanding. Just results. Steve and the instructors will applaud their course design, but those who know Daryll know better.

It's a measure of the man, not the training.

DURING A WEEK of relative calm around Langley, we kill time until Christmas break begins. We cannot stay home unless we use vacation, but there is nowhere for us to go in the building. Our interim assignments are long over, and the officers in those areas have real work to do. Babysitting students is not a priority.

Some folks find a quick, temporary-duty assignment or spend some time doing "free" work in the office they eventually want to be assigned to. Others roam the halls or congregate in the cafeteria in between runs to the Agency's library. We haven't had much free time to read as of late. Now is as good a time as any to catch up before we disappear for a while. Big Mike found his own way to pass the time: He let his creative juices flow and created the Class 11 logo.

It's an emblem reflecting our unique status as the 9/11 class. Images of the Pentagon and Twin Towers, though greatly overused, are nevertheless icons of that fateful day. *VICTORIA. PERSEVERANTIA. SACRIFICUM.* The Latin phrases convey our collective reasons for being here. He thought the emblem would make a useful class coin, similar to the unit coins given out by military personnel. We could use it for plaques, awards, and class certificates at the Farm. What he did not expect was the huge outcry against the idea.

Military unit coins are popular both in and out of the armed services. The coins are used for a variety of reasons, including as tokens of affection, awards for exceptional service, or as gestures of admiration. In corporate America we would call them a brand identity, each unit designing a coin that reflects its unique personality. There are a few students who do not understand this concept and want nothing to do with it.

This class is unusual, given that 70 percent of the students have no prior military or government service background. They are unfamiliar with the traditions of the armed forces. Some of the students who were Directorate of Intelligence employees before joining the Clandestine Service have heard about the environment at the Farm. They know each class leaves some sort of token, a reminder of their presence there. But many students look at this practice as egotistical, concerned it sends a message of arrogance to the staff. They cannot be convinced it is designed as much for us as for the Farm.

For a week the e-mails bounce back and forth, several students copying the entire class with their opposition to the idea. After a week of increasingly scornful e-mail, Big Mike decides to let the whole idea drop. It isn't worth the commotion it's creating. It is the only issue with which Class 11 has known any sort of disagreement during the first half of the program.

We are bonding well, which has been comprehensively discussed by the staff. The Directorate of Operations, like any large organization, has its stories and legends. Each class has a distinct flavor, a unique spirit and individual reputation. This reputation identifies the members not only within the Directorate, but also throughout the Agency. Class 4 is known as the party animals. Class 9 is known for outrageous stunts against instructors. Class 11 is also forming a reputation.

The instructors and staff have spoken about us to senior Bush administration officials. We are a serious class, a professional class, and a class where—thus far—nobody has been thrown out for doing something stupid. We are a competitive class. But instead of backstabbing one another to get ahead, we watch out for one another. Our inclination to socialize captures this attribute after one specific incident.

A group goes out to a local watering hole one night. Terry is standing at the bar enjoying a drink when she is groped by a patron. Half the bar descends on him with punches, kicks, and a couple of solid body slams. The poor bastard is lucky to escape with his life. Some students have to be restrained to prevent him from being seriously injured. How could he know this random woman would have a dozen or so big brothers standing around with nothing better to do than stomp the life out of him before ordering another round?

The incident turns into the hallmark of our reputation. Despite our record-setting number, we are not a random assortment of strangers. Class 11 is a family. These ties, this glue that holds the group together, will become more important during the second phase of training. December marks the end of Phase 1. We are halfway through the program, halfway to being case officers. We have a huge party to celebrate the milestone. But the celebration is offset by a touch of sadness.

Two students are released. Everyone is stunned. Both young men are popular students—one a prior soldier and the other an internal CIA transfer. They are told they would not proceed to the next phase of training. It was the staff's opinion that the pair should instead find "other opportunities." None of us has any idea what to say or how to help. For reasons that are never made clear, some hidden decision maker has determined that these two must go.

Over the next two weeks, prior to the Christmas holiday, the released students interview for jobs within the Agency. But, unable to secure a new position within the required period of time, they leave government employment completely. It's quite a blow. We've come to know one another's wives, husbands, children, and pets. The possibility we would not all finish together has not occurred to anyone.

During this same time a couple of other students voluntarily drop out of the program due to existing medical problems. They believe that the long hours, constant stress, and inability to safely handle routine medical needs could aggravate their conditions. Most of us recognize this thin bit of subterfuge; their real concern is their potential for affecting the rest of the class. The program at the Farm is heavily dependent on teamwork. Pulling your own weight is critical and occasionally pulling someone else's is often crucial. If you physically cannot do so, your entire team can be compromised.

Despite our pleas, impassioned by the involuntary and unexplained loss of two previous students, we are unable to dissuade them. Unwilling to be a burden or to limit the class in any way, they resign from the program, but remain with the Clandestine Service in support positions that allow them to address their medical issues. We are sad to see them go, but happy they will be there when we return.

As the year's end nears, Dottie herds us into the auditorium and encourages us to take time off. She instructs us to prep our families for the upcoming prolonged absence. She goes over lists of items we will need with us, as well as items we must leave behind. No cell phones or free e-mail services like Yahoo! or Hotmail. They can be traced back, destroying our cover. The Farm is like a convent or monastery. We are to be cut off from the outside world.

She also encourages us to work out, doing push-ups, sit-ups, and running in preparation for the Special Operations Training Course fitness test. Though it is cold and miserable outside, there are exercise facilities in headquarters and there is a large gym at the Farm. Get into them and use them regularly, she advises us. We should plan to pass the first physical fitness test if at all possible. By the time the subsequent tests are given, we will be too busy to train. Earlier is definitely better. Are there any questions?

Smilin' Brian raises his hand. This is his nickname for reasons that are obvious when you meet him; the guy is always in a good mood.

"Yes, I have one. When will we decide what assignment we want?" he asks.

"That will be worked on at the Farm. During the last phase of training, you will be allowed to make a wish list, ranked in order of preference. Your first-, second-, and third-choice assignments," she replies.

Brian nods his agreement but isn't finished yet.

"Yes, so I've been told. But I understand Class 10 did the same thing, yet they were all appropriated into one-year assignments in the Counter Terrorism Center. No matter what job they picked or which offices selected them, they have all been hijacked to CTC. Should we expect the same thing?" he asks.

It's a question we are all asking ourselves. We met with some Class 10 students the week before, and they gave us some kindly advice about surviving at the Farm. But Class 10's sage advice did not include how to evade the fallout when Dottie explodes.

"IF YOU DON'T LIKE IT, YOU CAN QUIT!" she roars. "This is no different than any large corporation. I can hire you for one thing and move you to another position as I see fit. This isn't Disneyland, people. The needs of the Agency come first. We will send you wherever we want. If you don't like it, find a job elsewhere. Any other questions?"

Nope.

Rick and I are sitting together along with a few other former corporate hacks. Rick sums up our collective assessment: "You hire me to be an accountant, and you put me in marketing," Rick says. "Yeah, you can move me. Three things will happen: I'll quit. Your shareholders will get wind of how you are pissing away money and people, so they'll fire you. I'll come back and take the job I originally signed on for. What a bitch." We nod our agreement. Then somebody notices Brian.

He's not smiling now.

Poor guy. Shock and bewilderment are plastered on his face. He's reeling from the stage-based detonation. But his question was perfectly legitimate. We're tired, and the prolonged absences from family haven't even started yet. How do we make it through six more months if it has already been so difficult? A few people are already on the fence about staying with the training. Dottie's tirade only brings morale down even more. If the reward is not getting the job you want, the job you were promised, many people are second-guessing coming into the Agency at all.

ALONE IN MY APARTMENT, I too second-guess my career choice. It's not only my own future that must be considered. There's Cathy's, too. She has had to adjust to doing a lot of things alone. Then there's the steep learning curve of being an Agency spouse. The bureaucracy, restrictions, and rules involved in every part of our lives are beginning to take a toll. Our conversations are demonstrably clipped. Edgy. To top it off, I am about to become even more distant. In just a couple of weeks I will depart for the Farm.

There I will be cut off even more than I have been over the past six months. The workload is alleged to be insane. We will be watched and evaluated nonstop for the duration of our stay. Only when we take weekend leave to return to Washington does the scrutiny take a break. We'll have a fish-eye view of what life is like inside the aquarium, with instructors walking around us, tapping on our glass, and deciding what to do with us next.

We've lost five people, wrecked half a dozen cars, and averaged twenty thousand miles on the road and two hundred miles by foot. All of this was to get us up to a minimum standard. What will it be like down there? Is it everything alluded to in the movies? Was the reverence paid to it within the halls of Langley truly earned? Can we justify being away from home and family, essentially disappearing for a few months?

Is it worth the price we must pay?

As I sit back and reflect on the past six months, I recall other moments of doubt. But now, halfway through the program, I look at Big Mike's banished Class 11 emblem lying on my coffee table.

VICTORIA. PERSEVERANTIA. SACRIFICUM.

Victory. Perseverance. Sacrifice.

Only now do I notice the other text in the emblem.

ANSWERING THE CALL.

Now I remember why we're here.

Dead Drops and Signal Sites
January 2003

THE CHRISTMAS HOLIDAY had been a refreshing break from the cold, the program, and the separation from Cathy. She had been busy preparing our home for sale, and we completed the closing as the year came to an end. The distress of selling a home was an emotional exclamation point to the commitment of the life we have embraced. This dedication is further tested as Class 11 departs for the most nebulous training program in the entire federal government.

We've been given no time lines, no phone numbers or points of contact, only a day and time to show up. We were provided with a list of items to bring: clothes, toiletries, and a very limited number of personal items such as photos. Isolation and immersion; we will be cut off from our normal world in order to more fully accept the simulated world created for us. But until we arrive, it remains an obscurity, cloaked in secrecy and silence. We don't know what we don't know.

On January 6 I report to headquarters and park my car in the West parking lot, the most distant patch of asphalt on the compound. I trudge through the snow to the main building and stop by security to get a placard for my car. When leaving vehicles inside the perimeter for this long we are required to give security personnel our contact information and a car key in case they need to move the vehicle in our absence. I drop a key with the desk officer and take out a five-by-seven card to place on the dash with my relevant information. I make a quick run downstairs for coffee and stop in to say good-bye to a few people in the Counter Terrorism Center. Walking down the corridors I link up with other students who are engaging in the same ritual.

Everyone is on edge. Nervous. Moody. We are halfway through the course, now going to one of the most infamous places in the United States. It ranks up there with the White House, Area 51, and the NORAD Command Center. We toggle between dread and breathless anticipation.

As we pass through the parking lot, a car door opens. Ahmed steps out into the midday air.

"What's up, kiddies? Are we ready to play?" he asks.

Sara's eyes roll back.

"What's got you in such a good mood?" I ask.

"What's not to love?" he asks. "We are getting paid to sneak around and do stuff that other people have to do for free."

"And not go to jail for," I remind him.

"Yeah," Sara teases, "maybe this time you won't get arrested and you can ride back in the buses with us!" A thinly veiled reference to his arrest during the border-crossing exercise.

"Nice! I'll try to forget that when I become Director of Central Intelligence," Ahmed retorts.

We pull the luggage out of our cars and load up the bus. When the driver comes over to wave us in, I stop to take one last look at the main building.

CIA headquarters is a typical government structure in many ways. It is concrete and steel, with wide pedestrian channels and well-lit parking areas. At the same time, it has a certain shadowy mystique. You know you aren't looking at the offices of the Commerce Department or the Department of Agriculture. You know that whatever goes on inside this fortress must be special. The main compound is actually two buildings in one.

The Original Headquarters Building was constructed in the mid-1950s. A cafeteria jutting out of the backside became a conduit for the add-on, the New Headquarters Building, or NHB, which was added in 1991. The NHB reflects everything that the United States has learned about designing a facility to thwart electronic intrusion. It is essentially a building under glass. The entire seven-story structure is housed under a permanent layer of thick glass plates. The design is unlike any other in the U.S. government.

The glass defeats laser microphones, which can pick up the minute vibrations of window glass that come from conversations going on near them. It also defeats overhead peeking by satellites or low-flying aircraft equipped with other listening devices. Any and all of these methods have been employed by foreign intelligence services operating in the Washington area. Standing in the parking lot with my friends and classmates clambering to get past me and escape the cold, I am silently appreciative of the privilege of being here.

Once inside the bus, we settle in for the three-hour ride to the Farm. I sit down with Jed and Daryll. Hal and Betsy are across the aisle from us. When the bus exits the compound and turns onto the highway, a tiny voice sings softly. Building in volume, the words become more and more distinguishable. Additional voices jump in as people recognize the tune and the irony. Hal, ever the cutup, slowly builds to a screaming crescendo before we pass the Pentagon: *"We're off to see the Wizard, the wonderful Wizard of Oz!"*

It has the desired effect. Everyone relaxes. We laugh, throw a Frisbee, and yes, even sing for much of the way down there. The banter bounces back and forth on the bus, a caravan of craziness barreling down the interstate to a facility that, according to official U.S. government position, does not exist. That its location and details have been repeated in books, magazines, and movies is irrelevant. As far as the government is concerned, we are disappearing into thin air—a terrestrial Bermuda Triangle in the Virginia countryside.

Exiting the highway a little more than three hours later, the bus takes a long oblique turn down a secondary road. Daryll pokes me in the side and points out the window. A high fence with five strands of razor wire whizzes by the window. Beyond the fence, a blacktop road evens out the rolling hills and disappears ahead of and behind us. Whatever we are next to, it's big.

Every one hundred yards, a large white sign appears on the fence. In big red letters it ambiguously identifies the site: USG FACILITY. NO TRESPASSING. DEADLY FORCE IS AUTHORIZED.

A dark-green Humvee with two armed men is parked behind the fence at the intersection with another road that leads to the interior of the property. The men are holding Heckler & Koch MP-5 submachine guns. There is a larger weapon mounted on the top of the Humvee. They watch the bus go by. One of the armed men speaks into a radio.

Looking ahead of and behind us, I note out loud that we are the only traffic on the road. Daryll turns back to where Hal is staring wide-eyed out the window.

"Toto, I don't think we're in Kansas anymore," he quips.

ENTERING THROUGH THE FRONT GATES of the Farm is roughly akin to going through Checkpoint Charlie, which separated East and West Germany for so many years. There is an enormous amount of fencing and barricades. There are heavily armed personnel with canine and electronic sniffers. There are cameras and sensor arrays of every sort. A guard speaks to the bus driver while another steps into the bus to confirm that we are who we purport to be, then steps back to wave us through.

As our caravan rumbles past the pine trees, every student's face is pressed to a window. Instructors note the sudden silence and look back at us, smirking and whispering to one another. Despite our efforts, there is very little to see from the roads.

When we leave the entry gate there is a small handful of buildings nearby, but no signage. The scenery is asphalt and trees for five minutes before cresting over a small hill. Below us, another clump of buildings emerges from the green blanket. There are signs for the fire hall, a post office, a recreation building, a gas pump, and a convenience store. We slow down but rumble past the entire scene, continuing deeper into the base. Up ahead is a fork in the road.

We see a neighborhood in the distance off to the right. An actual neighborhood. It appears to be a good size—at least a dozen homes visible. They are nice houses too, not the old government block homes commonly seen around government facilities. A sign designates this area as restricted to residents only. We take the left fork, passing a sign that reads SPECIAL TRAINING AREA.

After another mile or so we enter a compound of about a dozen buildings. Pulling all the buses into a large parking lot, instructors confer for a moment before giving us our orders. We are to get out of the buses quickly, take all of our belongings other than luggage with us, and go inside the building marked ADMINISTRATION. Our luggage will be offloaded while we are inside, and we can pick it up on the way out.

Daryll and I step off the bus. Nicole and Annie follow close behind.

I hear Hal's voice behind me. "Holy shit!"

He points at a building across the street. It has an overbearing presence—a concrete and steel fortress. Strong and imposing, it dares us to walk near. A circular driveway snakes through a tall concrete fence with iron spikes. A sign posted on the street clearly designates its purpose: a CIA station overseas. An American flag is raised to the top of the flagpole.

Hal brushes past us to the administration building. Daryll and I both hear his quiet comment: "God, I love this job."

Inside the auditorium the walls are a bizarre peach color, something I've never seen in any other theater environment anywhere. A gentleman walks up to the podium and introduces himself.

"Good afternoon. My name is Tom, and I will be your host for the next six months. Welcome to the Farm."

Behind us, several rows of staff and instructors applaud. Taking a hint, we all join in.

"Congratulations on making it this far. I am so sick of hearing about how wonderful you guys are that I am ready to throw you out of here right now. The HR staff at Langley, instructors in the training center, and even from your interim supervisors I heard nothing but glowing remarks. I only hope what I have been told is true. Again, welcome and try to relax. Get comfortable. Your first exam isn't until tomorrow."

Silence.

"That's a joke."

More silence.

Tom cranes his neck toward the back of the room. "Did you tell them to leave their sense of humor in D.C.?"

Instructors yell yes, no, and several variations on each.

Tom turns his attention back to us. "Seriously, everyone relax. This is the easiest part of your entire stay. What I want to do is walk you through some dos and don'ts and get you settled into your rooms. OK?"

Dottie, now referred to by students as the Wicked Witch of the West (parking lot), parks her broom and hands out white envelopes. Each one has a student's name on it.

"These are your room assignments. You can look them over while we talk. I'd appreciate you paying more attention to me, however. I've got what you really want to know."

The theater screen lights up behind him. It's a satellite photo of the area.

"This is the Farm. In addition to your training course, there are a number of other classes going on here as well. These are all CIA projects and classes. Everyone here is cleared and is cognizant of what this facility is for. There are two exceptions to this. One, there are construction workers. They don't know what this is and don't need to. Secondly, the children in the camp. Most of the older ones have been told by their parents they are Agency officers and are living at the Farm. Those too young for that conversation just think they are on a government facility. Do *not* tell any of the children you encounter you are CIA or that this is the Farm. You should not interact with them much, since you will not be venturing into the residential areas without permission. Everyone nod that you understand."

We nod.

"Good. Nobody goes into residential areas until told. I'm glad that's out of the way. By way of background, the SPOs—the Special Police Officers—you encountered when you came through the gates, they can be your best friends or they can cause you irreparable harm. I suggest you try the former. This is one of the most secure pieces of real estate in the United States. The SPOs are armed, as I'm sure you noticed, and quite authorized to protect this facility and its inhabitants. If you screw up, if you ignore the posted speed limits, giving you a ticket is the nicest thing they will do. If they ask me to throw you out of the program . . . well, I've never refused them before. You sound like nice people, so I'm sure that won't happen, but be aware the SPOs aren't campus cops. They are licensed officers like you would see anywhere in the U.S. When it comes to speed, they can be sticklers. There are two hundred children here and over two thousand deer. That's way too many innocent lives that can wander into traffic on a dark and stormy night when you are tired from your SDR runs."

A groan ripples through the crowd. More SDRs.

"Oh, you don't like that? Get used to them, folks. You are to start casing the area this weekend. Most of your SDRs will be for operational activities done offsite. Others will be onsite and require you to get through roadblocks safely. Some of you will find that interesting."

Snickers escape from the back of the room.

"While you are here you will train as if you are already on station in the mythical country of Winnebago. The local citizens are anti-American, but don't take that too literally. The constabulary is looking for spooks because Winnebago has enemies. Terrorism is a real threat here. There are roadblocks. Searches and seizures that are not legal in the U.S. are commonplace here. This is not a democracy."

He flashes an evil, wicked smile.

"Do we understand each other? Winnebago is a world unto itself. When you leave the classroom every day, even when still on the training compound, you are fair game for the Winnebago authorities to watch, follow, arrest, detain, or incarcerate. Are we clear?"

Everyone nods.

"OK. Let's start from the beginning. This base is somewhere around ten thousand acres. It was previously a military facility, as I'm sure you are aware. We are here." He aims a laser pointer on the diagram now splashed across the screen behind him. Beginning with the administration building we are currently sitting in, he shows us the locations of the cafeteria, the gym, the indoor pool, and the parking area for the rental cars assigned to us. There are two residential dormitory buildings. One is located down the road. Building two is located next door to the administration building we are sitting in and immediately next to the Student Recreation Building, or SRB.

He also points out the instruction building where we will attend classes and have offices. There are eight students in each office, with a mentor for every two students. Any problems we have go through the mentor first, the office chief second, the course chairman third, then to Tom.

"Oh, yeah. Let me go back to the SRB for the moment. I understand this class likes to socialize. The Student Recreation Building is just that; it's for students. Staff and instructors go there from time to time for a beer, but it is mainly for your use. It looks and feels like any sports bar out in the world, but there is no waitstaff, only a bartender. You mess it up, you clean it up. If the bartender reports any trouble, well, the SRB is not a part of the curriculum. That means we don't have to keep the building open if we don't want to. Understand?"

We understand.

"Good. Before I send you out to get your gear, I need to introduce you to some students that will be joining you. Will the DOD students please stand up?"

Nearby, a couple dozen people stand up. It's mostly men, though there are a few women. None are in military uniforms, and their civilian clothing looks brand-new, as if recently purchased.

"These are officers from the Department of Defense. We made a strategic decision a few years back to train DOD personnel alongside Agency intelligence officers. Except for one or two specialized classes that differentiate you legally, you will enjoy all of your training together. There are no special privileges for either group. I suggest you learn to get along. Rapidly."

By now we all have our envelopes. They contain our residential and office assignments.

"You have the next two hours off. Go get your gear, square away your rooms, and call home if you need to. Assure them you have not disappeared into a black hole. That actually happens later. I will see you in the training building at five p.m. tonight."

With that, we head out to retrieve our luggage and find our dormitory rooms. I'm in room 15 at the end of the hall, the second floor of Residence Two. On the downside I am right next to a staircase leading to the outside. On the upside, my room and the one immediately below it are closer to the SRB than anyone else's at the Farm. You find your positives where you can.

With only a roller garment bag it doesn't take me long to unpack. We are told we can bring other items back with us after returning to Washington this weekend. Since I've got some time to kill, I decide to wander around a bit.

It really isn't bad. For a former military base, it's actually quite impressive. I spend a couple of hours creeping around both residential buildings. My building is the better of the two as far as amenities go. Everyone in Residence Two has televisions in their rooms. Residence One's residents do not. There is only a central television downstairs in the common area. It's very similar to the dormitories in college and reflective of the typical demographic the Agency hires for the Clandestine Service.

There is a small kitchenette downstairs with a refrigerator and a microwave. A bank of soda and candy machines is nearby. There are small common areas upstairs and down, but the noise level is much higher than the other residential building due to construction next door. Another dormitory is going up. More and more Americans will be gracing this expansive campus to participate in the war on terrorism.

My room is very much like one you'd find in any large chain hotel suite: a double bed, a table with two chairs, a bed stand with alarm clock, and a low dresser spanning one wall. The television sits on the dresser. There's a closet by the door and a reasonably good-size bathroom. This is home for the next six months.

The cafeteria looks like it is gearing up for the dinner hour, so I walk to the gym. It's a very expansive facility. Weights, treadmills, bicycles, exercise machines, and a full-size basketball court. Connected via a hallway is an Olympic-size swimming pool. That will be nice. I have been slipping on my exercise regimen recently. The first SOTC physical is not far off. I need to hit this every day if I can.

I wander back out on the street. There is a shuttered pistol range on the other side of the new residential construction. Even on the Farm, suburban sprawl is a problem. The real estate goes for miles in every direction, but most of the property is trees—a buffer from the outside world to guarantee our isolation. This is our little corner of the world, hidden away from external influences and distractions.

A little before 5:00 p.m. I wander into the instruction building. I am assigned to East group again, but Daryll, Mary, and Big Mike are in the West group. There has been a real mixing of the students. Someone said that this is to force us out of our comfort areas, to keep us from relying on the student ties we made while training in Washington. Add in the new DOD students, and we are, in effect, starting all over again.

Walking into the East Side auditorium, there are name placards at each chair. Assigned seating. I wander down the aisle stairs one by one, reading names. All the way down to the bottom. Damn! I'm in the front row, second from the end.

Students continue to pour in from every door. Instructors and staff also enter and line the rear wall of the auditorium. Eventually, everyone is seated. A staff officer walks up to the podium and introduces himself as if he were at an Alcoholics Anonymous meeting. His head is bowed.

"Hello. My name is John, and I'm a spy."

Several students recognize the monotone expression and play along.

"Hi, John."

"OK," he says playfully, "some of you recognize that a bit too well. Maybe our vetting process isn't so good anymore. Listen, folks, I am your East Side course chairman. I want to try and get you out of here as quickly as possible and let you see your offices before we head to dinner. You are sitting next to your officemates. Counting off every eight students, you can figure out who your seven new best friends are going to be."

The guy on my left is student 006, on my right is student 008. What are the odds I would be student 007? Can this get any more surreal? I decide it's probably best not to play it up. There are two women and five men assigned with me. I met Terry earlier in the program, and I recognize the other woman as being a friend of Daryll's, though I don't know her name. Two of the guys I recognize but don't know well. The other two are strangers. They must be DOD students.

"Listen up, folks. Time is our enemy at this point. We have a lot of instruction to give you and damned little time to do it in. That means you must be good time managers. Especially toward the end of the course, the material starts moving real quickly. You can't get behind, you can't avoid evening and weekend work, and you absolutely must be in your seats on time for classes at eight a.m. We cannot keep to our schedule if we get a late start every day. So please, please, please! Set the alarm clocks an hour early if you must, but make sure you are here. Coffee or cokes are fine, but let's not get any three-course meals in here."

We are limited to two specified areas of the building, the common areas around the auditorium and the student office areas. We cannot go into staff or instructor areas without an escort. Anyone who tells us otherwise is wrong. Make them come greet us at the door and walk us to their office and then walk us back out. They know the rules, but we can expect them to test us. There are some other restricted areas of the base too.

We are not to drive aimlessly around. In addition to the residential areas there is a deployment area for the surveillance teams. Anyone found back there is automatically assumed to be looking for surveillance cars to get their type, color, and license plates. That's an automatic out for the course, no discussion. If we are driving around and run into red barrier gates blocking the road we should turn around and go back the way we came. This is a live-fire base. There are several gun ranges as well as facilities for testing firearms and "kinetic toys." We have no reason to be there, so don't be.

Once we are dismissed to go to our offices, we meet the other students and our office mentors. Our office chief's name is Mark. Though he has spent most of his time in the Middle East, he is enjoying his second tour as an instructor at the Farm. Assisting Mark in his first tour as a Farm instructor is Dwight, who had been an instructor at the training center in Washington. It was nice to see an instructor's face that we knew and liked. At the opposite end of the table is Gavin. Gavin is a military instructor who is the mentor for the two DOD students in our class. Gavin did little more than grunt his hello. Finally, Mark introduces Al.

Al is a retired officer with thirty years' experience, now back as a contract instructor for the Agency. He will be my mentor, my conduit into the management structure of the Farm. Any request goes through Al. Any condemnation of my actions comes from him. He is at once an advisor, counselor, teacher, sage, and guru while I am here. We shake hands and exchange a few pleasantries. Then it's time to meet my officemates.

Terry is seated at the corner of the large conference table in the center of the room and starts off the introductions, followed by Daryll's friend Wendy. I recognize one guy named Dave who graduated from West Point, so everyone calls him West Point Dave. I also recognize a guy named Matt who was a college football coach only a couple of months ago. Then there is the guy who'd been next to me at the lecture hall, Mike. He had been a Wall Street broker, so everyone called him Wall Street Mike. That rounds out the six Agency officers.

Across the table two Army officers eye us cautiously. Adam is a Hawaiian-born counterintelligence officer from the West Coast. Travis is a Special

Forces soldier. This is the sum total of their self-congratulatory introduction. I guess they won't be breaking their arms by patting their own backs.

This is my team.

TRUE TO HIS WORD, John starts at 8:00 a.m. sharp the next morning. This will be our routine, John opening each new day of training with a quick, fifteen-minute briefing on relevant news, updates or changes to the schedule, and any heads-up items we need to know for future projects. At 8:15 he hands the class over to the first instructor of the day. Today's course is on impersonal communications.

The title means precisely what it says. Communicating with a foreign-based asset without actually seeing the person face-to-face. An instructor named Roy pulls out a remote control and flicks on a movie clip to make his point.

The grainy image is actor Sean Penn walking down the street. It's a clip from the movie *The Falcon and the Snowman,* a 1985 film based on Robert Lindsey's book chronicling Christopher Boyce and Daulton Lee's sale of secrets to the Soviets. Roy notes Christopher Boyce, played by Timothy Hutton in the film, is due to be released next month after twenty-five years in prison. We watch Penn (as Daulton Lee) walk up to a mailbox and strike it with a piece of white chalk before throwing his mail in and walking away.

Turning the video off, the instructor asks what we think of the scene.

"Isn't he defacing federal property?" Hal asks.

"Good point," Roy replies. "Not exactly what I was looking for, though. What else?"

"He's walking around in broad daylight. There are a dozen people around. Isn't leaving a mark like that, even an innocuous one, kind of foolish if everyone and their sister is walking by?" Sara chimes in.

"Precisely!" Roy says. "He's got the right idea. In the film, and in reality, his Soviet handlers gave him good lessons, but they didn't follow through. Chalk marks are a fine recognition signal. So are stickers, paint, and a half dozen other things, but you don't want to do them in front of an audience. You know the difference between clandestine and covert, yes?"

We nod, recalling our first day of class with Steve.

"Good. Do you recognize this was neither of those? This was 1985 when the film was made. The actual incidents were much earlier. Given today's high degree of observation by the common citizen, anyone doing something like this might as well hold out a bullhorn and announce to the street 'I'm leaving a signal for someone.' It's too obvious, too high-profile. There's good traffic through the area, but too many people are walking around when he does his operational act."

For the next three hours Roy shows us how to make our chalk marks less obtrusive. We have to do them without stopping or otherwise drawing attention to ourselves. Unlike Sean Penn's clear marking on the side of a mailbox, we want to place marks in less obvious places. Still where they can be seen, but not where they are out in plain sight.

Signals like this are used in impersonal communications to indicate that a dead drop has been made. Dead drops can be anything. Documents, money, film, instructions, a passport, any relatively small item or items a case officer and agent need to exchange.

Signal sites are prearranged, typically along a route both parties can reasonably take without drawing attention. If I as a case officer leave a signal for my agent, a chalk mark on a mailbox or a remote street corner, he can drive by it on his way home and see that there is something for him to pick up. Maybe some instructions or his monthly compensation. He will then drive to a prearranged location and collect the dead drop.

When he has collected the materials left for him, the entire procedure is reversed. He can put something in the dead drop for me and leave a similar signal along my route to the office or home. I will then know it is time to go pick up my dead drop and either retrieve the materials he left me, or simply remove them from the area before a random passerby finds them.

Dead drop containers take a number of different forms. Devices intended for real operational use are crafted in the Agency's fabrication laboratory by a full-time staff. The range and depth of their skills is awesome. The laboratory analyzes the operating environment in which the agent and case officer are working and custom builds each piece. These environments can vary wildly. Extremes in temperature and humidity must be accounted for. The duration onsite must be evaluated. The time available to service the dead drop is also a big consideration. An animal carcass can't lie around on a street for six weeks, but a fake handrail on a staircase probably can last that long.

Complicated lock mechanisms aren't much good if the agent must service the drop while walking. Case officers are first trained in how to complete such actions while not drawing attention. In the field we are also responsible for training our agent to do this. That can be risky. The entire reason for using impersonal communications is so the case officer and the agent are never seen together at any time.

Our first exercise is an impersonal communications exchange, but it's not local. We are bused in small groups to another city a couple of hours away. There we are driven around by a couple of instructors and given a quick bit of area familiarization. Follow-up casing is up to us. We must find signal sites for our agent and ourselves, as well as somewhere for a dead drop. Oh yes—we are to manufacture our dead-drop object on our own.

This is going to be fun.

The following day Wall Street Mike and I go to the fabrications shop and look over the options for our dead drop. Whatever method we choose must be fitting to the location where it will be dropped. Changing the location means changing the dead-drop device. At the end of the day we are mentally drained. The adrenaline rush of being here has crashed.

It's like being in classrooms in Washington, only we don't know one another as well as we knew our officemates there. We meander to the office and mull over what to do next.

It's snowing and sleeting outside. Not the best time for casing. Terry looks over an area map. Mike is reading some class notes. Wendy is on the computer. Nobody is talking. Nobody is even making eye contact. For a bunch of type-A personalities, it's awfully quiet. Leave it to the infantry to come up with a solution.

Adam decides what we really need is to sit around and have a few beers, talk, and get to know one another a bit. He goes to his room and comes back with a twelve-pack of beer. We haven't gotten the fourth bottle out of the pack when two SPOs barge in.

"There's no drinking in the instruction building. The beer needs to go back to the residences or to the SRB. Otherwise, it has to come with us," the shorter of the two says.

I start to make a joke, but it's apparent they aren't kidding. Everyone looks around a moment, hesitant to do anything. Adam quickly grabs up the bottles and puts them back in the container. Having torn off the handles to open the carton, he is fumbling to hold the twelve-pack together when he stops at the doorway.

"Anyone for a beer at the SRB?"

We have work to do. There is map casing to be done, office supplies to be found, and document templates for agent meetings that need to be made.

"No, thanks," I say. "I'm gonna stay here and get some stuff done."

Wendy, Mike, Dave, and Terry all decide to stay too. Travis goes with Adam.

Matt, who we affectionately refer to as Coach, is staring above our heads. He hasn't said a word. His eyes are transfixed on the camera mounted to the wall.

"Guys. They are watching the offices right now. They are freaking watching us right now! Do you believe this shit? Our first week, and they are already watching us, busting our chops over some measly beer?"

I look over my shoulder at the camera, letting my gaze move to the microphone dropping a foot out of the ceiling and into our midst. Every conversation, every exercise, and every time we are at our desks, Big Brother is watching. Critiquing. Judging.

I'm still staring at the camera when I speak again. "I think Coach has a point, guys. We'll be under the microscope for six months. I don't think one twelve-pack is going to set us back too far. We may as well score some points for office unity while we can."

They all look up at the camera. Everyone then closes up desks, shuts down computers, and follows a hundred yards behind Adam and Travis on our way to the SRB. On the way, safe on the open streets, we discuss the SPOs' rapid entry after Adam's beer run.

"That was pretty quick," Wall Street Mike says. "I wonder how they watch every office at the same time."

"Probably circulates among them," I guess. "When something looks interesting, they stop switching and watch one office for a while. I guess when Adam walked in with a twelve-pack, it must have been the most interesting thing they had going on."

"I still can't believe it," Coach fumes. "I'm pissed! You just don't expect a couple of storm troopers to come crashing in on your first week. I nearly broke out in assholes and shit all over myself."

Wall Street Mike gives me a funny look, and I glance behind him to see how Terry and Wendy react. I see cringing. Apparently they aren't used to collegiate locker-room vocabulary. He's going to have to watch that. If the powers that be react to beer in the classroom, they are probably going to react to bad language too.

The profanity police may be listening.

VIRGINIA LIVING MAGAZINE has a special cover feature this month. It's on Virginia's extensive history with espionage. It even has pictures. We find this highly amusing, and many of us buy single copies of the magazine in nearby bookstores on SDR runs the first few days it is out. There are several articles inside; one of the more interesting ones is on the new movie *The Recruit.*

Starring Al Pacino and Colin Farrell, the film has had buzz building for months. At the Farm, which plays such a pivotal role in the film that the original title was, in fact, *The Farm,* the excitement is almost tangible. It isn't just instructors and staff. The cleaning crews, the cafeteria staff, the audio/video technicians—everyone is counting down the days until the movie opens locally. This excitement, however, is tinged with a measure of anxiety and bad memories.

The Recruit is loosely based on one of the worst security breaches in the history of the CIA. Harold J. Nicholson, an officer with extensive field experience, sold out the Agency and its employees to the Soviet Union. Nicholson was born November 17, 1950, in Woodburn, Oregon, and entered the CIA on October 20, 1980. He specialized in Russia and the Soviet Bloc, chasing this target set in several overseas assignments.

He worked in Manila from 1982 to 1985; Bangkok from 1985 to 1987; Tokyo from 1987 to 1989. In 1990 Nicholson was a station chief—the highest-ranking spy in a country—in Bucharest, Romania. Then he served as Deputy Chief of Station in Kuala Lumpur from 1992 to 1994. In each of these countries, he targeted Russian intelligence officers for recruitment, until the roles were inexplicably reversed. In the summer of 1994, as his tour was drawing to a close, Nicholson was recruited by the Sluzhba Vneshney Razvedki Rossii (SVRR), the successor to the KGB.

In 1994 Nicholson accepted a two-year assignment as an instructor at the Farm. From there he was sent to Langley, where with his GS-15 rank he was a branch chief for the Counter Terrorism Center. For the two and a half years that he was a Soviet agent, Nicholson received three hundred thousand dollars.

Many of the Farm's instructors and staff knew Nicholson well and liked him. He visited their homes for holidays, birthday parties, and sporting events. He was around their children and taken into confidence with their personal problems, professional doubts, and concerns about the U.S. government's position on world affairs. Everything told to him was now in the hands of the Russians.

In addition to hundreds of classified analytical papers, national assessments, and operations reports, Nicholson sold the name of every student who came through the Farm during his tenure. Among the many procedures put into place as a result is we do not use our real last names here. We have been given false ones to keep the instructors from knowing who we really are.

Course Chairman John addresses the movie's impending release in his morning brief.

"OK, folks. I'm not going to waste my time and breath telling you to not go see *The Recruit.* I'm only asking that you don't make it a spectacle. There are a lot of you. Break up into small groups. Blend in with the crowds. Don't draw attention to yourselves. Don't go en masse. And don't correct the material on the screen in the theater."

From the back of the room a voice pipes in. "And don't acknowledge any of the instructors you see there."

Wall Street Mike, West Point Dave, Adam, and I check out the film and have a few drinks afterward to talk it over. We find an Uno's Chicago Pizzeria on the way back to the Farm, and sit inside for an hour or so. We discuss the storyline, the marginal acting by several key people, and the somewhat lackluster ending. We hope our stay at the Farm turns out much better. The conversation soon turns to another drama-filled event, the first "spouses function" back in Washington.

A number of wives and husbands decided to get together regularly to help one another deal with the separation problems. Loneliness—especially in weather like this—and having no one else to care for young children is a real burden for spouses. Something the Agency is still perfecting: how to deal with students with families.

I wish Cathy were there to attend the Spouses Night. When we get back on base, I return to my room and give her a call. It's still early. She should be up. She answers the phone at my mother-in-law's house.

"So, how's the first week?" Cathy asks.

"It's got its ups and downs. I'm freezing to death. Everyone keeps saying this is an unusually bad winter. They can kiss my ass. Every winter up here is probably like this."

"Have you seen much of Daryll or any of the other guys?"

"Yeah, Daryll said to tell you hi. And Jed's wife wanted you to call her."

"OK. So are you learning much?" she asks.

We go back and forth for about fifteen minutes. How is your week? How's your mom? Are you settled in there yet? How's the job going? When do you think I should move up to Washington? The exchange a husband and wife would be expected to have under the circumstances. Then someone coughs. A male someone.

"Who was that?" Cathy asks.

I was about to ask her the same thing, when I realize who it is. Or, more correctly, *what* it is. Big Brother listens as well as he watches.

I know I can't bullshit her on this. She'll know I'm lying. Better to come clean than attempt anything else.

"The phones here are monitored. It comes with the territory. Three square meals a day, a clean room, and chaperones on the phone. Nice, huh?"

"You're serious?"

"Yep. You should see the camera in the office. Another in the classroom. I have a new respect for the critters at the Florida Aquarium. It's a tough way to live."

"Oh my God! You have to be kidding me. Those assholes don't have anything better to do than listen in on conversations with your wife?"

"I'm sure calling them assholes will do my career a lot of good, honey. I don't pretend to like it. I just have to live with it. Keep in mind, this place isn't designed for midthirties professionals. They're accustomed to young, unmarried soldiers who might be a bit loose-lipped on the phone. Just forget they are there."

I didn't buy that statement, and I sure as hell didn't sell it.

"Is there a camera in your room, too?" she asks.

That came up during the briefing yesterday. John swore on his mother's grave there aren't cameras in our dorm rooms. I remember hearing about a student a few years back who was convinced there were. He tore the place apart looking for it. Every piece of furniture. Every fixture. When he disassembled the smoke detector, it triggered the alarm. A dozen SPOs and several staff members responded to find his room destroyed and the smoke detector in bite-size pieces. He is no longer with the Agency.

"No, there's no camera in my room"—my eyes slowly scan the walls—"just a monitoring system for the phones. It's no big deal."

I'm a big fat liar.

We finish our conversation, and I tell her I love her. I go to bed but can't sleep. I know there aren't cameras in the walls, and even if there are, there's not much I can do about them. But I'm not too concerned with the cameras. I'm still thinking about *The Recruit*.

It was a mediocre movie, but I recognize a lot of similarities with the real Farm. The psychological games. The harassment. The uncertainty over what happens next, next week, and next month. We are plebes, neophytes who must earn the right to be here. I can't think of any management-training program that even vaguely resembles this. Monitored phones. Cameras in the offices. Perhaps youngsters require a certain measure of control. But it seems the Agency is stuck in yesteryear. We are not recent college grads, prone to silliness. We are professionals. Most of us have families, responsibilities. I wonder if the original training model from the early 1960s is still being used today?

Certainly our rivals have learned a few new tricks. Enemies of the United States are no longer limited to state actors. The concept of borders and sovereignty do not apply when dealing with a transnational foe such as al-Qaeda.

The influence of NGOs and powerful individual citizens sways world financial markets and political activity. As P. J. Singer points out in his book *Corporate Warriors,* Osama Bin Laden privatized terrorism. Instead of a nation-state funding fanaticism, the fanatic funded a nation-state (Afghanistan) to provide him refuge. As an individual he fluently intermingles explosives and expressions, depending on the message he wants to convey. His perception-management acumen is unmatched. He understands that perception can alter the course of society faster and more efficiently than military power. I am troubled that our training has not yet addressed this increasingly dangerous trend.

* * *

ONE ADVANTAGE that Bin Laden has over previous enemies of the United States is a well-designed and highly committed network. Simply stated, networks are the patterns of social relations among individuals based on their preferences and characteristics. People know one another through relationships based on a particular context. Being a corporate lawyer is a context, as is being a soldier, a chef, or an elementary schoolteacher. So is being a terrorist. A context can also be geographic in nature. I'm a Floridian, which is a context. All the various matrices of our daily lives from jobs to hobbies to familial responsibilities put us into distinct contexts. From these contexts we surround ourselves with like-minded individuals.

Bin Laden's network allows him to put a lot of obstacles in our way as we attempt to track him down. Given their blind obedience to him, his followers create a highly effective means of distancing him from the consequences of his actions, regardless of how brutal these actions may be. Though many of them carry guns and openly take to the streets in demonstrations, far too many more do not. They are hidden away from easy public view. They're not on the nightly news and not on the diplomatic circuit. They are the financiers, couriers, and a host of other logisticians who are as important as his shooters. Perhaps they're more important. Without this behind-the-scenes support, there is no money for propaganda and no weapons to march through the streets with. Though a network is a formidable shield, it can also be used as a direct pathway to the leadership when attacked in a logical and methodical way.

Everyone of a certain age is familiar with the game Six Degrees of Kevin Bacon. It's a silly time killer developed by three college friends as a variation on the Six Degrees of Separation theory, which states that everyone on earth can be connected by linking up the people they all know. For instance Elvis Presley's childhood friend Joe (1) grew up and married Helen (2) whose cousin Lynn (3) is the financial advisor for Ben (4) whose sister Lisa (5) was my college roommate's (6) prom date in high school. There. I am now directly linked to the King. We're practically brothers.

Mathematically speaking, the six degrees of separation does link everyone on earth. It's actually fewer than six. The overwhelming majority of earthlings can be linked, particularly in geographic terms, in about four links. The human race is a multitude of repeatedly overlapping social, economic, ethnic, religious, geographic, and political networks. This interlinking among members means wildly different people are actually closely linked. What does this have to do with espionage?

When we are recruiting potential agents, we have to operate in situations that are awkwardly unfamiliar. We may stand out from others in the room. Betsy, for instance is a young, white female of Western European ancestry. She can target and assess a wide variety of people. But how will she recruit them? She can't recruit without getting close, and that can be difficult.

How will she get close to a sixty-year-old Chinese diplomat in the Washington DC area, for instance? She could "accidentally" meet him at a diplomatic party, but that's about it. He's not likely to enjoy the same things Betsy does. His age, position, and profile will be radically different from hers. How, then, does she target such a person? It may be that she can't, but it doesn't mean she packs up and goes home.

Every prominent person in the world is encircled—in fact, even more so with the prominent people. Sometimes this circle is family and friends. Eventually it includes staff, assistants, and other people with whom the prominent person interacts. The relationships among them are based on a particular context—in this case, the diplomat's support and professional staff. They embody a spectrum of ages, backgrounds, hobbies, interests, and aspirations. Instead of one target, there are now dozens of potential targets, many of whom are likely to be easier to make initial contact with. The odds of finding someone with whom a case officer has more in common is much, much higher. What we must do is map out the people around the target.

We begin by mapping ourselves. How many people are in our immediate circle? How many are arm's length from us for whatever reason? Family, very close friends, colleagues we have a special bond with, they are our immediate circle. Outside them is a larger circle with a larger group of people with whom we have less contact or less tight bonds. Beyond that another circle, perhaps an occasional class of friends, more acquaintances than friends, but still people with whom we keep a tie professionally or personally. From a targeting standpoint, we have hit the mother lode.

Instead of a single sixty-year-old Chinese diplomat, Betsy would now have his family, friends, staff, colleagues, and professional contacts as potential targets. Any one of them could provide unwitting assistance in learning more about him through an innocent conversation. Maybe, just maybe, somewhere in these concentric rings of people is someone willing to turn on him for money. All she has to do is find this person and begin the game.

I'VE LOST MY MIND. Who ever heard of holding a physical fitness test at 6:00 a.m. when it's twenty-two degrees outside? I'm too old for this.

I have managed to squeak out a few trips to the gym this week, but nothing that could even remotely be called "training." I haven't even tried to run the two-mile course down Range Road. Right now, I just want to get my clothes on and get across the street in time for the test.

Everyone splits into pairs for the push-up and sit-up series. Daryll and I hook up for the duty. He goes first and drops down for his push-ups. In quick order he has them pounded out. I then drop for mine. Neither as many nor as fast as Daryll, but not too shabby either. We reverse positions for him to do his sit-ups. He pounds those out even faster. He's showing off for someone here, but I haven't figured out yet who she is. When we reverse, I get off to a great start, but then feel a familiar pang. My lower back.

I've had trouble with it for years. It tends to go out from time to time, and it is devastating. People who don't have back trouble can never understand just how debilitating it is. You cannot walk, stand, or lie down without pain. I'm fighting through it, but I'm sweating a little too. Everyone is watching the old man (me), and I am slowing down.

I make it past twenty-five with another minute to go, but my back is killing me. I can't stop on the downside of the sit-up. I can only hold at the top. I am at the bottom of number thirty when I manage to haul myself up one more time and hang for a moment at the top. Daryll understands things aren't going well.

"Shake the sticks out of your head, and polish these off. You've still got to run," he says, holding down my ankles.

"Shit! I think I may be hosed. My back is killing me. Why can't the military get with the modern age and do crunches instead of sit-ups?" I gasp.

"Twenty seconds," the timekeeper calls.

"OK. Drop. Let gravity take you down. Use muscle to come back up. Three seconds each. Let's go."

I drop.

I manage to pull up in a timely fashion and succumb to gravity again to get back in position.

Thirty-two.

"Atta-baby. Keep it going," Daryll calls.

"Fifteen seconds."

Thirty-three.

I bang my head on the ground when I drop. Stars are floating in front of my eyes.

"No stopping on the ground," the instructor yells.

I pull my head forward to shut him up, but it takes another two seconds to understand what I've just done. On the plus side I forgot about my back for a moment. I heave up.

Thirty-four.

I ease back down. Big mistake. Stomach muscles are a very unforgiving muscle group. Too many high-fat meals and not enough working out. I pull with my legs, forcing Daryll to lean in over me more.

Thirty-five.

"Ten seconds."

"Hold again for a two count," Daryll says. "Then pound out two really quickly, without even thinking about it."

I drop and immediately try to bounce up. My hands are pulling my neck forward. I strain to fight three opponents at once; gravity, age, and a sedentary lifestyle.

"Five seconds."

My head is pounding from the impact on the gymnasium floor. My back is killing me. To make matters worse, I may well pass wind in Daryll's face at any second. That should foster a lifelong friendship.

"Time!"

I drop back down again, my hands cushioning my head's drop to the floor. I only needed one more. Now I have to do the entire test over again in a few weeks.

"Son of a bitch!" I whisper.

"Dude, that sucks!! You were so close. You almost had it," Daryll offers.

I don't reply because I have rolled over in order to get up. Once I stand I am fully three inches shorter due to my stoop. My lower back is in spasms.

My own fault. I should be in the gym regularly kicking it up to 20 percent more push-ups and sit-ups than I need. I hobble around the gym watching other students go through the same exercises. Like Daryll, most of the military people pound through both tests before they are even fully awake. They start every morning with much more exertion than this. Maybe I should work out with them.

I know better than to sit or lie down. My back will seize up like an unoiled engine and I will be screwed for weeks. I've got to keep moving. That means doing the two-mile run, even in this weather.

We have fifteen minutes to fully warm up and get dressed before going outside. I can't believe I caved on the last sit-up. Wendy, Terry, and Coach find me on the way out, asking how it went.

"I get to do it again," I reply.

All three passed, as have Adam, Mike, Dave, and Travis, who we find outside. Letting them muscle their way into the pack, I move off toward the back, where I won't interfere with anyone else's run. I know I can't make it in the required time. No speed records for me. I'm just trying to get my back to unclench.

* * *

AFTER A COUPLE OF DAYS in a funk over my poor performance in the SOTC test I perk up. Every Sunday afternoon I'm a little happier at being alive and a little sadder at not being at home. I haven't been able to pay as close attention, given my distance from Florida, but every now and again there is a reason to hope: My beloved Tampa Bay Buccaneers are in the Super Bowl for the first time in their twenty-seven-year history.

Cathy is a longtime season ticket holder and provided me blow-by-blow descriptions of all the parties I am missing in Tampa. Super Bowl excitement builds to a feverish pitch. I've met a student named John who was born in Tampa, and we commiserate on our poor luck of being away when the team finally makes it to the big dance. When the appointed hour for the pregame show begins, Tampa John and I hold court in the SRB.

There is quite a crowd. The staff and instructors had held a chili contest earlier in the evening and begin trickling into the SRB with leftovers. From the opening kick to the final tick, Tampa John and I don't budge from our perch dead center in front of the television. We watch the postgame show and the presentation of the Lombardi trophy. When Head Coach John Gruden lifts that sacred chalice over his head, we jump up and down with a million loyal fans at home in Tampa. But none in the SRB.

We are alone.

The SRB has cleared out, leaving the two Buccaneer diehards behind to clean and close up. Everyone left the mess for us due to the Bucs' win. We clean up the paper napkins and plastic plates, throw out the empty beer bottles, and straighten the tables. On our way out we kill the lights and lock the door.

For twenty-seven years Buccaneers fans have dreamed of this day. Cathy had mailed me a couple of cigars from Ybor City—the historical Cuban enclave east of Tampa's downtown—to commemorate the Bucs making it to the finals. We cut the tips, light up, and walk out into a foot of freshly fallen snow, reveling in our victory.

Reaching the end of the sidewalk we stop. Neither of us knows what to say. Tampa, no doubt, borders on anarchy. Our team's greatest victory, and we are unable to share it with families or friends celebrating eight hundred miles south. Instead, we are sequestered away in a government training facility that officially doesn't exist.

We shake hands, shake our heads, and turn in opposite directions to our respective dorm rooms, trails of cigar smoke following behind. In many ways, this is indicative of life overseas.

Case officers cannot reveal their real college or hometown professional teams. They cannot have photos from their wedding or their children's school pictures in their homes when undercover as unattached, unmarried sales executives or government secretaries.

They must adhere to their cover identities. Distance from our own histories, motivations, and beliefs is part of the sacrifice. A part of you is stripped away, or perhaps more correctly stated, hidden away. Just as we will use any small part of an agent's personality to pry into their motivations, groups like al-Qaeda will use similar tactics to pry open our cover identities. In a world of rich fanatics, Internet searches, and suicide bombers, the stakes are too high to be careless.

Celebrations and personal triumphs are internalized. Pride, delight, and even sorrow on the most mundane of everyday topics reveal too much to our enemies. Case officers must be dispassionate, focused only on the job, the agent, and the information.

Everything else is secondary.

A Death in Afghanistan
February 2003

SINCE I FAILED the running portion of the SOTC test I am trying to be better about working out. Our class and casing time tends to take up most every waking hour. The only way to get it done is to pirate some of my non-waking time. Hence the early hour. It's 5:30 a.m. At least I won't be alone.

Coach is here for me every day. The man is a machine. I'm still not where I can run the full course nonstop, but I'm building my strength up quite nicely. I prefer to be in the gym on a treadmill like a sane person, but Coach says no way. Treadmills are crutches; you don't get the same workout. Besides, distance isn't my problem. Temperature is.

It is still in the single digits outside. Nine degrees on the thermometer hanging next to my window. I'm going running in nine-degree weather. This is insane.

I roll out of bed and brush my teeth, noting the clock creeping toward six. Coach is a stickler for punctuality. He'll be out there tapping his foot if I'm even a moment late. I grab socks, hat, sweatpants, and a thick pullover before tying my shoes and going downstairs. One last breath of warm air before I step outside.

Coach is not standing across the street, but I do see him coming down the road from Residence One. He's got company. Mike is running with him. They aren't coming off an earlier run. They are still building speed. I can tell because there aren't mountains of water vapor from heavy breathing. They arrive at Residence Two while I'm still stretching.

"OK, guys. Tell me this," says Coach. "What happens if I just tell an instructor to blow it out his ass? What can they really do to me?"

Mike rolls his eyes. "Well, Coach, I think they'd probably toss you out of the program and most likely out of the Agency. Why?"

Coach had a run-in with an instructor. Nothing serious—not yet anyway—but it's bugging him. As we trot down Range Road, he gives us the scoop on his problem.

I'm listening, but the heartbeat pounding in my ears interferes. This is crazy. How the hell do these guys not feel how freaking cold it is out here? I can't feel my feet. The cold moves right through both pairs of socks and deep into the bones of my feet. I'm going to have pneumonia the entire time I'm here.

"What do you think, Tom?"

I have no idea. I'm not even sure he's speaking English. I can't think straight when I'm freezing to death. I'm funny that way. All I can think of is getting down Range Road and back without dropping in my tracks. With the snow, they'd never find me before the spring thaw.

"Well, Coach, I think it's a little early to be pissing anyone off right now. Don't you think you should tone it down a bit?"

"What? Are you shitting me? That miserable asshole . . ." I've no cognition of what he said. My brain is frozen. I only remember I must keep moving. Coach is on one side of me, and Mike is on the other. It's the only way I can run in a straight line. Keep moving, keep moving, keep moving. I've never been this cold in my life.

After we get back to Residence Two, I haul myself into my room and step into the shower fully clothed. I don't care. As long as I am warm, everything else is secondary. Leaning my head against the tile walls I feel the warm water cascade down. My first coherent thought is that Mike and Coach are maniacs. This is a hell of a way to start a Saturday.

Because every classroom, exercise room, and meeting room in the training building is wired, the technical engineer is one of the most powerful people in our little world. He controls the information we see. He controls what channels our television gets, when we can watch them, and when we can view one another's exercises on a closed-circuit monitor. What we didn't know until today was that this person could also turn the television on or off remotely.

Everyone jumps in his or her chair when the televisions pop on. We are in the office at 8:00 a.m. and have a full schedule of casing and SDR planning for next week's exercises. A breaking news story is not part of our schedule. But like the rest of the country we are shocked by the images we see. The space shuttle *Columbia* is returning to earth, but something has gone horribly wrong.

An instructor walks in when he notices our television is on, and he watches the coverage with us. He says spy satellites monitor shuttle operations during liftoff and return—a practice that has quietly occurred for years. We wonder if they captured *Columbia*'s reentry and can explain what we're seeing. We watch silently as hope continues to fade. Some take it especially hard.

It was easy to recognize the pilots in the class. Pilots are a unique fraternity. At first, they don't perceive everyone's concerned looks and sympathetic distance. Class 11 has civilian and military pilots, fixed wing and rotor, men and women. Being in the class together is a secondary bond to them. Being a pilot will always come first.

After enough hours behind the stick, every pilot has a moment when a mechanical or electrical problem arises and for a split second they sense a meeting with the Almighty may be at hand. Several of them quote for us the pilot's creed, John Gillespie Magee's "High Flight." President Ronald Reagan cited the little-known sonnet after the *Challenger* disaster when he said the astronauts waved good-bye and *slipped the surly bonds of earth . . . and touched the face of God.*

Drew and Kirsten crowd around a television with others, a private bit of counseling from one sky jockey to another. They discuss how the crew might survive if the main cabin remains intact, or perhaps the shuttle can restart an engine and return to space. Maybe it can dock with the International Space Station and await rescue. But they know none of these scenarios will play out. They simply refuse to acknowledge there is nothing to be done.

Pilots believe in pilots, even as the debris trail widens over the Texas prairie.

AT THE CONCLUSION of yet another exercise practicing recruitment techniques, the instructor gives me an evaluation to sign. We can now have a simple conversation as adults rather than as instructor and student, so we chat a while. Unlike most of the Clandestine Service, he doesn't work overseas. The conclusion of our class closes out his second tour at the Farm. He's based in a large U.S. city and is looking forward to returning to his domestic assignment. He encourages me to consider a similar career track. Though not as sexy as the typical overseas work, it has taken on new significance since the 9/11 attacks.

"It's not the same anymore," he says. "Partly because of September 11. I want to get back out and catch bad guys. Plus, my kids aren't having as much fun as they did the last time I was here. We aren't in the haunted house anymore."

Whoa, did I hear that right? "The Farm has a haunted house?" I ask.

"Oh, yeah. Ask around, do some research. The haunted house is famous in the Agency. That's how they get a lot of the instructors with families to come down. Everyone wants to live in the haunted house."

"What makes you say it's haunted?" I inquire.

"Oh, it's not me. Ask anyone who's here. The house is famous," he says again.

He has another exercise to conduct with someone else, so I let it drop. I'm not entirely sure I believe him. Legend and myth are trademarks of the Farm. As it turns out, however, he isn't pulling my leg. The house *is* haunted.

It's a two-story, three-bedroom Cape Cod on a hairpin turn. It sits on the main road running through the base, about three miles past the entrance. I doubt that too many parapsychologists have stopped in lately, but the house's eccentricities are well known: furniture moving when no one's around, strange noises at night, and lights that go on and off randomly.

Before the CIA converted it to a training facility this campus was owned and operated by another government agency. An audit was performed of the site's accounting. Discrepancies were found. Those discrepancies turned out to be fraud. A government officer was accused. He confessed. He'd stolen money and cooked the books to cover it up. His wife was an accomplice. Prosecutors prepared their case. When he learned he was to be arrested he went home, killed his wife, and committed suicide. Authorities found their remains the following day. People have reported strange activity occurring in the home ever since.

When the Agency took over the facility as its training location, the bizarre acts continued. No one has ever been injured or threatened by whatever resides at the home. Teams of CIA technical and countermeasure specialists have measured and monitored every inch of the structure. They can offer no legitimate explanation for the manifestations, including the ones they saw firsthand.

Many Agency employees (who have not been to the Farm), don't believe it or call it a joke or hoax. Others chalk it up as another bit of mystique about the Clandestine Service and summarily dismiss it as such. But when we ask prior residents of the Cape Cod house, they assure us it's real. They too moved in with a healthy portion of skepticism, only to move out as true believers.

These officers have been around the world enough, seen enough ugliness of what man can do to man that a few odd apparitions aren't going to scare them off. They don't conduct tours or draw attention to the house. It's become something of a perk, a point of honor to be assigned to the haunted house, and they prefer to keep the specifics about paranormal activity to themselves.

As corny as it sounds, there was only one conclusion everyone could draw: The house is genuinely occupied by an entity, a spirit, or a poltergeist (depending on their religious predilection). Perhaps the apparitions are the tragic couple who ended their lives here, captivated by the humorous irony of their eternal presence.

A haunted house at a training camp for spooks.

OUR PERSONALITIES are emerging now. It took a couple of weeks to feel one another out, but now we are watching out for our officemates. If someone has trouble finding a drop site or needs help with report writing or just needs an ear to bitch to, we always seem to be there for one another. Other students have told us their offices don't seem to be as well meshed as ours. They keep coming over and hanging out with us to do map work or finalize reporting. I guess we just have a very eclectic group. Every person's strengths seem to cover someone else's weaknesses. The team's advantage is in our diversity.

First in the batting rotation is our single mom, Terry. Terry's gifted writing skills served her well in the first half of training and will likely keep her from too many late nights in the office. She is also the resident worrier. She makes sure the rest of us haven't forgotten anything. Will we have our reports ready on time? Does everyone have an SDR ready for tomorrow? What about the next day? How are you going to befriend that Albanian terrorist next week?

Next is Adam, the court jester. Given any subject matter, Adam can find a way to make a joke out of it to relieve the tension. He works in Army counterintelligence, so I guess a good sense of humor is a necessary part of the job. How he ever attends funerals is beyond me. I can only imagine him up in front of the casket and telling his latest yarn:

> *Three friends from a local congregation were asked, "When you're in your casket, and friends and congregation members are mourning over you, what would you like them to say?"*
>
> *Answer: "Look, he's moving!!"*

Wendy is the trooper. The woman can handle anything. She is fearless. She is committed. She will work until she absolutely drops before she hands in something that is not flawless. Her work ethic is the highest of any person I have ever known. But she is also shy, easily embarrassed, and uncomfortable in the spotlight.

Travis is the realist. He is a loner—not uncommon in Army Special Operations—but able to work very effectively in a team when called upon. He pulls no punches. If he sees bullshit, bullshit is what he calls. He will not interfere with someone's plan, but if that person asks for his help, he gives 150 percent. He is the quiet one in the office, accustomed to relying only on his own skills.

Dave is our deep thinker. A West Point graduate, Dave's technical background makes him a good analyst of problems—someone who can dissect the details very quickly but then reassemble them into a cohesive picture. He is not comfortable taking the lead, though. He's not a pound-the-podium kind of guy. He prefers to keep to himself, forcing us to call him out. If Travis is the tactician, Dave is the strategist.

Coach is our competition junkie. His sports and psychology background give him a considerable advantage in agent meetings. It's frightening. He rips their minds to pieces while making them laugh. He calls someone a son of a bitch, and they want to name their children after him. He is the consummate seller. He could sell anything anywhere. Just as someone is on the brink of walking away, Coach will reach over and pat their elbow, touch their knee, or take them by the arm. The sale is made. Nobody can resist.

Wall Street Mike is the practical one. He doesn't put on airs and is very self-deprecating. If there is anyone in the group who can pull off the "Aw shucks, I didn't really do nothing" routine, it's Mike. He is mischievous; his outward demeanor belies the internal computation his brain is performing. He is quick on his feet and able to adjust his appearance and speech to reflect the needs of the moment.

I am something of a cut-up. I like to joke and laugh. I don't think twice about making a well-timed joke at my officemates' expense, but I'm just as quick to make one at my own as well.

Al, my office mentor, is very quick with puns, and when I engage in some playful back-and-forth with him one day, it only encourages me to do more.

If Al says, "He who casts a friend aside like an old *shoe* is a *heel* without any *sole*," I might reply, "No more *cobbling* around together."

"His friend should *sock* it to him."

It goes on until someone finally interrupts us: "Are you guys done yet?"

Then either he or I will innocently say, "Sorry. A little too *tongue*-in-cheek?"

"I was feeling down in the *mouth*," the other would reply.

And the whole ridiculous bit goes down an entirely different path.

It is a way of having fun and taking advantage of the growing camaraderie in the office. We genuinely like one another. We realize how important our time together is once we understand how easily we can lose someone in this business. The *Columbia* disaster made us think about death, but only in a remote, esoteric way. But death soon came calling a whole lot closer to us, underscoring the life-and-death game of espionage in an age of terrorism.

John didn't need to call us to order the next morning. Word had spread like a California wildfire. Another case officer has died in the war on terrorism. Another recent graduate of the Farm lost in the line of duty.

Helge Boes, who completed training barely a year ago, was killed in Afghanistan yesterday. Helge was fatally injured during a training exercise when a 40-millimeter grenade went off accidentally. This was someone who was literally just here. He was only a couple of classes ahead of us, having joined the Agency in early 2001. Helge was a Harvard Law graduate working in private practice before joining the Agency. He could have made a fortune in the commercial sector, but chose to serve his country instead. He is the eightieth CIA officer to die in the line of duty. Like Mike Spann, he was only thirty-two years old.

There is a profound effect on the staff. Several walk through the training center openly crying. Everyone is drained. The war in Afghanistan has now claimed two young Agency lives. How many more will be lost? How many in Class 11 might also make the ultimate sacrifice?

A memorial service is held at Langley. Most of the instructors plan to attend, so a few meetings are adjusted to allow them time to drive up, pay their respects, and drive back to the Farm by tomorrow. Before leaving, however, Helge's mentor comes to the morning brief to say a few words.

With Helge's picture on the screen behind him, he tells us what a dedicated student Helge had been. Intelligent, articulate, and dedicated to the work. He was not thought to be a "lifer" in the Agency—someone who will spend his entire career here. He would have eventually returned to the private sector where he would, no doubt, have had a monumental impact. He then read Helge's official evaluation, the final assessment students receive before being shipped off into the field.

It feels like the air has been sucked out of the room. The instructor is sobbing when he finishes. Wendy and Terry are crying. Even Coach is subdued, and Adam isn't smiling for the first time since I met him. I've got a lump in my throat. This poor man is pouring his heart out a mere three feet from us. It is difficult to not share his pain. It's impossible to overlook the fact that any of us might be in that same region a few months from now. But the threat from al-Qaeda isn't just overseas.

On Monday, an increased level of terrorist chatter intercepted by U.S. intelligence has led the government to conclude that an attack may be imminent. The national threat level is elevated from yellow to orange. Homeland Security officials issue guidelines on how families should protect themselves in the event of a biochemical attack on Washington DC or New York City. Given the difficulty in responding to an attack with weapons of mass destruction, people may have to fend for themselves for the first forty-eight to seventy-two hours. The public are encouraged to equip themselves with the necessary supplies. A CBS News/*New York Times* poll shows fear of another attack is at the highest level since immediately after the September 11 attacks. The entire Northeast coast goes into a tail-spin.

Hardware stores report massive runs on duct tape, batteries, bottled water, and plastic sheeting. Citizens of the two major cities seem to take the Homeland Security warning at its word. Many people keep their children home from school. Absenteeism is rampant in offices throughout both New York and DC.

On Tuesday the warning appears to be all too real when George Tenet and FBI Director Robert Mueller speak to the Senate Intelligence Committee. One attendee calls it the most sobering national security briefing he has ever heard. Director Mueller finally articulates publicly what has been whispered in government circles for months: Al-Qaeda is inside the United States, and the Bureau doesn't know where. These sleeper cells could be quite literally anywhere.

Director Tenet warns that in addition to the potential of an imminent terrorist attack, the United States also faces a new nuclear arms race, calling it "a new world of proliferation." North Korea, Iraq, Iran, and Libya are trying to acquire nuclear weapons through black markets, which may not be under U.S. scrutiny.

Vice Admiral Lowell Jacoby, head of the Defense Intelligence Agency, rounds out the unholy trilogy by voicing his concerns over attacks with surface-to-air missiles, the so-called Stingers, against civilian airliners. Escalating the uncertainty, Osama Bin Laden releases a tape calling for more attacks. It makes for a very bad week in the intelligence community, even for us newbies still in training. Specifically, it makes it real hard with respect to the families left alone in Washington.

Students with wives, husbands, and children spend a lot of time on the phone, trying to calm rattled nerves. Others simply tell their loved ones to get out. Book a flight or train or simply pack up the car and take an unscheduled vacation. Take unpaid leave if necessary. Get out of Washington and go to the home of a family member or friend in another city.

In the event of an attack, the Farm will be locked down. Nobody will be allowed to leave. The entire facility is equipped to be self-sufficient for an extended period of time. We are not happy about this. But the reality is, there is nothing we can do if there is an attack. Washington will be in gridlock for hours, perhaps a couple of days. We will not be able to get to loved ones to assist. It will make the transportation standstill on September 11 pale in comparison. This time, people will know it's an attack. There's no standing around in a daze. They will run, and God help anyone in the way. It will be unbridled pandemonium, a panic in the streets that has only been seen in movies. This is what has students upset: our families facing this prospect while we sit several hours away, safe from harm.

I call Cathy. She is scheduled to come up for a visit for Valentine's weekend. I suggest that this is not the best weekend to come. I am juggling a growing caseload, preparing thousands of miles of SDRs, and to top it all off some Middle Eastern radicals are threatening to blow up the only home we have. Not the most warm and fuzzy Valentine's Day. She insists she's coming, so I meet her at Reagan Airport as usual.

What is unusual is the amount of snow the region receives. There is a good eight inches of the slop still on the ground. The drive to Langley on Friday is not especially treacherous, but it is nerve-racking. I don't have much experience in this weather. When I finally get into the compound, I see my problems are much worse than I expect.

The snowplows are digging out the parking areas, trying to keep the pavement clean. Even with salt and chemicals to melt the snow, there is still an enormous amount that must be plowed and piled somewhere. Someone has made the decision to pile it in the West parking lot. I can barely find my white car. Snow is piled all the way to the roof. Getting my rental car into the West lot is impossible. I park it in the garage and wave down an SPO making his rounds.

Explaining my problem and pointing toward where I think the car is,

I start walking that way, carrying dirty clothes and a weekend bag over one shoulder. It's fifteen degrees, and I am walking out to the West lot in ten inches of snow on top of a thin layer of ice with water running underneath it. My shoes are soaked completely through in minutes.

When I finally get to my car, I can't get the electronic key to open the doors. They are frozen shut, as are the keyholes on the doors. I scrape carefully to clear one keyhole and manage to get a door open. I open the trunk, stow my gear, and pull out the one object I have to shovel out my car. An ice scraper. For an hour I clear a path immediately in front of me while a snowplow finally responds to the SPO's call and clears a lane out of the parking area and onto the main road leaving the compound.

While I am racing to pick Cathy up, my feet feel like solid blocks of ice. I walk into the airport dripping water, drawing stares from everyone inside. I force a smile when Cathy comes out of the gate area, but she sees how cold and miserable I am. Fortunately she has her bag with her and we can immediately depart and go home. The next day we walk down to Old Town Alexandria and see the snow on everything along the waterfront. Despite the bitter cold blowing off the water, it is a spectacular sight. Most of the river has frozen over—something we just don't see in Florida. We duck into Union Street Station, our favorite local hangout, for some dinner.

"How are you folks tonight?" the waiter asks.

"Doing great, how are you?" I reply, opening the menu. I'm thinking about their chili. It's pretty good, especially on a cold night like this.

"I'm not bad. It's pretty quiet tonight, so I don't think I'll be making much money."

I look around. The place is largely empty; only a couple of other tables are taken.

"Yeah. You guys are quiet. This place is usually rocking on a Saturday night. I guess everyone's worried about being home if there is an attack. Personally, I refuse to seal myself up in my apartment without a final meal. I'm going to get the chili."

"Great," Cathy mutters. "Just what I need. Plastic sheeting to make the place airtight, and you've had chili for dinner. I guess the gas attack threat is real after all."

It is nice to make light of the serious nature of the threat. You can't keep dwelling on it. You'll go crazy.

"Actually, I think it's the weather that's got people scared tonight," the waiter says.

We look out the window.

"It's plenty cold," I agree, " but the streets are clear. We had no problems getting down here at all."

"Oh, no," the waiter replies. "It's OK now, but they are expecting at least a foot of snow overnight and another foot tomorrow."

I stare at him over my menu.

"Don't even joke," I warn.

"Seriously. Haven't you seen the news?" he asks, pointing to a television over the bar.

I can see someone standing in front of a map, but I can't hear him. I rocket the chair into the wall when I jump up to walk to the bar.

Yep. Twelve to eighteen inches by midday tomorrow. What we've had all week will more than double in the next few hours.

I am totally screwed.

Sitting back down at the table I pick up my menu again. Cathy asks what the reporter said. I ignore her and call the waiter back over.

"Sir, we will take two of your largest steaks. Baked potatoes as well. The lady will have a salad, and I'd like a bowl of soup."

Cathy looks at me like I've lost my mind.

"What the hell? I don't want steak."

"Yes you do. It may be the only food we have for a couple of days. We will get a foot of snow overnight."

"Oh my God."

"At a minimum."

"Oh my God."

"And let's face it: There's not a lot to eat in the apartment right now."

I pour two large glasses of wine for us.

"That's not the worst part," I said.

"What's the worst part?"

I take a long sip before answering. This is going to be ugly.

"I can't stay. I have to go back."

"You can't go if the weather is bad. You just have to miss a day."

"No, baby, I can't. Weather is not an excused absence. If the weather turns bad, we are to leave immediately and return to the Farm. No exceptions and no excuses."

Our Valentine's meal goes on largely in silence. The food is excellent and the service wonderful. But we are watching the satellite image on the television screen as a large white mass creeps closer and closer to Washington DC.

We walk back to the apartment from Old Town. I had thought about hailing a cab, but I figure I will spend more than enough time in a car tomorrow trying to get back. As we walk down South Washington Street and cross over the Woodrow Wilson Bridge the snow begins falling. Huge snowflakes shimmer in the electric daylight of fluorescent streetlamps. Behind us, Old Town resembles a Norman Rockwell painting. For a moment I forget how the snow will make my life miserable tomorrow.

Back in the apartment there is a phone message from Marty, another student who happens to live at my complex. He has also seen the weather report and is debating going back right now. With Cathy here, that's not really an option for me. I call Marty and tell him I'm waiting until morning to see what the situation is. Right now the ice trucks will be salting down the highways all night. They should be fine. If it continues to come down during the day I will go ahead and cut out early too. We agree to check with each other in the morning before heading out.

The next morning the area is not covered with a blanket, but more like a parka. I have never seen this much snow in my life. Cathy's flight home has already been canceled, as has every other flight out of the area. All three Washington airports are closed. She is here for the duration.

When I call Marty, I get a rude surprise.

"I'm sorry, Tom. Marty got up and left early this morning," his wife says.

"What?!" I yell. "We were going to reexamine our plans this morning."

"I know. He debated calling you at five, but it was coming down so hard, he just wanted to get on the road. He figured if he really had a problem you would be coming by in a few hours."

"And what if I have a problem?" I growl into the phone. I shouldn't yell at her. It's not her fault he's already gone.

"Gee"—she giggles—"he didn't really think about that. I guess you don't have as much experience as Marty in driving in snow, do you?"

"No, I don't. I'm going to get moving, though. If you hear from him, tell him I'm on the way."

"OK. Tell Cathy to call me later. Maybe we can find something to do tonight since you guys are gone."

I hang up the phone really annoyed. Cathy is not in a better disposition. She has to call her office and let somebody know she will not be at work tomorrow. She also will be doing some laundry downstairs, as she only brought clothes for a quick forty-eight-hour Valentine's weekend, not an extended stay.

I pack up my gear and bring along a sleeping bag in case I get stuck along the highway. I promise to call her from the road. It takes the better part of three hours to get to Langley and switch cars before I can get out of town. I-395 is crawling despite how few cars are out, and the radio announcer says police do not want anyone on the roads except for emergencies. Great. How am I going to explain to a cold, overworked police officer why I am driving in this snow with clean laundry and a sleeping bag? That should make for a fun conversation. It takes me more than eight hours to get back to the Farm. For the last two I have my cell phone turned off, so I don't give any record of where I am traveling. I call Cathy as soon as I get to my room.

She and Marty's wife spent the afternoon together watching movies and are now combining their pantries to cook a potluck dinner. The airport announces it would remain closed on Monday as well. Cathy calls her mother to say she is snowed in. My mother-in-law thinks it's wonderful, the two of us snowed in together on Valentine's Day after all the time living apart. What a great way to spend some time together. I hang up the phone repeating my mother-in-law's words: What a wonderful day.

COURSE CHAIRMAN JOHN briefs us as usual, then clears the auditorium of staff and instructors. He leaves us with no adult supervision, save for a man sitting off to the right next to Wall Street Mike at the end of our row. The man walks up to the front of the room and introduces himself. His name is David, and he is a professor from a prestigious university, specifically the theater arts department. I can hardly believe what is happening. He's here to give us acting lessons.

When we are undercover, when we are pretending to be someone we are not, we are actors. We must be like any other successful actor. More important, we have to also be directors, producers, and writers. We are engaging in theater and are responsible for everything our target will see and hear. If we are to do that, we must understand what theater is.

"Theater is the vicarious enjoyment of manipulation," he says. "When you go to a play or a movie, you know it's not real, but it's still worthwhile. The actor's job is to manipulate the audience. That's why people are willing to pay for the experience."

He waits for someone to comment. No one does.

"You are deceiving the people you are trying to recruit. If they really knew what you were at the initiation of your relationship, do you think they would continue seeing you? Of course not! You are manipulating them. This is what actors do. Actors are what each of you must become."

I can't believe this is going on. Acting lessons? I ask Mike if he thinks the guy could introduce me to Michelle Pfeiffer. He mumbles something about a double date with Angelina Jolie.

"But you can't just recite your lines and expect an agent to follow you anywhere," David says. "You have to set the proper stage. You are operating alone out there. If you try to let just your words carry you, it will fail every time. Let me show you. I need two volunteers. I know better than to ask for any, so I'll just volunteer you. How about you two?"

He points at Wendy and Coach.

They go to the front of the room, where David gives them a script to read. From opposite sides of the room they walk toward each other and stop.

"Hello."

"Oh, it's you."

"Yeah, look, we've got to talk."

"I know, but not now."

"Yes, now."

"No, I can't. Look, I've got to go."

"Really?"

"Yeah. Bye."

"Bye."

"So, what did we have here?" David asks. "Quarreling lovers? An investor and his broker? How about a pair of long-lost siblings disagreeing?"

David picks two other students, Caroline and Kirsten, to come up. Like before, he places them at opposite sides of the room and gives them a script to read.

They exchange funny looks before starting.

"Hello."

"Oh, it's you."

"Yeah, look, we've got to talk."

"I know, but not now."

"Yes, now."

"No, I can't. Look, I've got to go."

"Really?"

"Yeah. Bye."

"Bye."

"Notice anything?" David asks. "You can't concentrate on the words. That was the same set of words for both pairs of actors. I don't know what the hell this was. Two coworkers talking about a project? How about two sisters talking about an ailing parent? Over the years my students have identified over twenty-five different scenarios that could be taking place here. The problem is, you can't tell which scenario it is based upon what is being said. There was no setup, no context to what is taking place. You must not only be actors, you must also handle staging and directing and producing the recruitment scenarios you are running."

Despite our initial disregard for the concept of acting classes, they are very good and very well received. The exercises leave many students taken aback. We have a newfound respect for Hollywood, but also new concerns at how easily the mind is manipulated.

I keep David's acting instruction foremost in my mind when I begin the next exercise. I am operating in a safe house, a secret apartment used only for meeting with agents. In a few weeks we will use real hotel rooms and apartments "out on the economy" for expanded exercises, to mimic the real thing. Right now we are trying it in-house so to speak, practicing in the controlled environment of the Farm. The safe house is my dorm room.

I conduct a ninety-minute SDR to get here, but manage to miss the roadblock set up down the street. There are so many of us coming through, there are simply not enough instructors and staff to manage all the cars coming in. While the early birds get pulled into an actual inspection, the rest of us are waved on through to continue on our way. It seems a little too easy.

I am meeting in the safe house with Jeffrey, the Minister of the Interior for the country of Winnebago. Minister Jeffrey and I have had a splendid time for weeks now. I have already successfully pitched him on the idea of working for the U.S. government, but this was our first time to meet and discuss how it will work. I explain to him how the Agency will compensate him and make sure the nature of our relationship remains confidential. If I ever thought he was in danger, I would find a way to take care of him.

"Trust me, Minister. The U.S. government has been doing this kind of work for sixty years. We are the best in the world. Everything around you is set up a certain way to protect you from any innocent or not-so-innocent prying eyes."

He sips his coffee. "Thus far, I can't complain. But I am wondering what if—"

He is interrupted by a knock at the door. We've got company.

I hurry him into the bathroom while calling toward the door, "Who is it?"

"Fire marshall. I need to inspect the smoke detector."

Nice. Not controversial, appears to be in my own best interest to let him in, but since he's a Winnebago government official, it wouldn't be a stretch for him to question the Minister of the Interior in an American's apartment. I stall for time.

"Can you come another day? I'm a bit busy at the moment."

Minister Jeffrey is having a panic attack performance worthy of Meg Ryan's restaurant scene in *When Harry Met Sally*. I go into the bathroom and turn on the water to mask any further noise.

Putting both cups of coffee in a nearby dresser drawer, I take one quick look around the room for any contraband. Jeffrey didn't bring a briefcase, and he took his suit jacket into the bathroom with him. I make sure the bathroom door is locked. I'm about to take a real risk, and it will be embarrassing enough if it works. If it fails, I'm in real trouble.

In 1999 Showtime broadcast the first movie ever embraced by the Agency. Entitled *In the Company of Spies,* it starred Clancy Brown, Tom Berenger, and Ron Silver. Brown played the part of a CIA case officer in North Korea. He was in a safe house meeting an agent when there was a knock at the door. His female North Korean agent, aware that her country's intelligence services might intrude on a suspected foreigner, peels off her shirt. She lies suggestively on the bed in a bra with her skirt hiked up.

Brown opens the door to a shocked but otherwise innocent chambermaid. It's a great scene and an excellent tactic. If only I had a female agent. Then again, maybe I can work around that.

I get undressed.

Throwing my clothes haphazardly around the room I reach between the mattress and box spring and pull out one of Cathy's bras. I stole it on one of her visits, and I have other plans for it besides the theater I'm making up off the top of my head.

I drop the bra on the floor. Unlocking the door to my room, I pull it open and peer around, not letting my uninvited guest see anything other than my hair and eyes.

"What's this about? Your timing is really bad," I venture.

My left heel is directly behind the door. If he tries to push or kick his way in, I should be able to hold him off even barefoot.

I recognize the instructor, though I don't know his name. He has on a fire marshall's hat and badge and is holding a clipboard.

"Good afternoon, sir. How do you do? I'm Lawrence with the Winnebago Fire Marshall's office. We are inspecting smoke alarms in the building today. You received a note in the mail, correct?"

"No, I'm afraid I didn't. I'll have to speak to the landlord about that. Could I ask you to come a bit later, sir?" I ask. I know the answer is no, but I have to make the effort.

"Ah, no sir. We've got to get them all done today. It won't take a moment."

"No, I'm sure it won't. Still, I'm quite busy."

"I'm sorry, sir. Is there a problem of some sort? You haven't been tampering with the smoke detector, have you? You realize that's a serious offense?"

"No, I wouldn't think of tampering with a safety device. I swear I haven't touched it."

"Oh, I'm glad to hear that. Still, you seem nervous."

"Nervous?" I ask. Maybe he'll give me the opening I need.

"Yes. Everyone else has let me in. You are still standing in the doorway. Are you sure there's no problem?"

"No, I just don't like interruptions. I'm a private person, you know. I thought I made that clear to the landlord."

"Well, sir, the landlord must still abide by the fire code. We have to inspect these units once a year. Today's the day for this building. I'm afraid I can't really do much about it. Still, your face is flushed. Are you sure there's nothing wrong?"

"I'm sure you can understand. I'm a foreigner with an unannounced stranger at my door. I pay a premium for the privacy afforded by this building. I'm sure you are who you say you are, but I would be more comfortable if my landlord had said something about it to me."

Without warning the toilet flushes. Jeffrey is throwing me a curve.

"Is there someone else with you, sir?" the inspector asks.

Ah! Here's my chance. "I'm not sure that's any of your business! What does a fire marshall need to know about my private life?" I demand.

I take a half step to the right and allow the door to open all the way to the length of the chain. The bra under my foot is now clearly visible, and I am no longer hidden behind the door.

I am wearing nothing but boxer shorts.

"If I may!" I exclaim, "I am only asking that you service this apartment in a little while. I am spending some time with a lady friend, if you know what I mean."

Fire Marshall Lawrence steps back.

"Oh, my!! Why didn't you say so? I'm so sorry, sir. Uh, yeah. Why don't I come back after a while?"

He chuckles the entire way down the hall. He probably knows which instructor I'm conducting the exercise with.

I close the door and get dressed. I am buttoning my pants when the bathroom door creeps open and Jeffrey walks out. I'm barefoot and still standing on the bra.

"Who was that?" is out of his mouth before he realizes the state I'm in. "What happened to your clothes?" he asks.

"It was a fire marshall's inspector. Not a problem, Minister. He'll come back another time." I ignore the underfoot undergarment and put my shoes and socks back on like it's the most routine action in the world. "I'll see you again next week, yes?"

"I guess you were prepared for anything, huh?"

He is trying hard to not drop character, but he won't stop grinning at me. I can't tell if it's the Minister of the Interior or the instructor asking the question.

"I'm no Boy Scout," I say, picking up the bra, "but I'm always prepared."

PTA Mom and the Goth Queen
March 2003

WHAT DO A USED CAR SALESMAN, a teenage girl's father, and an intelligence officer have in common? The smart ones are practiced in elicitation, a linguistic judo that answers questions without having to actually ask anything. Car salesmen want to know their customers. Fathers want to learn a young boy's intentions with their daughters. Intelligence officers want to know what kind of access a target has and how they might best approach this person.

Elicitation is a carefully measured means of gathering information without raising suspicions. Instead of asking direct questions and causing a person's mental defenses to jump into high gear, elicitation appears to be an innocuous conversation. It's friendly, relaxed, and, when done properly, focused in such a way that the targeted person believes he or she is in charge. It is perfect for the espionage trade.

It is nonthreatening, easy to disguise, and very effective. The techniques involved are as varied as the personality types that people have. The tactics that work for an extrovert like me will be different from those of an introverted accountant. A woman's methods will be different from a man's, and so on. The instructor walks us through the psychological mechanisms of how this simple methodology works and outlines some specific techniques.

Want someone to talk with you about a topic? Naiveté works nicely. Don't act like an idiot, but if you carefully articulate your position, someone with a different (and to their thinking, better) position will be only too happy to describe it to you. Act interested, and they will throw in more and more detail, right up to a point where more than half will say, "I shouldn't tell you this, but . . ." and proceed to tell you anyway.

Ego and flattery are related methods that also work quite well. If I say to a potential target, "You must have an extremely important job in the Ministry," the most likely response will be, "That's nice of you to say, but in actuality my job isn't all that important. All I really do is . . ."

Deliberately misspeaking is also quite effective. If I say, "Well, everyone knows the Cayman Islanders have secretly been plotting the overthrow of Castro," it isn't a stretch for someone to say, "Actually, the Caymanis are far more interested in opening official channels there by . . ."

If I walk through downtown Kabul and ask questions about the Defense Ministry Building, I'm going to be in big trouble quite quickly. If I can elicit the same information as part of an innocuous conversation, I am able to complete my mission with little time, expense, and risk. Elicitation's power is such that the person being elicited will most likely not remember the conversation an hour later.

We practice elicitation during a diplomatic party specifically set up for this purpose the following night. The bash is held at the Base Club, a very nice conference and gathering facility overlooking a lake. Though not in formal wear, everyone is dressed nicely, and the food is outstanding. This is what we would expect when on the diplomatic circuit overseas. These are opportunities for the upper crust of society to get together. The food, drinks, and entertainment will be the very best available.

I have been told to find a particular Bulgarian official at the party. I have a very sketchy description of him: late fifties, balding, a paunch, and very gregarious. This description fits about half of the male instructors here. I'm searching for an individual tree in a human forest.

Working a party like this is similar to the thirty-second elevator pitch we had to do in graduate school. If you stepped onto an elevator with Warren Buffett and had the perfect investment opportunity, how would you pitch it in the thirty seconds before the doors open and he disappears? At this party we don't have an elevator, but we do have a multitude of people walking around with their own agendas. Both scenarios require you to get to your point quickly in a fashion that hooks the target's attention. He or she must want to follow up with you to learn more. The goal in both scenarios is the same: *Get a second meeting.*

We quickly learn to bounce information off of one another. It's the only way to cull through all the possible targets in the brief period available. "Have you seen my guy?" "No. Have you seen this other one?" "Yes, he's in the corner talking to Jim." This is our first graded exercise. Everyone, including the instructors, wants to make it a successful one.

I am chasing down another faux Eastern European diplomat when a student abruptly stops in front of me. I don't know Audra well, but she seems nice enough. Not wanting to be rude, I ask her how her night is going.

"Fine," she says, "are you having fun?"

"Not really," I reply.

"Well, maybe you should get a drink and try to relax a little," she suggests. Not exactly an epiphany, but it's not a bad idea either.

"Sounds good," I reply, gesturing toward the bar. "What can I get you?"

"Oh, a glass of merlot would be wonderful. Thank you."

She has a beautiful smile. These guys don't have a chance.

I collect our drinks and scan the room for my target. I finally see him in a corner, but he's not alone. He's being double-timed by two students; one an accountant and the other a tax attorney. Should I go save him or let them all drown in their collective misery? Hard to decide.

"You must have an important position in the Interior Ministry. The host seems to think very highly of you," Audra says.

It takes me a moment to realize she's speaking to me.

"I'm sorry. What was that?" I ask, leaning over to hear. It's really loud in here.

"The Ministry. I'm guessing this is not your first dip party."

I stare at her for a good two seconds, trying to think of a witty reply. I don't get it. I continue to stand there, puzzled. Coach walks by and says something about the Canadian ambassador and sheep. I smile and nod toward him while not taking my gaze from Audra.

She sees Coach go by. She hears the collegial comment. Her mental gears are running so hard, I can almost hear them. She shuts her eyes.

"Oh my God," she almost yells. "You sit next to him. You're a student!"

She scrunches her face tight. It looks like her neck is going to swallow her head. I touch her on the arm to try to quiet her down, but it doesn't work. Coach has that gift. I don't.

"I'm so sorry . . ." she covers her mouth with her hand. The remaining words are unintelligible. She tears away and makes a direct line to the ladies' room, knocking aside the Consul General of Kazakhstan.

It's a textbook application of flattery or ego stroking. She was setting me up, thinking I was an instructor, her target. Ouch! Once again I am reminded that I'm the oldest student here. I've got some gray, but I never thought about coloring my hair until this moment. I reluctantly walk toward my target to end the evening as quickly as possible, but the damage is done. My motivation is shot to hell.

Do I blend in better with the retirees than with the students?

AFTER EVERY EXERCISE we sit down with the instructor we are roleplaying with to get their feedback. What did we do right, wrong, or indifferently? The feedback we receive can be direct. Some of it can be downright nasty. The feedback Helen got this morning was like that.

She had had enough. The criticism she received was a little too personal. Someone in the hallway outside her room overheard her crying and called the office to tell Terry. By this time we have enough training to know that this is a situation best handled by a good friend. Helen and Terry are certainly that.

On the surface they have nothing in common. Terry is a thirtysomething divorced mom. Helen is a married twentysomething with no kids. Terry is prim and proper. Helen likes the gothic look. Yet despite their cosmetic differences, these two have a bond. Now Helen is ready to call it quits.

She is talking a mile a minute when Terry walks in. Helen doesn't normally raise her voice, but she is on an adrenaline-fed tirade and is just getting started. Terry takes her by the hand, clears a space on the bed, and sits her down. She then does something I would never have thought to do. She tells Helen to cry.

Don't just cry a little. Cry a lot. Wail if it makes her feel better.

Helen continues sobbing, complaining bitterly about the evaluation she received. The remarks were not kind: She wasn't cut out for this line of work. She should never have been allowed in. How did she get this far without being cut? Etc. It's pretty rough language for an official U.S. government document. Terry takes it all in and motions for more.

"What else did they say? Did they say you are stupid, too?" she asks.

"What?" Helen said. "No, they didn't, but they may as well have. 'I shouldn't be here'? Maybe I should just go!" She turns to pack some more.

Terry cuts her off. "That's it?" She jumps up. "You're in here ready to bail for that? I've had much worse. They've called me every variation of incompetent there is. One guy asked how I dress myself every morning. You've got one bad evaluation, and you want to quit? Forget it!" Terry flops down on top of Helen's suitcase.

"What difference is it to you if I quit? I miss my husband. I'm tired of this shit. I want to go home. I didn't come here to be a case officer. I want to drive a desk and have a normal life!" Helen screams.

Terry grabs her shoulders, her own resentment beginning to rise.

"You can't quit, because if you do, we *both* have to leave." Terry is in her face now.

Helen blinks.

"What are you talking about?" Helen asks as she wipes away tears.

"This job is about more than these idiots! Their time has passed. We are the future of this Agency. Women weren't allowed in the program when these guys came through here. It was a boys' club only!! We have to stay. We have to take it. If we have to do twice the work for half the credit, then that's what we'll do. I know you aren't going to be a case officer. Neither am I! But we will be trained as case officers. When they come in the office and spout some nonsensical bullshit about how this or that is done, we can call them on it because we were here. We know the tradecraft. We know how all of this works. You can't leave now."

Helen shakes her head. "I didn't come here to represent all women. I just came here for me." She stares at the ground.

Terry presses forward on her, tears in her eyes now as well. "I don't need you to stay for all women. I need you to stay for me. I can't do this alone. I can't do it without you. We're in this together. They may throw me out, but I won't make it easy on them. You can't either. You have to stay. If you leave, I have to leave with you. I need this. My son needs this. What am I going to do if I don't finish the course?"

Both are crying now, holding each other in Helen's room. The noise has not gone unnoticed by their neighbors.

Terry pulls back after hearing someone in the hallway. She looks toward the door.

"Don't do this. Don't do what they want you to do. Stay. If they throw us out, fine, we'll go home. But don't do their dirty work for them. You've been around the Agency long enough to know the mindfuck that goes on down here. This is the equivalent of boot camp. They tear you down to build you back up. Stay. Whatever it is you need help with, I'm right here for you. We have to make it so we can come back here, become instructors, and make sure this kind of instruction ends. This place is not designed for women, married people, or students with children. We can't change it unless we complete it."

Helen takes five minutes to herself. Terry maintains a respectful distance.

"Talking about your kid was a cheap shot," Helen mutters.

Terry smiles. "You use what you've got. He's all I've got without you."

Helen stays. She accepts her poor evaluation and puts it behind her. The next exercise goes perfectly and her evaluation reflects it. The bond between the two women grows stronger. They become inseparable.

Everyone in the office notices something new between them. They aren't just colleagues anymore. Each has shared with the other their private fears, hopes, and dreams. Each will know the other's life as closely as they know their own. The goth queen and the PTA mom. They are flip sides of the same life choices. Wall Street Mike and I assign them code names:

Leather and Lace.

A COUPLE OF DAYS LATER we learn during the morning brief that roadblocks can begin at any time. Not just during exercises, when we are easy to catch. They will also appear during our evening runs out to practice surveillance, during weekend trips back up to Washington, and when we are moving around the base for classes.

Roadblocks are every bit as ugly as you think they might be in a hostile foreign country. The thirty participating instructors are in costume and in character, acting out the part of the bastard child conceived from the mating of a testosterone-fueled SWAT team officer with a politically connected bureaucrat. The resulting progeny is dressed in black, armed, and carrying a clipboard with far more information about you than any foreigner should ever know.

They tear apart our stories, our cars, and any materials they find on us. They yell at us, each other, and cars passing by. There are K-9 patrol dogs. Police sirens and flashing lights add to the confusion. The point is not to find contraband but rather to get us to misspeak. What we don't learn until after it is too late is that the roadblocks are videotaped.

At first the cameras are fairly discreet, but as we progress through more and more roadblocks, from static ID and sobriety checkpoints to rolling "What are you doing here?" stops, the camera becomes more intrusive. On the flip side, this makes for great film the following week in class debriefings.

One of the early incidents involves a student named Tim. Instead of taking the correct action of talking his way out, Tim decides to play the indignant American diplomat. He flashes his diplomatic passport and refuses to get out of the car. Instructors and staff beat on the car for half an hour until finally Tim's counselor comes to the window, motions him to roll it down, and gently whispers that if his ass isn't out in five seconds, he fails the entire program and will be sent home. Other people also have problems.

A young woman is found with notes from an agent meeting. Apparently it has gone very well. A little too well. She has notes of the debriefing, which is damning enough. She also has the schedule for their next two meetings, the times and locations, and, to top it off, her agent's name, address, and phone number. The following day she receives a note that her agent has been found shot at his home. This is precisely what would happen in a number of countries. Even though it's only a training exercise, it has the desired effect.

I am not without my own problems during the first roadblock. I had switched cars earlier in the week due to a mechanical problem and had not conducted a complete "clean sweep" to make sure there were no compromising materials in the car when I left the compound for my agent meeting. Feeling a bit cocky about how well my meeting went, I didn't do a subsequent sweep after dropping my agent off. I am therefore very surprised when, at the roadblock, an inspector reaches into my trunk and finds a laminated map of the entire area.

We use laminated maps because we can mark our routes with a grease pencil to practice and time them. It's a good system because, with practice, we can memorize the route and the approximate times it should take to hit every landmark. What we should not have, however, is the map in the trunk when we are stopped by a foreign intelligence service. My evaluation is properly uncomplimentary. I feel like a complete idiot.

The best roadblock scene doesn't involve a student, however, but instead turns the tables on the instructors. A nearby military unit specializing in urban security is invited to conduct the roadblock. It gives the unit additional training at little expense and forces us to go through a roadblock with authority figures we do not know. This time, however, it's the military inspectors who are under the gun. Again, cameras capture the entire scene.

Gavin, the quiet instructor from my office, is an Army colonel and a tough instructor, but extremely well liked by everyone in the program. I've gotten to know him fairly well. When I get through the military roadblock and make it safely back to the office, everyone is buzzing about Gavin.

The unit's commander asked Gavin, an old friend of his as it turns out, to go through the roadblock as a student. But instead of talking his way through, he asked Gavin to make a run for it or become combative and see what happens with the soldiers. Gavin is in excellent shape, a five a.m. workout fiend, and not someone who shies away from a fight. He jumps at the chance.

About an hour after I return to the office, Gavin comes in behind me. His shirt is torn, his face badly scratched, and he is covered in dirt and mud. He has a smile bigger than the all outdoors. "Wanna watch?" he asks, producing a VHS tape from behind his back. He pops it in the VCR, and we watch the exercise unfold.

It starts off like any other roadblock, until the bomb-sniffing dog goes nuts going through Gavin's car. Gavin takes off. He clotheslines the first poor slob he reaches, then disarms and drops the second soldier a half second later. It takes four armed soldiers to chase, catch, and contain him. After he is finally subdued, they put plastic restraints on his wrists, which he promptly removes in less than thirty seconds. He glances around several times, apparently planning to make a run for it again.

Instead, he is concerned that one soldier will go too far. Gavin pulls out his identification, and the soldiers holding him down quickly jump back and salute. Like the professional he is, he shakes each of their hands, tells them how well they did, and gives them some pointers for "the next time."

Everyone got something out of it, including Gavin.

ON MARCH 17 we are riveted to our chairs as President Bush announces Iraqi President Saddam Hussein has forty-eight hours to leave Iraq or face military assault. The Defense Department students, some of whom had been working up battle plans a couple of months ago, knew it was coming. Now that CNN is broadcasting it live, it's all too real. They are depressed. Soldiers train for one thing: war.

We are very close to the military students in the class. Although still different in many respects, we treat them no differently from our fellow Agency students. We work shoulder to shoulder in all weather and at all hours. I am particularly close with Adam and Travis, though we have only known one another for three months.

They had lived and trained with their unit buddies for years. They have dodged bullets and cleared minefields with them. When necessary they have carried them to medics or carried messages back to their grieving families. That bond is not easily ignored or replaced. They feel they are letting their friends down by not being nearby when the bullets are flying. The temptation to drop out and come back in another class is very strong.

The military students now keep to themselves in their off hours. They are not as social as they previously had been. When we inquire why, the answer is simple enough: When shit hits the fan, military personnel rely on the only thing they have—one another. They know that some of their friends will not leave Iraq alive. They didn't have a chance to say good-bye. As the war spills out on the screen this conflict between duty and training becomes more and more apparent. Travis and I go out for a beer one night, and he explains how military bonds form.

Travis is an interesting guy. The Navy SEALs in the class treat him with respect. Not like you see someone defer to an elder or even a commanding officer. It is . . . well, different.

Lots of people talk about honor and duty. Travis exemplifies it. Gavin had brought him into the program and didn't share Travis's reluctance in bragging about his abilities. Travis has gone to most of the trouble spots the United States has had in the past decade and served his country admirably in all of them. He is an accomplished peacekeeper, paratrooper, and discretionary warfare soldier. He has killed our nation's enemies from a distance and up close. He has assisted refugees and briefed high-level officials. You would never know it to talk with him.

Travis is not tall, not particularly muscular. He wears glasses. He does not run very fast, nor is he an outwardly aggressive sort of guy. He is not loud, not boisterous, not one you will see bar-fighting on the weekends. He lives quietly and simply—a homebody when off duty, spending time with his wife and son as much as his specialized profession will allow. What he does very well, however, is complete his mission.

He understands the big picture and doesn't waste time on actions that don't support the task at hand. He doesn't complain, nor does he seek accolades or medals. He is a soldier because that is his calling. He says his Special Operations experience is as much luck as any particular talent on his part. Gavin begs to differ. Gavin and other Special Operations commanders want every Travis they can get their hands on.

Travis makes no apologies that the military students are closer to one another than they are to the Agency students. Though we have mutual adversaries in the instructor ranks, he tells me the military students will never view Agency students as equals. Not that they view us as having a lesser stature; we are simply different. Our roles are different, as are our skills, abilities, and responsibilities.

Soldiers like Travis get the job done. They don't make up their own rules, don't cause a commotion, and don't praise the business of killing. They are soldiers. They do what they must in the service of their country. They earn the respect and trust of other military professionals, like Navy SEALs. Travis is here because Gavin wants him here and has made sure Travis's application was approved.

There's little doubt that Gavin has plans for him when we're done.

TODAY WE GET A BRIEFING from the Directorate of Science and Technology (DS&T). One could argue these are some of the most dangerous people in federal government. Case officers get all of the glory, but when it comes to *Mission Impossible*–style projects, it's the DS&T engineers and technicians who make the "impossible" merely an opportunity to shine.

It is DS&T officers who design new technologies for sophisticated spy satellites that peer through clouds at enemy sites. They were responsible for the recently revealed program the CIA worked on with Howard Hughes, creating a cover story for commissioning a huge ship known as the *Glomar Challenger,* allegedly designed to harvest mineral deposits in the deepest parts of the ocean. In actuality, the ship was designed to recover a lost Russian submarine and hide it so that engineers could dissect and reverse-engineer Soviet technology.

But not every project is as large as the *Glomar Challenger.* The DS&T staff is known in the Clandestine Service as the Toy Makers—makers of the tiny hidden cameras and microphones used in covert spying operations. All of us assumed the Toy Makers were just a bunch of geeks. Well, the geeks came in to tell the big-shot case officers how things really are.

DS&T officers are every bit as trained as we are. It's just that instead of learning how to manipulate minds, they are taught how to manipulate locks. Or alarm systems. Or computer systems. As the details of their unique specialty come tumbling out, every student in the class suddenly feels like we are transported to an adult version of Disneyland. We complain about our one-year training program? Theirs can be up to three years long!

We tour through a special house across the compound that showcases the exceptional skills of this group. Every room of the house is wired. There are pinhole cameras hidden in the suspended ceiling tile and in the cork of the kitchen bulletin board. The furniture is custom-built with special hiding places, the size restricted only by the case officer's requirements. What needs to be hidden? A camera? A briefcase? A family of four? All of these and more are featured in every conceivable way. It's as if Ethan Allen hired David Copperfield.

To our surprise (and to Hollywood's ongoing discredit) we learn that case officers don't ever enter a building and place a bug or steal an item. It takes weeks of planning by a team of technical specialists to plan entry into a room.

Which rooms have motion sensors? Locks? Cameras? Every problem is handled by a different specialist, whose only job is to tackle that single piece of the puzzle, then step aside. When the alarm guy is done, the lock picker is up to bat. When he is done, the camera guy will tackle the cameras. It goes on and on like this until the entire team is confident it can enter a room and conduct the business necessary to complete the task. It was a pretty fun day all around—a nice break from the hectic pace of the training. So I am surprised and disappointed when I get word that Crystal has decided to leave.

Granted, I barely know the woman, but after nine months in training, it's odd that someone decides to pack up and head home. As I am walking between the cafeteria and the instruction building, I see her loading up her car, and I walk over to chat for a few minutes.

She had come to the conclusion that being a field officer was not her forte. She is returning to headquarters to pursue a career in the Directorate of Intelligence. She doesn't like the back-slapping of recruitment, the subterfuge of deception, or the hidden cloak of cover operations. She wants to contribute to the mission, but she's ready to go home.

I wish her well and return to the office. I have an exercise with Crystal scheduled for tomorrow. It's designed to practice the critical skill of handing an agent over from the recruiting officer to a new case officer. This can be a difficult transition period for agents. What began as a personal relationship must eventually be accepted as a business relationship. While routine for Agency personnel, this is frequently a traumatic experience for the newly recruited agent. The wool is no longer over the agent's eyes. The bond with the new case officer is the espionage equal to an arranged marriage; swapping spouses in such an unholy union can be dicey.

Having another student pick up Crystal's role means doubling their workload on an already busy week. Course Chairman John comes to the rescue. We reverse the scheduled roles. I take over as Crystal's case officer character handing off the agent and John takes on my role, taking on the receiving case officer. Crystal's instructor on this exercise was Bruce, with whom she's had four meetings and a considerable body of reporting. I read up on all of her reporting on the exercises and felt comfortable that I knew her agent as well as anyone could.

The agent is an atomic physicist, a father of two, and a ranking member of the nation's ruling elite. He likes tennis and American NCAA basketball, and is a sailing fanatic. He has two key criteria for working with the Agency: his concern over his nation's growing nuclear arsenal and the desire for an American education for his children. I must speak to both of these motivations when we meet. I also read up on the winners of the America's Cup should his favorite pastime come up in conversation.

Our meeting goes off like clockwork. John and I speak eloquently about the agent's critical efforts to minimize the arms race. By the time the meeting is concluded, I have bonded with him, been debriefed on new intelligence he has acquired, and arranged a follow-up meeting in a new safe house across town. It is after the meeting that everything unravels.

Per standard practice I go to Bruce's office for my evaluation the following day. He and I chat for a few minutes and he hands me the evaluation for my review and signature. I notice a minor typo and highlight it. Then I see another.

And another.

And another.

I begin the evaluation from the first page and reread it once more. "Student conducted meeting in safe house, student was prepared with relevant background on case, student built rapport with agent." These were all positives. Then there are some other notes. "Student did not ask agent about his kids. Student did not provide amenities for meeting. Student did not have good description for next car meeting." This is odd. We had discussed the potential for his son to play basketball at Georgetown. We enjoyed Starbucks coffee and bagels when I showed him the location of my new safe house on a map. What gives?

Even more odd, Bruce is apparently confused about my gender.

Every reference was to "her" or "she." The evaluation is written for a female student. I am not aware that I've had a sex-change operation, so I reread the document once more.

"Any questions?" Bruce asks.

"Um, yeah. Just give me a second to look it over again," I reply.

I read over the document a final time. The exercise name is correct, as is the date and the training subject we are practicing. The final paragraph refers to a prior evaluation on another exercise. That's when it hits me: It was written before Crystal quit two days ago. Bruce wrote the evaluation *before* the exercise actually took place!

It's a complete fabrication.

He forgot to change the pronouns when a male student replaced her. I have no idea what to say. I hand the document back, uncertain how to handle the situation.

"Um, Bruce? I'm not a girl," I finally manage to say.

"What?" he asks.

"I'm not a girl. This evaluation is for a female student. I'm a guy. I pee standing up, and I scratch myself in the morning. Also, some of the meeting references are not accurate."

Bruce snatches the evaluation back, taking notice of where I circled each *her* and *she*. His face turns a deep shade of crimson.

"Well! I—that is . . . I uh, I'm not sure what to say."

Good. That makes two of us.

"I'm pretty embarrassed by this."

You should be.

"Tom, why don't you give me a couple of hours and let me retool this a bit? Can you come back on your way to dinner tonight?"

Do I have a choice?

I excuse myself and walk outside. I don't feel like going back to the office. Instead, I walk back to my room for a few minutes of peace and quiet.

He wrote her evaluation before the exercise even took place. I wonder how often that goes on. I wonder if that's the reason she quit. I wonder how many other evaluations are not worth the paper they're printed on.

Are we simply going through the motions? Is the training process merely a formality of government bureaucracy? Are some of the instructors coasting toward retirement so quickly that doing the job is no longer important? Are our lives and careers that meaningless? Is national security no longer a concern?

Doesn't he give a damn?

Finding no answers in my room, I take a walk down Range Road to clear my head. No wonder she quit. I doubt if anyone could have talked her out of it. She never had a chance. This guy just didn't like her and was determined to run her out. Well, he succeeded. Who knows what Crystal might have accomplished if she had remained in the program. Why is one instructor allowed such latitude in deciding that a student should be removed?

For the first time I'm immune to the cold. I'm furious, with the instructor and with the Agency for allowing him to teach here. Who does he think he is? Who made him an expert over this young woman's career? He has no other way of counseling her, working with her to bring her performance up to his "standards"? After all the time, effort, and money it took for the CIA to get her here, he has elected himself judge and jury. Sentence passed. This is not the CIA I wanted to join.

How is it that someone like this works alongside highly professional instructors who only want the best for students? Is the selection process for independent contractors so radically different from the criteria for students that this many bad apples are allowed in? Is there no oversight? Is there no formal process for dealing with situations like this? Where is the accountability?

He didn't have the guts to express potential concerns on Crystal's performance through official channels. Instead, he predisposes her to failure before she begins the exercise. He's so smug and content with himself, he forgets to change the pronouns on her evaluation when a male student is substituted at the last minute.

I wish I could have captured the look on his face, the shock and uncertainty of what to say, the realization that his disloyalty against a CIA officer is suddenly thrust into the light of day.

Not as deadly as Nicholson's treachery, but certainly no less a traitor to the Agency.

I TELL AL about the exercise. He looks up Bruce's evaluation on his computer and notes it's extremely complimentary of me. I'm sure that's just to placate me and keep me quiet. If I weren't seriously questioning the training already, I sure would be now. As if there isn't enough fuel on my attitudinal fire, someone leaves a newspaper clipping on my desk.

The Washington Times publishes a blistering piece about the Agency and its shortcomings. Highlighted in bright yellow for my review is their opinion on how the Agency's age restrictions on entering the Clandestine Service should be lifted. I agree with the paper's position, but I can't tell from the highlight if my anonymous deliveryman agrees with the idea or not. I probably don't want to know.

The remainder of the article is brutal. It makes the obligatory reference to our class being the largest in Agency history, but also points out how such drastic action was necessary after eight years of budget and personnel cuts. Though the article defends our ability to recruit persons of different races and cultures it also suggests the Agency's entrance requirements had to be dumbed down to meet politically correct recruitment quotas. Lest we feel they are only picking on us, the article also seriously questions Jim Pavitt's ability to lead the Clandestine Service. The article makes many of us question whether we've made the right decision in coming here.

The CIA has always operated with a level of autonomy unparalleled elsewhere in government. They routinely call the shots, direct their own programs, and lead the intelligence community from a high and heretofore irreproachable perch. September 11 strongly calls that position into question. If the Agency was unable to perform its job because of its own bureaucracy when the world was relatively calm (before the attacks), what is it going to be like in the years to come? Was, as the article clearly suggests, the relevance of the CIA so inescapably lost that it should be replaced by another organization more capable of responding to modern threats?

We view this question with obvious concern. We moved our lives and livelihoods to this profession, but have we chosen the wrong organization through which to express this commitment? The Agency's geopolitical structure appears tragically mismatched to the transnational threats to our nation. As so many of us learned in business, the world is an increasingly smaller place. Global finance, travel, and communications mean that people affect and are affected by pressures across the world as sharply as those across the street. But we've not heard any discussion of these points in our training here.

Much of what we practice is old-school—old enemies and old thinking. Perhaps it will fall to us to create new ways of fighting our new enemies. While the techniques are old and proven, their new application is uncharted territory. The Agency only knows the diplomatic circuit, officers under government cover. Non Official Cover officers have never been considered mainstream intelligence operatives. That must change. The agents of the future will be targeted, recruited, and run by officers in the private sector. The question we are all wrestling with is can we do this within the CIA as it currently exists?

I'm dissatisfied with how and where our training is going, this most recent incident simply becoming the icing on a long-baked cake. I've met few Agency staffers capable of running a private firm, conducting business that could provide cover for intelligence officers to launch recruitment operations. This is what I expected to find here. These were not the defenders of my country I had planned to join. The Farm resembles an out-of-control high school when the principal is away. There is backstabbing, sniping, and rumors churned out by the hour, only it's by the staff and instructors. Fortunately, things are about to change. There will be some supervision at the Farm this weekend, albeit temporarily.

Friday afternoon, our last exercise is completed around 2:00 p.m. We are still responsible for getting all of our reporting in by 8:00 a.m. on Monday, but many of us will be busy this weekend. The boss is coming to town. It's Spouses Weekend.

The Agency is trying to be more family friendly, and Spouses Weekend is one of the smarter parts of this new direction. It allows wives and husbands to come to the Farm and see what we have been doing for the past three months. Our spouses stay with us in the dorms for the entire weekend. Not only do they stay with us, they essentially become the students, while we take more of a backseat role. All other course exercises are suspended for the weekend, and the unmarried students are free to return home or to simply hang out and enjoy a free weekend.

The spouses arrive around five on Friday afternoon. Many of them have still been meeting monthly in the Washington area as a means of coping with the long separation. This will be the first extended bit of time we will spend together. After a quick Friday night social gathering at the Base Club, everyone is free to roam the compound and see the lake, shooting ranges, and aircraft hangar. We can even venture into the residential areas—in part to convince our spouses to consider an assignment here at some point in our careers.

Because so many Class 11 students have young families, the base is besieged with children. The infrastructure of the Farm has not kept up with the new pro-family strategy. There are no playgrounds, no play sets, and no facilities for children whatsoever. The first hint of trouble comes Saturday morning.

The cafeteria was aware that there would be a large number of families here over the weekend, but the schedule didn't change to reflect this. Nor did the menu or capacity. As a result, the limited amount of adult food quickly ran out, and a number of spouses were late to their first activity—the morning brief. It was a logistical oversight that puts a bad taste in everyone's mouth. Things don't improve much over the course of the day.

The brief is held in the same auditoriums where we have been for our daily morning briefs. Unfortunately this left the (overwhelmingly female) spouses unavailable for their young children. The instruction building is designed for training spies. It is not designed or furnished for entertaining children. Exacerbating this problem was the kids have essentially been raised alone for the last three months. Seeing Dad in a strange building with an incomprehensible number of strangers does little to settle the poor breakfast. Loud and continuous screaming is the order of the day.

Wall Street Mike has the foresight to ask his wife to bring some Nerf balls with her. His two boys are toddlers—a fun age to be with on a Saturday no matter where they are. He grabs both boys and signals for me to join them. We got three or four good tosses in before the rain hit.

Now we had *wet,* crying, screaming, hungry children in an environment not conducive to them. We needed a plan B, a fall-back position. Markers! Drawing! Mike suggests taking the kids to our office and letting them play with our pens and markers. An excellent idea.

Mike's boys are working on their third series of abstracts when Travis walks in with his son. Travis's boy is older than Mike's kids—around ten years old. Markers and coloring books aren't going to cut it. Fortunately, he is aware of what his dad does for a living and, though he doesn't know what kind of facility he is in, he knows Dad does some pretty cool things and wants to see where it all takes place. Travis has something more for him though. Travis pulls out his wig.

He eventually pulls out his entire disguise kit and outfits his son with a wig, mustache, glasses, and various cosmetic accoutrements. It only takes a few minutes of silliness before we are trying all of our disguises on Travis's son. He is wearing a long blond wig and trying out earrings when his mother walks in. She'll never leave Travis alone with the kid again.

The spouses break from their briefing and board buses for a tour of the compound. We are still "discouraged" from going with them. The instructors want one-on-one time with our spouses to share (sell) stories about family life in the Agency. Mary is standing next to me when we wave goodbye to our respective husband and wife as the bus pulls away.

"Why do I feel like a mom sending her son away on summer camp?" she asks with a laugh.

"I don't know," I reply. "Seems to me like we're the ones who have left. At least they will get to have some fun."

That assessment turns out to be premature. As the bus lumbers through the Farm's expansive acres one young woman jumps up and screams, "What do you mean 'the CIA'?" Her husband had not told her where he was working! She goes into hysterics and has to be calmed by two staff members on board.

I take advantage of a couple of free hours to write up reports from Friday's exercise. I also have some casing reports to do. I found some new alleyways to use for dead drops and have to get the descriptions ready. Many students decide to do the same. We will not see our spouses again until the soiree later tonight.

The Agency is throwing a full-blown diplomatic party so the spouses can see what these functions are like. The instructors will perform their role-playing parts for targeting purposes so they can be chatted up for a second meeting. But the students won't be doing the talking. Our spouses will!

This is a stroke of genius. The spouses are a part of their mate's employment at the Agency. The risks, long hours, difficult working conditions, and limited opportunities for advancement are too stressful to not have an officer's significant other fully on board. They have to know what is going on. The best way to do that is to let them be a part of it. Tonight they are taking the lead, allowing us to be the supportive ones as they fumble around the Base Club looking for ambassadors, diplomatic officers, and local dignitaries of our fictional nation of Winnebago.

This is a no-brainer for Cathy. In our real lives, she is the social butterfly. I am the guy in the corner nursing his drink for three hours, people-watching. I like figuring out the personal dynamics in the room from a distance. Cathy likes to be in the trenches. Opposites attract, I suppose. Cathy is not at the diplomatic party for three minutes when she comes face to face with a military officer wearing a chest full of medals. Gavin extends his hand and says hello.

He is just being himself tonight, which many of the instructors are doing, giving spouses some wiggle room outside the artificiality of the training.

Gavin does an admirable job of socializing with her, talking about working with me, but remaining in the character context of the exercise. She got a real charge out of meeting him after I had told her about him on the phone. Unfortunately we need to cut the evening a bit short. We have another operational assignment elsewhere, one I have cooked up for one of my officemates.

Though the Agency is relaxing certain hard-and-fast rules on their definition of family, one area they have not acquiesced on yet is "significant others." In order to be cleared by the security office to attend Spouses Weekend you must be a spouse, a legally married partner of a student. That was a problem for our office. One of us is single. Though Terry and Frank are engaged, it is not enough to convince the 1950s legacy rulemaking. Frank can't attend any of the weekend activities.

I didn't like this and made no secret of it. I worked the instructors in our office, my counselor Al, and even Course Chairman John. I articulate my feelings about the situation in considerable detail in full view of the office camera and under the microphone. When this doesn't have the desired effect, I create a fall-back plan.

George, an instructor who lives in the immediate area off base, is sympathetic to our situation and suggests a local restaurant. He knows the place well—is a regular in fact—and is sure they will help us out. I use my newly acquired elicitation skills to learn Frank's phone number and give him a call. He will come to town, stay at a local hotel, and Terry will join him offsite. As far as she knows, they are just going to relax, forget about the Farm and training for the weekend, and enjoy some private time together.

I arrange for him to bring her to George's restaurant for dinner. What she would not know was that the entire team would be sitting there when they arrived. I send everyone an e-mail saying that if she couldn't bring him on base for our office party, we will move the party off base where he can attend. Unfortunately, Frank is not particularly good at security. The poor guy can't keep a secret to save his life. He tells her about the party.

We have a great time, though. We eat and drink for hours, toasting our friendship and our careers. George's restaurant certainly does the trick for us. A private dining room with fresh flowers, light appetizers, and a staff that knows when to be attentive and when to leave us alone. It is one of the high points of the year when I stand and toast my colleagues and our spouses. It is a delightful evening. When the evening slips into morning, we trickle toward the door.

Like the good case officers we are training to be, every one of us goes to the front desk to ensure the waitstaff has been properly compensated and to thank our hosts for a wonderful evening. We chat briefly with the staff, which is still taking care of us though the restaurant closed hours earlier. The owner shakes each of our hands in turn as we walk to the door.

That's when the bomb drops: "So, do all of you work at the Agency with George?" he asks.

The subsequent silence of thirty hearts stopping at once engulfs the room.

"The Agency?" Mike manages to squeak.

"Sure. I assume you all work with George at CIA. He's a great guy, that George. He practically lives here. He must really like you guys. He never uses my place for recruiting or work-type stuff. He likes to keep some of his life just for himself. To let you guys in, he must really think the world of you," he effuses.

I process the words but have no snappy comeback to distract him from the question at hand. When all else fails, fall back on our cover.

"Oh no," I say. "We work for other federal agencies. I've known George for years and he is always talking about this place. I've been browbeating him for weeks to share it with us. Nice to see for once everything he described is accurate. We appreciate your hospitality."

I open the door and we race for the safety of the night air. But our host isn't finished. He grabs my arm before I can let go of the door. "Don't worry," he says. "I'll tell him you stuck to the company line. I know how it is. You guys are under the microscope 24/7 while you're here. I know it's tough, but George said you were the best group to come through in years. Keep it up! Get through all the hoops they make you jump through, and get out there. Everyone in town—every shopkeeper and restaurant owner—is behind you a thousand percent. Don't get me wrong. I love George. I love him. But the Agency was asleep at the switch. We can't let September 11 happen again. We can't let those bastards win."

We stand there lost in our uncertainty when Coach steps up. He grips the man's hand with his insanely powerful handshake and immediately slips into case officer mode. Placing his other hand on the man's shoulder, he gives the restaurateur a deliberate nod and a wink before saying, "They may have scored first, but they won't score last."

Disguises Gone Wrong
April 2003

ONCE AGAIN WE PRACTICE crossing borders into a fictitious country. Our terrestrial "planes" bump and sway along the narrow asphalt roads and emerge at the Winnebago Customs and Immigration facility.

After disembarking we shuffle into a waiting area. Unlike the border exercise we had in Washington, the subterfuge here is more discreet. There is not much interrogation. We are supposed to be able to get past that by this point. This exercise is designed to let us practice our commercial covers as international business travelers.

But the exercise has a valid purpose. It gives many students their first exposure to international business travel. We carry brochures, marketing plans, company letterhead, and business cards for fictitious companies created last month. Today we must defend the deception, taking care to *sound* like businesspeople. No flashing government credentials, no "calling the ambassador," just us talking ourselves out of harm's way. This is how Non Official Cover, or NOC, operations work. The officer is on his or her own, jumping without a net.

When I am called into the interview room, my laptop computer is taken by the inspector and handed off to someone else. The computers have ingeniously designed encryption systems that allow us to communicate covertly while traveling. A sweep of the hard drive will not find it, nor will any of the more aggressive computer forensics tools. That is where my laptop is being taken—out for some exploratory digital surgery. Any compromising files, e-mail, or instant messaging that can be retrieved would be printed out and given to the inspector for a lengthy interrogation.

The inspector is polite and professional, asking me about my business in Winnebago and when I am leaving. I give him my doctored itinerary and conference brochure. Due to the large number of people entering the country for this conference, he knows quite a bit about it, and asks me a few questions. Any student who hasn't read up on the industry and its current issues is likely to get zapped right here.

I make it through the checkpoint in less than ten minutes and retrieve my laptop before departing for my faux conference. We pass the exercise if we are able to leave the border station and drive our rental car out onto the main road. I have no issues whatsoever. Really a rather fun exercise to me, but nerve-racking to others.

Some of the military students have no idea how to act as businesspeople. Several of them take the bad advice of a couple of instructors and create their own 10-K reports (SEC-regulated reports filed by every company listed on a stock exchange) for their fake companies. This was foolish and gave the student a meaningless false sense of security.

First off, no businessperson carries 10-K reports when traveling. The Securities and Exchange Commission is an American entity, so why would anyone carry these reports overseas? Secondly, anyone can take two minutes to look up the major stock boards and find that the alleged cover company is a fake. Better to say the firm is private and not publicly traded, but that's not what the curriculum says to do.

Back in the office we share stories about what happened during the exercise. A few students answered interrogators' questions when addressed by their real name instead of the alias they are traveling under. A male and female student had compromising e-mails from each other suggesting a merger that can only be politely described as monkey business. Finally, a few people just made simple mistakes like using spy lingo including "station" (refers to a CIA office), "per diem" (the government's daily allotment for travel expenses), or "headquarters" (instead of the far easier "home office"). But most disheartening, nobody was busted with embarrassing lingerie.

I had absconded with Cathy's bra—the one that came in handy during the safe-house exercise—so I could place it in Daryll's overnight bag. It would be found during this border-crossing exercise, and he would have no idea where it had come from. The downside of the plan was once he figured out it was me, he would crush me into pulp. Lifelong rehabilitation aside, it was a small price to pay to make the big guy squirm. I hated that I couldn't get to his bag in time to plant it.

The following day we are map casing in the office when Al calls for me to come upstairs. I walk in with our office chief Mark following behind me and closing the door. They are both solemn.

"Tom," Al begins, "we need to talk about the border-crossing exercise."

"Sure thing, Al," I reply. I'd had a blast.

"I know you like to cut the fool and whatnot, but this time things have gone a bit too far. Some people are very unhappy with you."

I'm waiting on Al's punch line.

"OK, Al. I can see how you might think that." I'm bluffing. I have no idea what's going on.

"Tom, I just want to try and understand what you were thinking. I know misdirection is one of the areas you have excelled at in this course, but this incident is way past that. We have a real problem here."

Al isn't joking around. Something is wrong. It's conceivable that he might pull an elaborate joke on me, but he wouldn't involve Mark, nor would he pull me away from real work to do it.

I know there's nothing compromising on my computer, because I've never done anything stupid with it. There are no porno or gambling sites in my Web browser, nor are there compromising e-mails between me and anyone else. I had taken classes on computer forensics for a previous job. The only way to get away with something like that is to not do it at all. Time to elicit more information from him.

"What exactly were you told, Al?"

"Well, Tom," he began, "I understand you sat down with the interrogator and everything was fine. Your cover story was believable, and you knew the conference material cold. That's great. It's what was in your computer bag that created the problem."

Mark just nods.

"I see. Go on," I say, volunteering no comment.

"When the computer inspector came back with your bag and gave it to the interrogator, you should have just stayed quiet. You were in the home stretch. But you screwed up by saying too much and saying offensive things on top of it."

Mark chimes in at this point: "Tom, the problem is the instructor you did the exercise with is pretty pissed off. All the good points you racked up during the interview you pretty much blew away when the computer bag came back."

Al picks the story line back up. "That's right. Again, we all like to joke and laugh in the office, and that's all well and good, but you can't pull this kind of thing during a graded exercise. I mean, come on, Tom, really! Would you do this for real during a border crossing? An inspector pulls a tin of Altoids mints out of your bag, and you tell him they're birth control pills? What the hell is that all about?"

I maintain a stoic expression, nod, and stare at the floor, working up the best guilty look I can manage.

"That alone might have been forgivable," Al says, "but following that up with how you were going to screw your way across the convention and wanted to make sure the women you were with are on the pill whether they know it or not . . . I just can't believe it. The instructor said you were so nonchalant about it. He was stunned. You've done so well in the course, he called Mark and I to ask if something traumatic has happened to you recently. Jesus, Tom! Birth control pills? Screwing the attendees? What the hell are we supposed to do with you? How do we defend this? There are people calling for your head right now. What have you got to say for yourself?"

I take a deep breath. Whatever is going on is way too screwed up for me to not be livid, but these guys aren't the ones who screwed it up. At least, I hope they aren't.

"Al, I appreciate you bringing this to my attention. Mark, I'm glad you are here too. It really means a lot for you guys to go to bat for me. What I would like you to understand first and foremost is, I don't have any *fucking* clue what you're talking about."

Mark jumps in his chair when I let the F-bomb fly. I thought it added the dramatic flair I need.

"Tom, now I don't think . . ." Al starts.

"Al, buddy, I think I should talk now," I interrupt. "I didn't have any type of incident during the exercise. Not with birth control pills or any other prescription products. I sure as hell would not tell an instructor, a border-control agent, or any other asshole I met that I was going to screw my way through a conference. But that's just me."

"Tom, the guy was very specific about the whole thing. He told us the story word for word," Al retorts.

"Al, I did the border-crossing exercise with Roger. I don't know the contract idiot you are talking about. Roger's office is two doors down the hall." I stand up. "Let's go. Right now. You might even say I insist."

Mark stands up, but he's not moving toward the door. He's facing me. "You're sure about this, Tom?" he asks.

"Mark, let's take a walk. Roger can tell you. We did the interview, I went to the rental car area, and Roger brought my laptop and briefcase out in about ten minutes. There was no incident in the interrogation room and no Altoids mints in my bag."

Mark and Al stare at each other, speechless.

"What the hell is wrong with you guys?!" I yell. "Some shit-eater independent contractor tells you I did this, and that's it? Have you packed my room up? Am I ejected from the program because some dumbass can't pick a photo out of the class roster?"

Mark sits back down and rubs his chin.

"That's how he picked me, right? Didn't know the student's name, so he had to go see the photo roster in the administration office? I know Roger, and he knows me. I'm not aware of any dementia problems *he's* having, so why don't you two guys get up, go chat with him, then go find this other idiot to get this straightened out."

"Now, Tom, if a mistake's been made there's no reason to start name-calling," Mark starts.

"What the hell do you think you two are doing?!" I roar. "You just said the guy was talking it up with other instructors, asking what should be done about it. Do you really want to tell me every instructor in the course doesn't know about this and assumes I'm guilty?"

Al holds his hands up. "Tom, we'll get to the bottom of it. If you were falsely accused, we'll make sure it's fixed."

"*If?* What's the '*if*,' Al? I just told you I did the exercise with someone else, someone you have been friends with for twenty years. I want this fixed now! This is the third time you guys have mistaken me for someone else. I'm tired of it."

Al is on his feet and opening the door. My last few words escape down the hall and several people stare at us. Al assures me they will get to the bottom of whatever is going on.

A couple of hours later, there's a note on my desk from Al. He writes that the contract role-player sends his apologies, that he had indeed picked my photo out from the student roster, and was sorry he caused me any trouble.

The guy is a retired case officer with thirty years' experience, and he can't pick out a student's picture? More important, he didn't give a damn enough to learn the student's name prior to the exercise, knowing he had to write an evaluation after it was over?

* * *

ON WEDNESDAY AFTERNOON I am trying out a new SDR route. Some new and, I think, innovative stops on the way and an easy sell to justify the route and the order of stops. This should work out well. I am on my way back to the Farm when Terry calls my cell phone.

"Are you busy?" she asks.

"Nope. I'm heading for the office, actually. Where are you?" I ask.

"I'm stuck and need some help. Can you help me?"

"Sure. Where are you?"

She gives me the address. "It's a shopping plaza. I've stepped inside a store to get out of the weather. I'm in Michael's when you get here."

"Sit tight," I tell her. "Help is on the way."

I find the shopping center in quick order and walk up to a small boutique named Michael's, not really paying much attention to it. Terry is not standing by the front door, so I take a couple of steps in to look around. Lots of people in here during the middle of the afternoon, but I still don't see her. Maybe there's a ladies' room in the back. I meander around that way. No ladies' room. I'm walking back up front when a voice calls out.

"What do you think?"

I spin around. A young woman is standing on a dress pedestal two feet over me. She is smiling. She is beaming. She is waving her cell phone at me.

Terry is trying on wedding dresses.

After taking a moment to recover, I address the most obvious point first. "I see you're working hard today."

"Oh, come on," she says. "I'm allowed a little time off. I'm barely able to plan my wedding with all the stuff they have us doing. Give me a break." She picks up her skirt with both hands, flipping it back and forth. "So, what do you think?"

"I think you look beautiful," I say.

"Really?" she squeals. "Hang on. I'm torn between this one and one other one. Let me change." She hops down and runs into a nearby dressing room.

I flop down into a chair. "This is the help you needed?" I call out.

"Yes. I can't decide which one I want."

How did I get roped into this? I didn't help Cathy pick out the dress for *our* wedding. How the hell do I help pick out a dress for someone else's?

Terry comes back out in another dress that is a distinctly different style from the first. Where the first one was stylish and elegant, this dress is more . . . well, suggestive. It's formfitting, shows lots of skin, and leaves little to the imagination.

"That's quite a dress," is all I can muster.

"Is it not me? Too much *Leather* and not enough *Lace*?" she asks with a glare.

I'm going to kill Wall Street Mike when I get back.

"Didn't think I knew about that, did you?" she asks playfully.

"Nope. So much for operational security. I hope his next career is more successful."

"Oh, relax. We thought it was pretty funny."

"We? So Helen knows too, huh?"

"Whatever I know, Helen knows. Now stay on topic. This dress or the other one?"

"I don't know. Seems to me this is not the image you want unless you're charging twenty bucks for table dances. I'd go with the more traditional one."

"OK. Just a sec." She disappears back into the dressing room.

Instead of coming out ready to go she's back in the original dress again. Everyone walking by comments or oohs and aahs at her. She is radiant. I hope Cathy's dress hunt was this much fun for her.

"Yeah," she says, "I think I like this one better too. It's more traditional. Tradition is good."

"Why don't I get a camera, and we can take a few pictures to show the kids back at the office? Don't you need Helen's input for this sort of thing?" I ask, desperate for an exit strategy. I don't like shopping, and the only time I can imagine where I might enjoy it is if Porsche decides to have a 50 percent off sale. Better make that 75 percent. I work for the government now.

"No, I think I like this one."

"Still, let's take a picture and get some other opinions. I don't know about any of this. Cathy can tell you. Actually, Cathy would probably love to tell you. I didn't do any of our wedding planning. It was all her. I was too busy getting ready to come into the Agency. All I did was show up."

Terry thinks this is hysterical and says she hopes her fiancé will allow her the same space to plan. Her soon-to-be mother-in-law has other ideas of what she wants the wedding to look like.

"Tell her to pound sand. It's your day. Whatever you want is what's important. Tell his mom to go plan her own wedding."

She changes clothes and purchases the dress. She thinks it could be difficult to explain why she has a wedding dress with her if she's stopped at a roadblock at the Farm, so she ships it home with Saturday delivery. When we get back outside, she stops me again.

"Thanks for coming out. I didn't want to do this by myself. All my friends had such big parties and stuff when they picked out their dresses. I just don't have time for that. I guess I was having a pity party and just decided 'screw it'; I'll pick out a dress now and have a party with my girlfriends after we finish in June. It's not exactly traditional, though." She pouts.

"No," I say. "Nothing is traditional about what we are doing. But look at the bright side. When you get married, you will be living with your husband right away. Look at how Cathy and I are apart after getting married a year ago. This way is better. Finish the program, then start your life together."

I'm riddled with guilt that I put Cathy through all of this. Talking about it makes me feel like an even bigger jerk.

"Did you guys have any trouble with the in-laws?" she asks.

"No, not at all. In fact, we all get along real well. Why? Are things bad?"

"Yeah, well, sort of."

I won't repeat the entire conversation, because it was personal and a difficult topic for her. What we did not know at the time was that there would now be an additional difficulty. While we are standing outside talking, Terry's cell phone is jostled in her purse. It redials the last call she made.

To her fiancé.

He isn't home, so naturally it rolls to voice mail and records a message. A twenty-minute message. She calls me later to relay her fiancé's distress over her airing his family's dirty laundry. He played the entire phone message for her, "refreshing" her memory about what she had said. They argued for half an hour.

The phone monitors hear all of George Carlin's seven dirty words tonight.

ONCE AGAIN we arise way too early in the morning for my taste. And once again I am flat on my back for sit-ups, then flipping over for push-ups. There are only a handful of students here for the test. In fact, there are more spectators than testers.

I complete the required sit-ups and push-ups this time with very little problem. When I walk outside to join the crowd for the two-mile run, a striking sight awaits.

My entire office is dressed to run the course with me.

They are out here at six thirty in twenty-degree weather to run because of me. There is not another student whose office has chosen to support him or her in this task.

We start off and Coach sets a comfortable pace. He runs this course several times daily and has milestones along the route to know whether he is on time or not. I've got twenty minutes and nineteen seconds to complete the run. Much longer than any of them, but still very aggressive for the corporate hack I have become.

I do very well the first half of the course. We are chatting but still keeping the pace that Coach has set. As we start the backside, however, I slow down. I've been concentrating so much on sit-ups and push-ups that I've slacked off on running. That, plus it has still been freezing outside with ice on the ground. That hasn't helped motivate me for additional practice.

Making matters worse is I've had a terrible pain in my lower abdomen. Adam tells me to ignore it, and Coach suggests it is just a "stitch" and will go away if I keep going. But the pain gets worse. I slow down to a walk.

"No!! Move it! Pick it up! You don't have time to kill on this!" Coach yells.

"Come on, Tom. Pick it up," says Adam.

"Come on, Tom, one more time and you're done for the course," says Mike.

I trot a couple of steps, but the pain increases. If this is a stitch, I have a solid respect for it. I come to a complete stop and bend over, touching my toes.

Someone kidney punches me.

"Move your ass!" Gavin is beside me, dragging me forward via my waistband. How great is an instructor to run with a student on a physical fitness test?

"Gavin, I'm hurting here. I would grab it, but you guys would just say I was playing with myself."

"You're running that risk either way, so get something out of it. This is bullshit. Come on, Tom!" Gavin shouts.

Adam and Travis are behind him, the Agency students a respectful distance back. Gavin's not an instructor now. He's just doing what I suspect he does in real life: He's being a leader.

I start again, but my heart and speed are definitely not in it. Gavin runs alongside me, with Travis flanking and Adam just ahead. Everyone else is close behind. One office rallied around one student. I've never experienced anything like it.

I make it to the end of the course, but miss my time by thirty seconds. I'll be doing the SOTC fitness test once more.

I walk around the outside of the gym, trying to walk off the pain. I can feel an abdominal bulge through my sweatpants. That can't be good.

"Hey, Travis!" I yell.

He walks up.

"You've taken that Special Forces medical course, right?" I ask.

"Roger that."

"What would you diagnose if someone gets a shooting pain from an unexplained bulge that appears?"

"What kind of bulge?" he inquires.

"The kind we would have to be married before you can see," I joke through clenched teeth.

He thinks for a minute. "I would call that a hernia."

"Would you call that a life-threatening problem?" I ask.

"Life-threatening? No. Damn painful, though, and it could get out of hand real easily if it's not taken care of."

"How simple is it to fix?"

"Pretty simple, if you have a hospital, doctors, and a real live surgical suite. If you just have a physician's assistant and some basic medical supplies like we have here, then I would call it a problem."

"So, this would be an automatic out from training, then?" I ask, already knowing the answer.

"Yeah, probably. If you do the arthroscopic, you can probably be back in a week or so, but you won't run for a while."

"Or finish the SOTC course?"

He starts to say something and changes his mind. He looks around. We are alone.

"No, probably not. They will toss you for sure."

"Gotcha. Thanks. I assume I get the same doctor-patient confidentiality anyone else would."

"You bet. But don't think you can hide that forever. You're old, pal. If it really is a hernia, it's only *started* hurting. Ignore it long enough and it ruptures? You will learn what pain is really like."

EASTER SUNDAY is our first anniversary. To say it has been quite a year is a gross understatement. I manage to hide the unsightly bulge from Cathy over the weekend, though I know that won't last long. She isn't blind, and she certainly isn't stupid.

We go to church at the National Cathedral in Washington, followed by brunch at the Four Seasons Restaurant in Georgetown. We spend the day together and receive countless phone calls from family and friends wishing us well. I hate to do it, but I've got to leave her again this afternoon to return to my dorm room at the Farm. I leave mid-afternoon and arrive just before six o'clock.

There is probably some long-lettered psychological term for the feeling you get when you just *know* someone has been in your living space. You walk in and feel violated before you have a chance to notice a door ajar or a missing item. I have that feeling now. Looking around my dorm room, it all appears in order, yet something is wrong.

I put the laundry down and quickly scan from one wall to the next. I had cleaned the place before I left because I have a safe-house exercise in here tomorrow. I didn't want to risk coming in late and not getting a chance to really prepare before Monday morning. That's when I notice what's missing.

My September 11 Tommy Bahama shirt, SHAKEN BUT UNDETERRED, is gone. I'm anything but deterred.

I tear the room apart. If there are cameras installed, I will certainly hear about this. I've worn that shirt twice since arriving and intend to wear it during a recruitment exercise this week. I had had it dry cleaned and put it in a specific place. It's gone.

This was a present from Cathy. This isn't just a theft. What was stolen was a gift from my new wife, commemorating my opportunity to come to the Farm. I would have preferred the entire rest of the room was taken and the shirt still remained. But that hasn't happened.

The doors to our rooms can only be locked when we are inside them. There are no keys available to students to lock up when we are out. On the one hand, it makes it easier for the housekeeping staff to vacuum or change our linens. On the other hand, it makes it impossible to secure the room when we are in class, on an exercise, or gone for the weekend. My room has been open and available to anyone for two and a half days.

I am furious, and now my room is not ready for the exercise tomorrow. I square the room away again, but vow to file a report with the SPOs in the morning. If I see anyone on this base with that shirt on I will go to jail to get it back.

Several other people report items disappearing from their rooms too.

A Walkman CD player, several pairs of sunglasses, and some jewelry just on the second floor of my building. It bothers me that someone was in my room. It bothers me that someone stole from me. But it infuriates me beyond mere words that someone has taken my September 11 shirt.

So much for the Farm's tight security.

WE PREPARE for our out-of-town field trip by wearing our disguises on an exercise in the local town. For the first time we will display our disguises in public, outside the sheltered protection of the Farm. This will give us a taste of what it's like to wear a disguise for a real operational act. We have to become the character we are portraying.

John finishes the morning brief, and the head of the Farm's disguise office addresses us. This exercise is external—that is to say, there is a whole lot more that can go wrong. John and Jane Q. Public are out there. They are concerned about terrorism, duct taping their homes, and snipers in their midst. Their radar is attuned to anything that seems out of place. We will be out of place.

We are to drive to a local shopping mall. We will go inside in disguise, ignore the other students walking around in similarly outrageous outfits, and engage shopkeepers in at least two different stores. After we have successfully conducted business in the two stores, we can break off, remove our disguises in an appropriately discreet location, and return to the Farm. Getting caught means failing the exercise. Lose, drop, or smear the disguise, and we fail. If we talk to another student, we fail. If we don't talk with at least two shopkeepers, we fail. Policing us on all these details will be a small team of technical officers.

The surveillance teams will be walking around in the mall or sitting outside on benches with covert video equipment. The entire exercise will be videotaped to show us what we look like—in appearance and mannerism—while we're in disguise. We will then critique our work with the instructors.

We depart in groups of four. Mike, Coach, and Dave are with me. Adam,

Terry, Wendy, and Travis are the other group. We all get into our disguises and load up into two cars. The exercise is to begin at 12:30, so lunch is thrown in for free by the instructors. Of course, we have to eat and drink in our disguises, just like we would do in the field. At least there is no SDR today, and we thank the espionage gods for the small favor!

Mike and Coach decide that a lunch at McDonald's, across the parking lot from our designated mall entrance, is the best venue for us. There is a high turnover of customers and lots of noise and distractions. We sit down with our burgers and try to eat lunch like everyone else.

I had a mustache from about age sixteen until I turned thirty, when I felt it had successfully completed its mission of making me look older. At that point I was going for the opposite effect, and shaved it off. I forgot how difficult eating with a mustache can be if you are out of practice. My three officemates have never had one, so we are going through napkins like life jackets on the *Titanic*, trying to keep ketchup out of our synthetic facial hair.

We are sitting in the back corner of the restaurant. My back is to the window, and we laugh and make comments at the people who are laughing and making comments at us. Mike and Coach are right about this being a good place to hide, but unlike adults, children stare at someone with an outrageous appearance. Four guys looking outrageous is almost circuslike.

Mike is sitting across the table from me and looks over my shoulder. He has seen an instructor's red pickup truck pull into the mall parking lot. Two men with shoulder bags get out of the truck and enter the mall.

"Hey, guys," Mike says, "the surveillance crew is in place."

We turn around and watch them enter. From our vantage point a hundred yards away we can see two different sides of the mall around a corner. Our entry point is opposite the entrance the instructors are using. We will stagger in behind Group 1. Ten minutes after they enter we will stand at the entrance and space ourselves one minute apart, walking into the mall and fanning out inside.

The video crew has gotten halfway across the parking lot when Group 1 exits the mall from the other set of doors. They are standing there, elevating their profile to allow the video crew and instructor staff to target them before beginning the exercise. Mike looks at his watch.

"What the hell? They're twelve minutes early. They can't go yet."

Coach looks at a little girl staring at him. She looks like she may start screaming any second.

"I don't think we can blame them for going early. I suggest we get out of here, too."

As we gather our trash and check one another's disguises one last time, Group 1 enters the mall.

The four of us begin a slow walk across the parking lot. We aren't supposed to appear to be together, but we didn't take that into account when selecting McDonald's for our lunch venue. We arrive at the mall entrance and stand at opposite corners for the prescribed time to attract the instructor's attention. Mike reads a newspaper, Coach goes through his wallet, Dave looks at the bus schedule, and I pull out my cell phone. It's not an Academy Award moment, but it's at least believable. I break off first and enter the mall.

As my eyes adjust to the light, one thing is immediately apparent: There are way too few people in here. There are only young mothers with children or retirees in mall-walking groups. Everyone else is outrageously dressed and trying desperately to look innocent.

I recognize a couple of instructors shopping in a store to my right, and I suspect that the woman on the park bench in front of me is probably taping me. When you think you're being watched, it creates a self-fulfilling prophecy. You think "they" are watching, so your mannerism is affected. You don't act normal. You fidget. As a result, people do watch you. This just makes you more nervous.

I decide the best tactic is to go on the offensive. I duck into a Levi's store. Two guys around eighteen years of age are working, though not actually doing anything.

"What's up, fellas?" I say loud enough for my antagonists outside to hear.

"Good afternoon, sir. What can I help you with"—his speech slows down as he gets closer to me. He can see my moustache is fake and I'm wearing a wig—"today?" he finishes.

"Oh, I'm just poking around. My wife dragged me in here to look at baby shower gifts for a friend, and I can stand only so much estrogen in that store. I had to get out before I started growing tits. What I really need is a gun shop, but failing that, jeans are going to have to do."

The kid finds this funny, but the other clerk eyes me like I'm going to jack the place.

"If we can help you with anything, don't hesitate to ask," the first one says.

"Thanks, fellas. If you were discussing hot women or cold beer, don't let me interrupt."

Another patron walks in—a man carrying a pilot's flight bag or similar case. Probably one of the surveillance guys.

"Hello, sir, can I help you find anything?" the second kid asks him.

The man simply shakes his head no and looks through the racks of clothes. Could it be he doesn't want his own voice on the recording? No, wait. Don't assume. There will be plenty of other people and voices on the tape. It doesn't matter if the instructor's voice is on there too. Quit trying to second-guess everything. Spend ten minutes looking around and get out to the next store.

I say good-bye to the two clerks and make my way back into the mall to find another store. If I can have similar success elsewhere, I should skate through this.

Ahead of me is another student named Tony. He's about ten years younger than I am, but also a good three inches taller than my six-foot-three-inch height. His disguise is not convincing and actually accentuates his height, making him stand out all the more. As he is walking by a jewelry kiosk, I notice the young clerk's eyes bulge in fright.

I slow down. This could go badly.

As soon as Tony passes her, she bolts from the kiosk and frantically waves at someone out of my line of sight. As I emerge from behind a column,

I realize what she's doing. She's talking to a mall security guard, one of those private company guys who don't carry guns but have radios and cell phones. I can't hear what she's saying, but she's pointing at Tony. The guard is speaking into his phone.

I can't get Tony's attention, nor can I walk up to an instructor to report what I think is happening. Now that I actually need one, there isn't one in sight. Are they avoiding the rent-a-cop, or are they following students in the stores?

I take a left at the center of the mall and continue down the next corridor. I need to find another store to hide in. First is a Victoria's Secret followed by a Pea in the Pod. Lingerie or maternity wear? Hard to make a legitimate case for either, especially looking like I do. I don't think I can pull off a cross-dresser persona.

I reach the end of the corridor just as a police car pulls up. Looking behind me, I see another policeman is already inside the mall and talking to the security guard. If I walk up there, he is just going to point me out unless there's another student nearby who looks more outrageous than I do.

Jed walks past the two police officers looking so normal, it takes me a moment to notice him grinning at me. He knows he is safe, the miserable bastard. Nicole is behind him, sitting on a bench with a mother and child. Very nice. Hiding in plain sight. They will both sail through this. I, however, still need an out. Better to fend for myself in the open parking lot. My hand is on the door when I see the police car has stopped and the officer has exited the car and is talking with Adam and Terry.

His right hand is on his gun.

He's probably not in the mood for any more company, so I go with plan B. I pull out my cell phone and talk as I stare out the window at the spectacle.

Another officer pulls up behind the first and walks around behind Terry.

"So, who would like to explain this?" the first officer asks.

"Explain what?" Adam replies.

Idiot! Never be the spokesman for a group, especially if you are doing something wrong.

"Who are you? Do you have any identification?" the cop asks.

"Sure. Here." Adam hands over his military identification. The picture is so old and his head so shaved, it's not unreasonable for him to look nothing like the photograph.

"And where are you staying, Captain?" the officer asks.

Adam gives him the name of a nearby military airfield.

"And who there could vouch for you?" the officer asks, smiling now.

"Um, actually, no one. I think they are probably all out here somewhere."

"Everyone from the base is out here at the mall, huh?" the officer looks at the cop behind Terry. "Are you on an exercise?"

"Yes, sir."

"Are you a military officer too?" the second cop asks Terry.

"No sir, I'm not."

"But you are out here with a military officer?"

"Yes, sir."

"Do you have some identification?"

"Yes, sir."

Terry hands him her driver's license, but unlike Adam's identification, hers is relatively recent.

"Well, we've dyed our hair, have we?" the second cop says.

"Yes, sir. Do you like it?"

"Sure, it's real nice. Did the dye job go bad, or are you enjoying wearing a twenty-year-old wig?"

Terry stands there, lost in her story. There really isn't anything to say.

"You guys wouldn't be staying at the Farm, would you?" the first cop asks.

"Yes, sir," Adam says. "We can't volunteer it, but since you asked I think I can get away with it."

"Well, Captain, that'll be about all you get away with today. What's the story with you guys? We don't normally catch you doing stuff like this. Are you just that bad? You have the entire mall spun up. They were expecting to be robbed at any second. You guys scared the shit out of them."

"Excuse me, Officer, may I be of assistance?"

Walking up from the parking lot is the head of the disguise office. Her hands are spread out in front of her, a nonthreatening gesture before approaching any closer.

"Are these people with you?" the first officer asks.

"Yes, sir. May I show you my credentials?" she asks, gesturing at her purse.

"Yes, please do."

She reaches in and pulls out her CIA identification declaring herself an Agency officer. She also produces an Endorsement Card from the local Sheriff's Department. Anytime she produces the card she is on a U.S. government–approved training exercise, and the inquiring official should cooperate to the fullest extent possible. More important, the names of any students are never included in any official document without prior review by the Agency's Office of the General Counsel. It is the mythical get-out-of-jail-free card people always talk about but never actually see.

On the other side of the mall, another group of students is rolled up before they even reach the mall doors. Like us, they had been having lunch across the parking lot, but they chose a more traditional sit-down restaurant. A woman sitting nearby looked up from her sandwich and saw four men in disguises. She's a teller from the bank next door and thought they were casing the joint.

She dialed 9-1-1 from the table.

Police surround the restaurant, and an entry team challenges the four students before they can stand up. In the woman's defense, her concern is understandable. All four students are elite military: an Army Ranger, two Navy SEALS, and a Special Ops helicopter pilot. They have the muscular, chiseled look of experienced combat veterans. Their attempt to blend in with their disguises in a nice restaurant simply didn't work, and the exercise is over before it can even start.

The next day we learn that Adam and Terry's episode is caught on tape when it is played for the entire morning brief audience.

THE MILITARY STUDENTS note each American death in Iraq with intense concern. These are not simply news items. The victims are people they know, people they work with, people they feel they are letting down by not being in the fight.

When service personnel are deployed overseas they must prepare a mountain of paperwork. Among these are their preferences for burial in the event of their deaths. Arlington National Cemetery is hallowed ground to the military, as it should be to all Americans, and is selected by many of the personnel called up for action in Iraq. While an average of twenty-five funerals are held there every weekday, most are elderly men. They survived Vietnam, Korea, and even World War II, and are now succumbing to the ravages of old age. Many have few friends and little family. But this week the crowds have swelled.

The week of Friday, April 25, Arlington National Cemetery buries seven soldiers, sailors, and Marines killed in Operation Iraqi Freedom. The men range in age from twenty-three to thirty-one, barely started in life's journey when they *answered a call*. On Sunday, April 27, the *Washington Post* prints a few of the last letters sent home from the soldiers who died. Reading the paper between classes on Monday, one soldier's story catches our attention. I hope the family of U.S. Marine Corps Captain Ryan Beaupre will indulge me in citing part of his letter.

He was killed on March 20 in a helicopter crash in Kuwait. Captain Beaupre wrote a note to his parents that would only be delivered in the event of his death. He told them to not be angry with the Marines, the nation, or the president. They were doing what they thought was right. He was doing something he truly loved, and doing it for a purpose greater than himself. He quoted a paragraph he carried with him that spoke volumes about the man and the Marine. That paragraph, written a hundred years ago by John Stuart Mill, reads,

War is an ugly thing, but not the ugliest of things. The decayed and degraded state of moral and patriotic feeling which thinks that nothing is worth war is much worse. The person who has nothing for which he is willing to fight, nothing which is more important than his own personal safety, is a miserable creature and has no chance of being free unless made and kept so by the exertions of better men than himself.

Travis shows the article to Adam. Both men speak eloquently of friends who have fallen in the line of duty. It really bothers Travis that he is not in Iraq when his friends are under fire. He's having trouble sleeping. He's distracted, and his overall performance in the program has slipped noticeably. He has almost quit twice. Both times Gavin has talked him into staying, though Travis is clearly torn over where he should be.

We are still talking about Captain Beaupre when we lock the office on our way to class. Taping the article to the hallway side of the door, Travis says out loud what we are all thinking: "He would have made one hell of an intelligence officer."

Blackmailed with Russian Porno
May 2003

BLUE LIGHTS in my rearview mirror. That's never good.

I am finishing up a ninety-minute SDR before returning to the Farm. This is my last onsite exercise. I'm sure I don't have surveillance, even though the teams are now picking us up randomly as we drive around the area. Like a foreign service will occasionally do, they sit at major intersections and traffic chokepoints, waiting for someone interesting to come by. Overseas they would identify us by our diplomatic license tags. Here, they just identify our car make, model, and license plates. We're fish in a barrel. Unfortunately, I'm now pinned by an entirely different service.

A local sheriff's deputy has nailed me speeding in a quiet residential neighborhood. The neighborhood is perfect for detecting surveillance. Lots of cut-throughs and dead-end streets. What I didn't expect was a speed trap, especially in a downpour.

Police rarely put up speed traps in the rain, because people automatically tap their brakes when they see an officer with a radar gun. Those who slam their brakes go into a spin and what begins as a traffic violation matures into an accident. What the hell is he doing out here now? I roll down my window and turn the car off. This will not be fun.

"Afternoon, Officer," I say as rain pours in my window. I'm wearing a coat and tie for today's exercise and don't have a change of clothes.

"Good afternoon. May I see your driver's license and registration, please?"

"Certainly. Here is my license. The car's a rental, but I have the paperwork."

He looks both of them over.

"You're a long ways from home. What's your hurry?" he asks.

"I'm here for a meeting at the base."

"Really?" He gives me a knowing look. "Are you military?"

"No, sir."

"Law enforcement?"

"No, sir. I'm running late, so I was moving a bit fast."

"Yes sir, you were. Just a moment, please."

The officer returns to his car and sits inside to avoid the downpour while writing out my ticket. No sense fighting it and delaying my exercise any longer than necessary.

"Here you are, sir," the officer says, returning my driver's license and handing me his clipboard to sign my ticket. I should at least find out why he's here.

"You guys don't normally set up in the rain," I say, handing back the clipboard. "Are that many locals hauling through here?"

"No, not exactly. Some neighbors noticed suspicious activity recently. Cars driving aimlessly, turning around in driveways, stopping for short periods of time before moving on. Things like that. They've been calling the mayor for a couple of days. He made us set up out here."

So much for clandestine activity.

"Wow," I say. "Do they think people are looking around hoping to rob someone?" I ask, hoping to point him in the wrong direction.

"Could be. I just know I'm soaking wet and haven't seen anything suspicious. But you need to slow it down. There are a lot of kids in this neighborhood."

"I don't suspect I'll be around again, but I take your point. I'll keep it to a dull roar."

"Have a nice day, sir," he says, returning to his car.

"Same to you, Officer." I roll up my window.

I'm now twenty minutes behind schedule. There's no way to make my meeting on time. I have the instructor's cell phone number, so I call, explain what happened, and push our meeting back thirty minutes so he isn't standing around waiting for me with no explanation. We conduct the meeting without further incident, and I return to the instruction building.

I stop by the surveillance office and tell the desk officer that I had been ticketed. She explains that even though I have the right to fight it in court, contacting the General Counsel's office for assistance on a traffic ticket will not be the best career boost I would ever have. I assure her I plan to pay the fine with no court appearance. I also tell her what the officer had said about the calls to the mayor. That gets her attention.

She takes me into another office, which is plastered with local maps. I show her my overall route and timing sheets and trace them out on the wall map. I outline the neighborhood where the police officer was set up. She says the surveillance teams have been through the area a lot in the past two weeks as more and more students found out what a perfect spot it is. Rather, it *was* a perfect spot. It's off-limits now.

The following day we complete the morning brief but are told to remain in our seats. Dottie has come all the way from Langley to see us. Today we get to select our assignments.

Forms are passed out with our names and other pertinent background information contained in a short biographical paragraph. We are to correct or amend any part of this paragraph that we want them to use for consideration of the area assignments we want. Then we assemble our wish list.

The wish list is our top three picks for assignments. Do you want to be a case officer in Dubai, a reports officer in Budapest, or a desk officer in Taipei? Is that the order that you want to be considered? We can also select an area of the world and take any position that comes available, say a position in Kuala Lumpur or Beijing. We could also just offer to take any case-officer position anywhere supporting the war on terrorism. We have two hours to complete the form before reporting to the administration building auditorium.

We wander back to our offices to complete the wish list. The DOD students are already there. They do not have a wish list; they simply go where and when they are told. They find our wish list activity amusing and help everyone fill out the forms. Travis suggests we might want a few beers tonight.

"How about seven o'clock at Uno's?" he asks.

Everyone agrees it's a good plan. We have no exercises on tap this afternoon, and we are sick of driving around. A night off sounds good.

"What's this auditorium thing today?" Wendy asks. The session was not on our master schedule but was added during this morning's brief.

Nobody knows. Adam and Travis have also been told to be there, so we walk over together. When we enter the administration building Adam steps into the men's room. He still isn't back when Course Chairman John takes the stage.

"May I have your attention, please?" he asks. The doors in the back of the room are shut.

Coach leans over to whisper, "Adam is locked out. He's screwed."

Travis nods but says nothing. He doesn't even turn around to look at the back of the room to see where Adam might be.

"I would appreciate it if you would all give Gavin your undivided attention for a few minutes," John says from the podium.

Gavin takes the stage in full dress uniform. We all look at one another in surprise.

"Good afternoon. The majority of you are civilians and have never seen a military promotion ceremony. You will see one today. This is the first military promotion ever conducted at the Farm. It is an honor to be officiating at such an occasion."

In a loud voice he calls out across the crowd.

"Captain! Front and center!"

Adam steps out from behind a curtain, also in his full dress uniform. He marches to the center of the stage and stops at attention.

Travis looks at the rest of us and grins.

"Boys, we've been had," I whisper to Mike and Coach.

For the next five minutes Gavin reads Adam's official promotion from Captain to Major in the United States Army. He removes the Captain's bars from Adam's uniform and replaces them with a wreath signifying the rank of Major. True to most field promotions, he doesn't pin the clasp on the back of the insignia. Instead, he slaps each one into place, driving the pin's stem into Adam's collarbone. It's tradition.

Gavin explains that under normal circumstances, an officer's spouse takes responsibility for pinning a new rank on their uniform. For single officers, it's a responsibility usually handled by their mothers.

"Don't even think about calling me Mother," he growls at Adam.

Adam salutes. Gavin returns the salutation. Gavin exits the stage, and the military students lead the thunderous applause. Adam makes a ten-minute speech about the military promotion process and how happy he is to be sharing it with us. He explains that out of respect to his Defense Department colleagues, he will wear the uniform for the remainder of the day.

That night he changes into civilian clothes, and our little office meets at Uno's per Travis's devious plan. We eat and drink, toasting both men's continued promotion through the Army's ranks. We return to the Farm and resume our celebration at the SRB with the rest of the DOD students. By midnight we are sufficiently emboldened to create some quiet mayhem.

Dave had begged off from the evening's revelry. He was behind on some paperwork and planned to catch up during this rare window of opportunity. We quietly case the instruction building. Our office windows are dark, so the doors must be locked and the alarm set. Dave is done for the night. Since he was not at the SRB when we left, he must be in his room.

We quietly slip across the dark expanse of the Farm into Residence One. There are students milling about watching television, talking on the phones, or sitting outside enjoying the night off. We work our way up the back stairs to Dave's room and huddle outside his door. He must be punished for not joining us tonight. He must be dogpiled.

"What's 'dogpiled'?" Wendy asks.

"We get the door open, throw him to the ground, and everyone piles on. Dogpile!" Adam explains.

"Oh. Back home we call that sport-humping," Wendy said.

Adam and Mike exchange looks, then look at Terry and me before busting out laughing.

"I thought sport-humping meant something else entirely," Travis says. "I like Dave, but not that way."

"Me too," I volunteer.

"Ditto," says Mike.

"Sport-humping does mean that!!" Terry ventures. "Are you sure you understood it correctly?" she asks Wendy.

Wendy's embarrassment makes it all the more amusing, and we were already making a lot of noise. A nearby door opens, and a student peeks outside to see what's up.

"Shut up! He'll hear us!" Travis insists.

We finally quiet down. We are preparing to make our entry when Adam holds up a hand signaling everyone to stop. He points to his ear.

Terry hears it. Then Mike. Then Travis and me.

Dave is singing in the bathroom. Frank Sinatra's "Come Fly with Me." He isn't half bad.

This starts the hysterics all over again. It takes Travis another five minutes to shut us up.

Adam tries the door, but it's locked. Dave is no fool.

"How do we get the door open?" Terry asks.

"Someone he knows has to knock so he won't be expecting any funny stuff," I reply.

"Sounds like he's getting ready for bed. What if he comes to the door in his underwear?" Wendy asks.

"Good point," Travis says. He looks at Adam and me. "Gentlemen?"

Adam links arms with Travis and me and we push Wendy to the front of the group, trapping her in the doorway. Mike reaches over us to rap on the door.

"Dave," Mike calls, "can I borrow your laptop charger?"

When Dave opens the door, he is indeed in his underwear. We pour into the room. Tackling Dave via Wendy, the human avalanche falls on the bed.

"Dogpile!" we yell.

Dave can't even yell for help. His toothbrush is still in his mouth. Terry, being the good den mother she is, jumps off the pile and takes the toothbrush from him, putting it in the bathroom sink. The noise brings several neighboring students to Dave's door.

"Pile on," Travis invites.

Students take running leaps onto the pile. Wendy is crushed between a mountain of men and Dave. We finally allow them both up and meander back into the hall. It's two in the morning.

Daryll pokes his head out of his room to see what the fuss is about.

"Oh, nothing," Wendy assures him. "I was just sport-humping Dave."

Daryll's face reflects his interpretation. Apparently sport-humping means the same to him as it does to the rest of us. Wendy is aghast, realizing she has done it again. She slaps a hand across her mouth, turning beet red. She tries to explain more clearly what she means, getting more and more flustered the longer she talks.

Daryll closes the door without uttering a word.

AFTER THE MORNING BRIEF, the instructors leave the auditorium. A lone figure walks down the left wall staircase to the podium.

"So. How'd that border-crossing exercise go?" he asks. David is back for part two of our acting classes. Once again, per his requirement, he is alone with his students.

Several people comment about how nervous they were for that exercise compared to the Washington version. They thought this one would be easier, but in actuality it was just the opposite.

"Hmm. I see. Can't quite lie as effectively as you could when you were a kid, huh?" he asks.

A student in the back points out that it is more difficult now than as a child because of the artificiality of it. As a kid you never had to pretend who you were.

"Sure you did," David interrupts. "You did it all the time. You just weren't believable."

He turns and writes LIAR on the board.

"This training will turn you into the best liars in the world. Seriously. When you finish this program, you should be able to withstand any short-duration examination, interview, or interrogation without flinching. What you must do is remember to tailor your language to your audience. You already do it subconsciously all the time. Now you must be able to do it on command, and sometimes with little preparation."

He describes a scenario and tells us to consider how our description of it would change based on the audience we are speaking to.

"Would you use the same language with your mother that you use with your best friend? Can the words used in a locker room be used with a priest? I'm guessing not. I'm hoping not! You have to tailor what you say and how you say it to your audience. Think about how they are taking in the information and evaluating it. If I describe for my wife, boss, mother, or a small child the same scenario I just described to you, it's possible that you wouldn't recognize it. Not because I gave you incomplete information, but because I gave you *different* information. What I told you was specifically formulated for your preferences, norms, expectations, and beliefs. Work within that framework, and you can effectively lie to anyone."

He pulls a wig out of a nearby box and puts it on, along with a pair of fuzzy pink sunglasses. He looks like a tall Muppet.

"That's the difference," he says. "Outrageous can look normal in the right context. If I'm Elton John, this looks normal. If I'm David the professor, it's not. Context is a central part of acting. I imagine that's also why some of you got wrapped up during the disguise exercise."

A murmur sweeps through the auditorium.

"I think this is pretty common knowledge, yes? Who got wrapped up? Where is the mall team?"

They are sitting beside me right in front of him. All four raise their hands.

"Great. And the restaurant team?"

The Special Forces veterans are more hesitant to hold their hands up, but neighboring students make it clear which ones they are.

"OK. Didn't go so well, huh? That's hard to believe, given the high quality of the disguises. So why weren't you guys believable? What made you stand out in an otherwise homogeneous crowd?"

He walks to a nearby blackboard.

"When you pretend as a kid, your focus is no farther than the reach of your own arms. If this is you" he draws an X—"the extent of your lie extends only here." He draws a circle around the X.

"That is the world you have created. You're a child. You don't know there's really much more out there. As an adult watching the child, you can see through it. It's transparent. There's no extended reach, no comprehensive thought on how the child exists in relation to the world around them. There is no world for them to consider. For a child, the world revolves around them. For an adult, it does not. That's one of the two points for the day. You have to have your story and understand its relation to the world immediately around you." He checks off the circle he has drawn.

He then draws another circle around the one that contains the X.

"Then you must decide where your character fits in with the world immediately around that. Why are you here, in this building? How do you appear to someone outside this immediate circle? How do you look to someone in this second circle? A passerby, a janitor sweeping up, a woman talking on the phone? How will they interpret what you are doing and saying? Are you believable? Do you blend in to their preconceived notions, or do you stand out for some reason? Standing out is bad."

He draws a third circle encompassing the previous two.

"How will you interact with the world at large if asked? This is where most of you had trouble with the border crossing. You can remember your character's phone number, but you can't recall the name of the next-door neighbor. Why? Because you didn't have one prepared. This poor depth of character is a sure way to fail when cross-examined. Keep these three circles in mind when you have to lie."

Nobody makes a sound. The students who had heeded David's earlier advice sailed through the border crossing. Those who didn't listen didn't make it. The type-As who spoke ill about acting classes a month ago are now paying rapt attention.

"Emotional commitment. That's the second key. I understand we have some Navy SEALs here. Where are you?"

A couple of hands rise.

"Gotcha," David says. "How about Army Rangers?"

A couple of other hands go up.

"Good, good. Any of you others just plain coldhearted sons of bitches that couldn't care less about anyone or anything?"

Armies of hands rise.

"You're lying!" David laughs. "How do I know this? Emotional commitment. You're here because of the emotional reaction you had to the 9/11 attacks. You wouldn't have joined the Agency otherwise. But you've got to put that emotional commitment to work for you. Let me show you what I mean."

David's example is less an exercise than it is group hypnosis. He asks us to recall specific incidents in our past. Our most embarrassing moment. Our saddest moment. Despite knowing absolutely nothing of the details of each student's specific memory, he succeeds in an emotional aggressiveness with everyone in the room. Every eye is shut. Several students are crying, reliving the death of a parent, sibling, or friend. In less than fifteen minutes, everyone is reexperiencing his or her own private hell.

Now that he has our attention, he brings everyone back to the here and now. He has made his point about emotion. It is a by-product of the character, not an ingredient of it. Character is something you control. Emotion is a result of the moment at hand. In order to use this, we must experience the life we are trying to create.

"How many of you saw Quentin Tarantino's film *Pulp Fiction*?" he asks. "There is a great scene early in the movie where Vincent (John Travolta) and Jules (Samuel L. Jackson) arrive for an appointment early, so they are chatting in the hallway outside the apartment. You see them engage in friendly conversation—two friends chatting about work. But what happens? Jules says, 'Let's get into character.' That's when they go inside the apartment, start smashing the place up, and Jules yells what has become the most oft-quoted Bible verse in modern cinema, Ezekiel 25:17."

David assumes Jules's posture from the infamous scene.

" 'The path of the righteous man is beset on all sides by the inequities of the selfish and the tyranny of evil men. Blessed is he who, in the name of charity and goodwill, shepherds the weak through the valley of darkness, for he is truly his brother's keeper and the finder of lost children.' "

He points at Coach. " 'And I will strike down upon thee with great *vengeance* and furious *anger* those who attempt to poison and destroy my brothers. And you will know my name is the Lord when I lay my vengeance upon you.' "

David delivers the verse with the same articulation, intensity, and rising volume that Samuel L. Jackson does in the film. It's a jolting scene for such an early hour.

Coach leans over and whispers, "I think he's seen that movie one too many times."

David continues. "What happens next? They kill everyone in the place except for one poor kid! He's beside himself with fear. But when the three walk outside, the two homicidal maniacs are lucid. They're simply Jules and Vincent again. I want to talk about this turning on and off of character and a concept called Violating the Fourth Wall."

He draws a diagram on the chalkboard of two stick figures standing on a horizontal white line. He adds two vertical lines, one on each side. It looks like a floor and two walls around the two figures.

"When you are in character you must never violate the Fourth Wall."

He connects the two walls with a line at roof level.

"I know that's a roof, but consider it a wall. Inside this box, you are in character. That's what we see Vince and Jules do when they walk into the apartment. They go from being themselves to being the characters they are playing for the theater inside this apartment. Their boss sent them there to teach these guys a lesson. How they do it is up to them. When they are in the apartment, they are in character. Jules tells one of the kids in the apartment that his name is Britt. He's in character. He's this other guy named Britt; he's no longer Jules. What he does not want to do is float up and become Jules again."

David draws an arrow from one stick figure's head to a point above the roofline that he added to his diagram.

"If he floats up for some reason, if he breaks character to become Jules again, it is virtually impossible to go back down and restart as Britt."

He draws another arrow back down to the original character.

"It doesn't work. You can't float back and forth. If one character breaks and violates the Fourth Wall, it pulls the other characters along with them."

He adds an arrow to the second figure.

"Now neither actor is able to maintain the illusion they created when they walk onstage or, in this case, into the apartment. If you remember the end of the scene, only after they leave the apartment do they become Jules and Vince again. This, ladies and gentlemen, is what you must do when undercover. Keep in character at all costs. Where many of you will be working, the penalty for being caught is death. Do not violate the Fourth Wall: It's impossible to go back."

ON THURSDAY JOHN FINISHES the morning briefing and immediately turns on the VCR. We see a man and a horse. He's not roping the horse, or chasing it, or riding it. He's simply looking at it. Then he turns his back on it. Caroline, a longtime horse wrangler, recognizes him immediately. Monty Roberts. The Horse Whisperer.

I remember the Robert Redford movie of the same name a few years ago. I didn't see it, but remember the premise. An old-hand horseman has an unusual way of breaking horses. Instead of a whip and bridle, he simply walks up to the horse and bonds with it. No yelling or threats, no wild shenanigans or hours of harsh treatment. The horse is free to walk away from him at any time, but it doesn't. Horses are usually broken and submissive in less than a half hour.

We watch a video of Roberts. The horse was not one of his, but was supplied by the organization making the video to ensure there was no funny business, that a tamed horse isn't substituted for a truly wild one. He forgoes the usual physical mistreatment and instead goes for an emotional bond with the animal. It is all based on nonverbal communication. Dr. Walsh, the Farm's clinical psychologist, provides some background on the technique and how we will be using it as a recruitment tool.

Nonverbal communication works as well on people as it does on horses. Seventy percent of all communication is nonverbal. Using nonverbal communication, we can induce the emotional reaction we want a target to have. Building on David's point of emotional content in our acting, Dr. Walsh tells us that we can induce an emotional response that will help endear us to them, making them more receptive to our eventual pitch. What we want is for the target to feel a oneness with us. She jokingly calls this "you-me, same-same."

The targets of recruitment must believe the case officer is exactly like them—a mirror image of themselves in a different body. This perception of diminished difference is the reason a young, white, civilian American woman can recruit an older, black, Egyptian military officer. Though their physical similarities are few, if the military officer feels and sees in the case officer what he feels and sees in himself, he is already halfway to being recruited. We will often spend months building the rapport necessary to achieve this level of comfort and confidence with an agent.

Each person has a subjective reality, an image of himself or herself that frames the way he or she perceives the world. It's sort of like a mental Wheel of Fortune. Instead of a wheel of dollar amounts, think of a wheel of personal categories. Every person is made up of such a wheel; it's the categories that are individually unique.

For me the categories could be things like male, brother, son, husband, diver, biologist, fraternity brother, college graduate, Protestant, boater, and martial artist. Let's not forget Floridian! A person's totality is the sum of all of these individual characteristics.

No one else I have ever known has these exact categories on their personality wheel. But a quick review of my closest friends shows that all of them share at least a couple of categories with me. Most of them share several. This is the basis for our friendship. Family we cannot choose, but friendships are built because people are like-minded with respect to our subjective realities.

Building a personality wheel for a potential target gives case officers the necessary entry they need in a conversation. If the target is a sailor, the case officer should read up on sailing. Does she like opera? Get two tickets for Pavarotti's concert. A golfer? Start hanging out at the driving range. Per the lessons we learned in Washington, have an interest in the target's areas of interest, but be prepared to share more than one trait. A one-trick pony is no good. You've got to go the distance.

When considering which personality traits to use, we must consider the entire breadth of personality categories. Physical and genetic traits, race and ethnicity, cultural and social status, hobbies and interests, politics and religion—all are fair game when trying to get inside someone's head. This is what Monty Roberts hit upon with the horses. Control their minds, and their bodies will follow. While Roberts can influence horses in as little as half an hour, humans take considerably longer.

Altering people's behavior means understanding their beliefs and values. When you can fully state a targeted person's beliefs and value system, you have an overwhelmingly powerful chance of recruiting that person to do just about anything. Values are our visions of ourselves, how we view the world. They are virtually impossible to change. Our national values of truth, justice, and the American Way are set early in life and strongly nurtured by our parents.

Beliefs are the means by which we organize our value systems. They create boundaries around our value systems, but the boundaries can be moved. There are a million different ways such movement can be done.

Looking at Osama Bin Laden, we can understand how he recruited people to give up their lives for his cause. He influenced them using these same techniques. He built on the value systems of Islam by manipulating the beliefs of his followers. He controls their access to outside information, intentionally misquotes pieces of the Koran to fit his needs, and assures them that Paradise awaits anyone who dies in the service of Islam. Manipulate belief by leveraging values. It served Bin Laden, David Koresh (the Branch Davidians), Marshall Applewhite (Heaven's Gate), and Jim Jones (The People's Temple) equally well. What we must do is watch the target's response and understand the subtle nuances.

Dr. Walsh pulls Wendy to the front of the class.

"When is someone lying to you? Can you tell?" Dr. Walsh asks. "We are teaching you how to do it, but understanding human nature can tell you a lot about whether or not someone is lying, just in the way they answer questions."

She walks to the board. "I might make a statement like 'I don't think we should have declared war on Iraq.' How many ways might someone agree with me that indicates their preferences in nonverbal communication?"

She starts writing on the board while Wendy watches.

- I *see* what you mean.
- I *hear* what you're saying.
- I'm in *touch* with that.

"Listen to how people respond to you verbally, and you can better understand what their preferential methods are. Obviously Monty Roberts is not using a horse's spoken response in creating an emotional bond. He is, however, watching what the horse does and effectively crafting the response he wants. The question for each of you is, can you recognize these cues when you see them? Let's find out."

Dr. Walsh sits Wendy on an elevated stool on the stage. She faces Wendy, her back to the class. From the back of the room a technician turns on a camera and aims it at Wendy, tightening up the shot to show just her face on the giant screen behind her.

"Wendy, I'm going to ask you some questions. It's up to you to decide whether to tell me the truth or lie. Ready?"

"I guess," Wendy says, clearly nervous.

"When were you born?"

"December 17, 1975."

"What is your mother's maiden name?"

"Paltees."

"Where did you graduate from college?"

"Wake Forest University."

"I think that's enough," Dr. Walsh said, jumping up. "You told the truth with two questions and lied on one. Is that correct?"

Wendy's eyes widen. "Yes, how did you know that?"

"You didn't attend Wake Forest University. Where did you really go to college?"

"Oh my God. That's so weird. I went to Penn State."

Dr. Walsh looks up at the video technician in the back of the room. "Can you rewind that for me, please?"

The video of Wendy's answers reruns on the screen.

"Watch her eyes," Dr. Walsh says. "A person's eyes are an easy way to monitor for deception. There is computer software that can do this during a monitored interrogation, but you aren't going to have that kind of gear in the field. You have to be able to do this on the fly. Watch her eyes."

Wendy answers the first question. Her birthday is December 17, 1975.

"Wendy's eyes go down and to the left. She is recalling something real, a fact stored in her head."

The second question plays on the screen.

"Here her eyes go up and to the right. She is recalling what her mother looks like."

Finally, the third question rolls.

"Here you see Wendy's eyes go to the left and up. She is trying to construct a new image, a new university to replace the real one she attended. Her eyes give her away, as they will often do when people are making something up."

She passes out a paper featuring a human face and six major regions where the eyes can drift when answering a question. Each region represents a recalled or fabricated memory combined with a visual, auditory, or kinesthetic sensory preference.

"Learn from Monty Roberts. He watches the horses' reaction to his movements and changes his methods accordingly. By using the reaction to choreograph his movements, he is essentially tricking the horse into providing him the means necessary to break him. You can do the same with the people you recruit. Horses or people, everyone responds to custom-tailored rapport. In essence that is exactly what you are doing. Customizing the pitch. An Arab tribesman or a Japanese businessman, you will use the same set of tools. But the choices you make must be tailored for them, not for you."

"TAKE A SEAT, folks. We need to talk."

Course Chairman John looks unhappy. Everyone sits. Something is up.

"I have news from Langley that you won't like. As you know, the SOTC program is a historical part of the curriculum here. We are serious about it and require a certain level of physical ability before people are allowed to attend. Unfortunately, we are going to have to cut the course short for you guys."

Dozens of students moan and mutter remarks under their breath. John holds up both hands.

"Getting mad at me won't help. I'm just passing on the news. Due to the need to get you out to the field as quickly as possible, and because we have a real shortage of equipment and instructors, the following changes are being made to your SOTC program: There will be no amphibious or helicopter assault training. Most of that hardware is in the Middle East. More directly, there will be no jump school for this class."

The students vent a loud outcry of disappointment. The Agency's jump school is one of the most sought-after programs in the CIA.

"I know, I know. This is a disappointment. Again, the equipment and personnel needed to conduct the class are overseas. The SOTC program will be cut to firearms, defensive driving, and land navigation. That's it."

In the back of the room a student holds up a hand.

"Does that mean we will not be doing a final SOTC physical fitness test? There's no need for a test if there is no airborne school, correct?"

"To be honest, the staff is just now learning this, so we have not really made any decision along those lines. Do we need a fitness test if there's no jump school? Probably not. Will we do it anyway? I don't know."

The conversations among students get louder and more obnoxious. John raises his hands and his voice.

"Listen up, folks. Complaining will get you nowhere. I didn't make the decision. That was done on the seventh floor at Langley. Complain to them. For the moment, until you hear otherwise, assume the final SOTC test will be conducted as planned. You never know. Equipment and personnel may be available at the last minute. In all honesty, though, those three sections are more about honoring our past than they are about preparing for our future. Under commercial cover I don't think you'll be jumping out of a high-speed boat or parachuting behind enemy lines. They are fun courses, and I hate that you are going to miss them. But we need you in the field more than we need you jumping out of planes."

Everyone has been looking forward to the boat and helicopter assault classes, and most of us could not wait to jump out of airplanes. For the military students that is just another day at the office. For Agency students, it's a once-in-a-lifetime opportunity. It was going to be the reward we gave ourselves for all the work, all the long hours. We are hardly in the mood for a class at this point, but like always, the course must go on.

WHEN WE ACTUALLY PITCH someone into becoming a paid asset of the U.S. government, there can often be a lot of give and take. Sometimes the potential asset is ready to be recruited, even hoping for it. Other times the case officer mistakes where the relationship is and makes a formal pitch—dropping our loincloth, so to speak. When a pitch fails, it can be embarrassing and dangerous. A potential recruit who turns down a pitch may report it to his superiors. This can mean as little as an embarrassing failure or as serious as a formal declaration of "persona non grata," requiring the case officer to leave the country within a few days. In some countries the offending case officer might simply disappear. To ensure that we are as prepared as possible for pitching our agents, we take a negotiations course.

Unlike most of the Agency's training programs, this one is not internally developed. This comes from the commercial world, where it has enjoyed great success in mergers and acquisitions, in purchasing high-ticket items like aircraft, and in lobbying on behalf of big business. If it can move Capitol Hill, it must be good. It applies the lessons learned from Dr. Walsh's nonverbal communications class and David's acting classes. We are starting to better understand how the individual pieces of instruction slowly intertwine as the training moves closer to completion.

The negotiations course is very straightforward and requires students to anticipate and outline what they think their potential target's reluctance will be based upon. Patriotism, religious belief, fundamentalist ideology, or something more basic like greed, revenge, or a need for adventure. Identifying what the target's needs are will ensure that a pitch is at least considered. What we must absolutely not do is use the words "but" and "however" when responding to a potential agent's initial reluctance.

Either word is guaranteed to harden the person's initial rejection of the idea. Reframe the statement, but don't even think about using blackmail or extortion—either in the pitch or in a request to not tell anyone about it if it fails. They make for good television, but in reality the case officer is entrusting his life to the agent as surely as the agent is entrusting his to the case officer. Blackmailing someone and then putting your life in their hands is not the best of ideas.

We practice our negotiating programs on one another using the closed-circuit camera system in our practice room. Terry squares off against Mark, who later also works with Dave. Al fends me off but acquiesces to Wendy's pitch immediately afterward. We go on for more than an hour, practicing on each instructor. After a short break, Mark suggests we practice on one another.

Dave successfully recruits Wendy in the first student-to-student exchange. My attempts to recruit Coach are miserably unsuccessful after he runs from the room screaming, *"Spy!"* We go back and forth for another hour, continuing to mix up students until finally Adam and I go at it.

I am the case officer. Adam is my target. I am waiting in my safe house for him to arrive. He knocks on the door.

"Hello, Adam. Good to see you. Please come in."

"Thank you, Mr. Tom. I appreciate being invited to your home."

"Let me get you something to drink. Do you like scotch?"

"Oh, yes. Very much."

I hand him bottled water.

"Thank you," he says.

"Adam, I've been wanting to talk with you about an opportunity. You are familiar with what a consultant is, and I've recently been made aware of a consulting opportunity that's right up your alley."

"Oh, that would be very nice. I could use some additional income."

"Yes, I know. That's why I wanted to bring this idea to you. Now, this would not be a consulting position in the traditional sense. It would be something else, something special, and something discreet. I—"

There is a knock at the door.

"Oh, that would be my friend," Adam says. "I hope you don't mind, I invited a friend of mine over."

I'm clueless of what's about to happen.

"Of course I don't mind if you invite a friend over. Who is your friend?"

Adam opens the door. "This is Sergei. My very good friend from Russia."

Mike is standing in the door, wearing a Russian army hat. I recognize it from Al's office.

"Good afternoon, Comrade Tom," he says. "May I come in?"

Oh, crap! I am about to get screwed on closed-circuit television.

"Of course, Sergei. Any friend of Adam's is a friend of mine. Won't you come in and sit down?"

I glare into the camera. I can't hear the laughter across the hall that I'm sure is taking place.

"Well, now. What shall we talk about?" I ask.

"I told Sergei about how we have become friends," Adam replies. "He said he wanted to meet you. He can always use a new American friend. I told him that you might have a job for me. He has one too! Isn't that incredible? He says he might have a job for you as well."

"Really?" I reply. "How very inventive of Sergei."

"Oh, Sergei will never admit it. He's very bashful. But he can be extremely persuasive when he wants to be."

"Is that right?" I ask. I wonder where this is going.

Sergei/Mike pulls out an envelope from his jacket. Opening it up, he places a picture in front of me.

"Do you recognize this woman?" he asks.

It's Cathy's photograph from the frame on my desk.

"Yes. That's my wife, Cathy. Is there a reason you have her photograph in your pocket?"

Adam is sitting across from me grinning, but Mike has not broken his stoic appearance in any way.

"Yes. Your wife. A lovely woman. Truly adores you. It's sad that you treat her so badly," Mike says with a thick Russian accent.

"Treat her badly? I've never raised a hand to the woman. I don't know what you mean, and I don't like your tone. Now, unless you have some other reason for being here I . . ."

Sergei/Mike pulls out two pink pages from his envelope.

"I believe you will recognize this woman as well. I believe her name is Ter-ry?" He pronounces her name phonetically. "From the photographs, you appear to know her very well."

Mike had taken two page breaks out of a three-ring class binder and drew stick figures on them. The couples are engaged in various graphic portrayals. I still have no idea where this is going, though it is pretty damn funny.

I look up at the camera and silently plead for help, a stupid smile on my face. Terry is no doubt horrified by all this, sitting with four instructors and the rest of the team.

Faked Russian pornographic blackmail is not a scenario I'd planned for. I try desperately to get back into character and quit smiling. I'm only half successful.

"Well, Sergei, you certainly have taken a strong interest in me. But I don't care what photos you have doctored up. I don't know that woman. She certainly appears,"—I am eyeing the camera—"friendly. But I don't think trashing her reputation is going to endear you to her or to me."

Mike dismisses my comments with a wave.

"Please, Mr. Tom. This woman has been in our employ for many years. If the photos are not enough, perhaps your wife would be more interested in video. I didn't think you would enjoy wearing a dog collar. Is this type of debauchery common in the United States? A very sick country you have, my friend."

Al and Mark have the decency to interrupt my slow death spiral before any more trashing of Terry's reputation is presupposed into the Farm's video record system. Adam slaps me on the back, and Mike breaks out into his trademark innocent grin while shaking my hand. I retrieve the pink-paged pornography and return across the hall.

We walk into the office and get a standing ovation, including from Terry.

THE ENTIRE CLASS is nervous. Fingernails are chewed. Tempers are short. We are haggard and sleep deprived. We've come to the end of the second part of the course. What comes next is legendary within the CIA: the Murder Boards.

The instructors and staff sit down and, one by one, vote on each student. Students who are approved can move on to the final phase of the program: Testing Phase. For those who do not pass, the months spent getting to this point are rendered moot. They are given sixty days to find another job within the Agency or are unceremoniously terminated.

The day of the Murder Boards we are kept busy in a counterintelligence brief, far away from the instructors and staff. No one is paying much attention, a fact acknowledged by the speaker. He had been much the same way, he said, when he was sitting here as a student twenty years earlier. It doesn't do much to ease the nerves in the room.

About midway through the afternoon Course Chairman John, accompanied by four instructors, walks to the podium with an announcement. After some chiding and comments about our frazzled appearance, he informs the room that the entire class has passed. This is a stunning achievement.

Approximately 10 to 15 percent of students typically wash out on the first Murder Board. The fact that everyone made it only reinforces what instructors and staff have told people at headquarters: This class is different from all that came before.

The parties run late into the evening. Some students get together with close friends they have made during the program. Others have more reserved activities in the homes of staff and instructors. I gather with my office and enjoy a few adult beverages at Pizzeria Uno. We remand ourselves back to the Farm to complete our celebratory assault in the SRB. As we come through the heavily fortified front gates, a guard waves us down.

"Congratulations," he calls out as several other guards smile and nod. "We heard all of you passed. Keep up the good work, guys!"

We wave back and tear off into the night.

At the SRB we continue our well-earned celebration. The end is in sight. We can just barely make out the light at the end of this yearlong tunnel. At one point Adam asks for everyone's attention and begins to speak.

"Ladies and gentlemen, I commend you on your accomplishment in reaching this milestone. You should all be proud."

The crowd cheers.

"At the same time, I must say that if you had paid more attention when you were children, you probably could have gone directly into the field. You see, everything I ever needed to know about espionage, I learned from watching *Magnum, P.I.*"

Another cheer erupts from the crowd. Though most of the students are too young to have seen the popular television series in prime time, everyone is at least familiar with it from reruns.

The show's title character is Thomas Magnum, an ex-Navy intelligence officer turned private investigator. He lives on the Hawaiian estate of writer Robin Masters for free in return for serving as the estate's security director. A couple of Vietnam veteran buddies make up his ad-hoc staff, and the estate's curator is his antagonistic overseer as Robin Masters's absentee landlord. The show's eight-year run won numerous Emmys and Golden Globe awards for its often complex story lines covering religion, politics, business and, of course, espionage.

"OK, class. Pay attention," Adam says, playing instructor. "Let's examine the cast and see what we have. First off is Thomas Sullivan Magnum. An ex-Navy officer. Apparently there wasn't a monkey available, so they got a Navy guy."

Howls erupt from the current and previous naval officers in the crowd.

I lean over to Travis. "Is he serious?"

"Ssh! He's been working on this for a week," he replies.

"Look at the setup Magnum has," Adam continues. "Higgins is the acerbic station chief. Rick is the reports officer—excuse me, *Collection Management Officer*—with the liaison contacts into the Hawaiian underworld. Mac is the desk officer with access to everything online, classified and unclassified. TC is the Special Ops guy. Zeus and Apollo (two Doberman pinschers) are the Marines. All the cool toys he has, like long-lens cameras, phone-tapping equipment, the expensive cars and all—we'll have that when we're out there. It's all preplanned. He was a spy from the beginning."

He takes a hit from a long-necked Budweiser.

"Now, most people don't know this, but the Magnum P.I. character was originally pitched to CBS as an ex-CIA agent. Sort of a James Bond of Honolulu. But it didn't fly. Then, someone at CBS grew a brain and realized that a *military* intelligence officer, now *that* was honorable. *That* was believable. *That's* when the show took off. It's a shame it had to be a swabbie [Army slang for Navy officers], but at least the military intelligence community got some decent PR for a couple of years."

He continues his alcohol-induced assault on the CIA as we party the night away. The whole class is in attendance, as are most of the instructors and staff. Most important, our office is sitting together. Eight bodies with one collective soul. We are as close as any eight people will ever be, celebrating an achievement few could ever understand.

We didn't know it was our last night together.

A Conjugal Arrest
June 2003

I WAKE UP like any other day at the Farm. A six o'clock run with Coach and Mike. After a quick shower, I meet them in the cafeteria for breakfast. We walk over to the instruction building in the early morning sunshine. We haven't felt this good in months. We are near the end. Last night's celebration was a release. No more instruction. No more classes. We're only a few weeks away from finishing the entire program. We are relaxed, comfortable in our roles and in our team. That's when everything changes.

At the morning brief Course Chairman John plays a video clip: the opening montage of the television series *Kung Fu*. Actor David Carradine plays the part of Kwai Chang Caine, a student of the martial arts teacher known as Master Po. Po's narration of the opening credits echoes through the auditorium.

It is said a Shaolin priest can walk through walls. Listened for, he cannot be heard. Looked for, he cannot be seen. Felt for, he cannot be touched. This rice paper is the final test. When you can walk its length and leave no trace, you will have learned.

"Folks," Chairman John says as he turns off the video player, "welcome to the rice paper. We've taught you all we can. Our work is done. It is up to you now, to walk the rice paper for the next thirty days and prove you can do this work. I'm sure you've all heard horror stories about this. If you are prepared, if you come to each meeting with only your agent in mind, you should do fine. There are neither trick questions nor any type of funny business. What you saw during training is exactly what you will see in Testing Phase. Good luck to all of you. This is our final meeting. From now on, you will be briefed in your offices, just as you will be in the field. When you leave the building today, you are stepping out onto the rice paper. I look forward to seeing you all at the end of it."

Our program of instruction is concluded.

In Testing Phase we operate as a real CIA station. We spend each day in character. Like a reality television show, we work in real time at a pace approximating that of a station working in a hostile nation. As we progress, our cases will intermingle. If we have not updated our colleagues as to what we are doing, the entire station will be at risk. We must keep our chief apprised of everything we do. The chiefs can be touchy.

The four instructors in the office are now gone. Al, Dwight, Gavin, and Mark will be busy in role-playing exercises full-time. Each office is assigned a new and unknown instructor to serve as station chief. We are to treat him like we would a real boss. He will treat us like real case officers. We cannot make any inquiries regarding training, but are strongly encouraged to ask questions as far as case and agent management. Our chief's name is Bill.

I recognize Bill from other parts of the program, though I have never done an exercise with him. He has a reputation for being difficult, but overall is well liked. Bill is only a couple of years older than me. Everything we do or say over the next month must go through him. No more mentors, instructors, or staff. As if we are already overseas, the station chief sits at the right hand of God himself. He owns that country and everything taking place in it from the CIA's perspective. I figure we'll have no problem working with Bill. I've got a good team here.

I should have seen it coming.

The offices are broken up and the students remixed and reassigned. Our eight-person office, along with all the other offices, is redistributed across the board. When we take our first assignment overseas we will be working in a country where we will not know anyone. Testing Phase re-creates that uncertainty and apprehension as much as possible. Every student will have to pack up and move his or her classified and unclassified materials from the current office into a new one.

We spend a few hours packing up our desks, shocked that our tight-knit team will be no more. We didn't expect this. It makes the next four weeks much more precarious. We have a good machine in place here. Everyone knows his or her role, the strengths and weaknesses of individual team members, and the tolerances for how much pressure people can handle. We will now have to relearn this operational awareness for an entirely different group of students during the most important period of the course.

I pack up my desk and find my new office assignment. I am now sharing an office with Caroline, Annie, Marty, Jed, Drew, Jim, and Allen. This may not be so bad after all. Marty and I have become friends since we live in the same apartment building in Washington. Annie and I had worked the scuba-diving case during our interim assignments. I met Jed and Drew through Daryll during the initial weeks, proving what we learned in our Six Degrees of Separation class—you become friends with the friends of your friends. In the pressure cooker of the CIA, we lean on those most able to understand and help.

I recognize Jim and Allen but don't know them very well. The team doesn't get time to become acquainted. Bill calls the station meeting to order and tells us about our first project.

We will fly on commercial aircraft to several East Coast cities. There we will spend one week operating under commercial cover on our own. We will have no interaction with Bill, with our new officemates, or with other students. We are to operate as if we are alone in a foreign city outside our country of residence. We will operate in alias, using the real cover identities the

Agency crafted for us last year in Washington. We're putting it all out on the line in the real world, far away from the safety and assistance of the Farm.

Our trips depart from a half dozen airports throughout Virginia. Bill hands out envelopes to each student. The Agency's cover office has been very busy. Inside is the alias driver's license we acquired six months ago along with a Visa or MasterCard issued in that name. There are memberships in libraries, health clubs, video stores, and other items to create convincing pocket litter.

We must go through airport security, arrive at our hotel, and check in with a local instructor using the covert software on our laptops. Only then can we begin casing the area to find signal sites, dead-drop locations, and SDR cover stops. We have two days to find everything we need. We are to carry out a series of clandestine meetings with instructors we do not know. In addition, we must conduct business with real companies that we will cold-call today. We are to get an initial appointment, conduct the meeting, and close it out so the company has no interest in following up with us. The purpose of this is to practice cover operations that mask our clandestine activities while operating alone. If we can pull this week off flawlessly, the rest of Testing Phase should be easy.

I immediately take to a phone and set up a couple of quick meetings. Having done this type of work before, I don't think much about it. I get two meetings booked quickly and turn my attention to creating the necessary props. Other students are extremely nervous about this exercise.

How do they act in a business setting? The border-crossing exercise gave them some feedback on how to look like a businessperson to a border-control agent for a brief few minutes. Conducting a real meeting in a potential client/customer's office is a different story, however. The first group of students leaves tomorrow. The rest of us will follow in a couple of days. Several of the military students conspire to practice with some of us who have real business backgrounds to make sure they can look and sound legitimate when they need to. For me the problem isn't the exercise but the isolation.

I call Cathy from my room and explain that I will be out of town for a week and unable to talk to her. We are to have no contact outside the exercise. My fake persona is single and therefore has no wife in Washington to call every night. I likewise have no brothers and sisters or other extended family. When the airplane goes wheels-up, we are on our own until we get back and switch our documents in the office. Only then can we return to our seminormal lives.

Cathy is incensed. It's bad enough that we continue to be physically separated during our first year of marriage. Forbidding any contact for a week adds fuel to the fire. She is starting a new job, excited to have a normal routine in Washington. She had not been expecting to be completely alone while doing it.

I remind her it's only for a week and that in a month I will be back up in Washington leaving dirty dishes in the sink and generally making a mess all over the apartment. That cheers her up some, but not as much as I'd hoped. I don't mention to her the last thing I will do before I leave.

I've only removed it twice since she slipped it on my finger a year ago. Both times were to show people the inscription inside. My alias persona is single, so I carefully pull my wedding band off. The skin on my newly uncovered finger reacts to the unexpected exposure. All the time it took me to get used to wearing it will be lost over the next week. I flip the ring over to look inside. Yep. The inscription is still there.

Carefully placing it on my personal key chain, I put them both in my luggage to take home upon my return. No matter how much of a hurry I'm in when I get back, I can't return to Washington without my keys. If the keys are with me, so is the wedding band. Showing up without it would not make the next three weeks go by any faster.

Flying into Knoxville I feel like a kid who successfully skipped Algebra class. I have no problems at the airport, and my luggage (complete with business card tag in alias), arrives safely. My rental car is ready, and I have a hotel that can't be connected to the real me. I'm living a spy movie. I expect to see Jason Bourne, Jack Ryan, or even Miss Moneypenny at any moment.

All I need is a wad of cash and a pocketful of passports to complete the subterfuge.

When I check into the hotel, the room is not ready. It's right after lunch and check-in normally doesn't start until around three. I need to kill some time, but I don't want to venture too far from my luggage at the concierge desk. Who knows what the staff has planned for us this week? If that's not enough of a threat, Daryll knows about my attempted bra caper. He's in town this week too and will get even if he can. I decide to kill some time in the hotel convenience store. Maybe buy a newspaper.

I pick up the current issue of *BusinessWeek*. A lot has been going on since I stepped out of the corporate world a year ago. I probably should buy a copy for the prop value and catch up on the world of big business.

"Looking at the pictures?" a voice asks.

I spin around. Adam is standing two feet behind me.

"What's up, buddy?" I ask. "What are you doing here?"

"I'm on my way out," he said. "This is a great hotel. You'll have a blast. It'll be a piece of cake for you."

"Glad to hear it. So you had no problems?" I ask.

"Naw. It was great. Did you hear about Terry?"

"No. What?"

"She broke her ankle!"

"How? Where?"

Adam watches someone walk by us and pulls me around the corner to a more discreet location to talk.

"She was on her foot SDR and fell down some stairs. Concrete stairs—it was a cemetery. She got banged up pretty good on the way down."

"Did she go home?" I inquire.

"Hell, no! Do you think she got this far into the whole thing to get sent home because of an accident on the last leg? Did you get that? *Last leg!*"

"Yeah, yeah. You're a regular Eddie Murphy. Is she OK?"

"Oh, sure. She's patched up and continuing on as planned."

"No more SDRs?" I ask.

"Nope. Maybe we all should have thought of it," he laments.

"No kidding. Must be nice to be able to forgo all that nonsense."

"I guess they figure she earned it. She was under surveillance when she fell, and the team saw the whole thing. She was a trooper, though. Hit the ground and hid her maps before anyone could see them. She even maintained cover when the ambulance crew showed up."

"Ambulance?"

"Yeah. I told you her ankle is broken. What do you think she's going to do? You've got to get the thing fixed. They hauled her off to the hospital and admited her using her fake identification."

"Good on her," I said. "That'll look good on her final evaluation. 'Maintained cover in the face of adversity and considerable physical pain.' She'll coast the rest of the program. Is she OK?"

"Yeah. She's on crutches and moves pretty slow, but she's all right. You should call her when you get back."

"I will. Keep an eye on her when you get back, will you? You've got a pretty easy week coming up. A bunch of computer training stuff in the classroom. Nothing external. No exercises or SDR bullshit. Relax for a week."

"Will do." He shakes my hand. "I'll see you back there. I think we need an old team evening out before Testing Phase has a chance to crank up."

"Damn right," I assure him. "You coordinate it with the guys onsite. I'll hook up with Mike, Wendy, and Travis on our way home Saturday."

"Cool. Keep your eyes peeled. They're everywhere out here," he says, slipping out a side door to a waiting cab.

I check into my room and fire up my laptop. Sending the city station chief a quick note, I confirm I am "in-country" and had no problems with my alias documents or travel activities. I am now clear to case the area and start my exercises.

Adam is right. This is fun. I case my way across town and back. I map out dead-drop locations and a couple of pedestrian signal sites I can easily service out of the public's eye. My first assignment is to meet a foreign agent who is in town for a conference. But we cannot be seen together at either of our conference programs. We must meet elsewhere. Somewhere out of the way.

I receive an encrypted note from him via disguised e-mail. After I decrypt the note it says to meet him at a local restaurant's bar. We have an expensive (corporate) dinner and agree to get together two nights later for dinner and drinks. In the meantime, I have the first of two cover business meetings to conduct.

I assemble my brochures and go to my appointment, a local Business Services Provider. These are popular facilities for individual lawyers and consultants who want a minimal expense for a presence in a major city. The provider gives them phone, mail, and e-mail/Web site service for a nominal fee. It's all on a pay-as-you-go arrangement, which works out well for my consulting cover.

I tour the facility and appraise the various amenities and services. At the end of our meeting, the manager hands me a price list and I tell her I simply don't anticipate having a clientele big enough to fund these types of expenses for a couple of years. She politely and professionally asks me to keep her firm in mind when my business reaches the appropriate size. Meeting over. Follow-up potential: zero.

With my cover activity concluded I prepare for my dinner and drinks meeting that is taking place the following night. This is a carryover exercise—started in one city and carried over into another. It mimics how an officer under commercial cover meets someone at a conference and follows up at another time. Conferences are crowded and loud, neither the time nor place to assess someone's potential as a recruited agent. Dinner and a couple of drinks, just two businessmen enjoying a night on the town, is a casual and relaxed means of building rapport while determining a person's suitability for espionage. The exercise is with an instructor named Dale.

I sit for several hours across the street from the restaurant he recommended, watching to see if anyone else is using it and to get a feel for the traffic. Nothing I see concerns me. I should be alone with plenty of time and adult beverages to promote an insightful conversation.

We enjoy a huge seafood feast. We talk about fast cars, fast women, and fast boats—the luxuries successful single men discuss most. Then we go to the cigar bar. Here we compound the two predinner beers and bottle of California merlot with single-malt scotch. We burn down two cigars sitting in a back corner of the bar. It doesn't feel like work. I genuinely like Dale.

I've been impressed with him since the first meeting of this exercise. I can see why he's such a good case officer. He puts you at ease in a moment and genuinely listens to what is being said. A guy you like to hang out with on the weekends or don't mind living next door to. Our conversation gets deep into politics and religion as the night goes on. Dale suddenly leans over to me.

"Hey," he says. "Don't you have a report to write tonight?"

Do I hear his head hitting the Fourth Wall? Is he dropping character? I can't tell. I glance at my watch. It's 2:30 a.m.!

"Shit! I've got to go. I've got a-a-a—thing in the morning. My friend, I look forward to seeing you on Friday. If you have any scheduling problems, you will give me a call. Yes?"

"Yes, buddy. I'm looking forward to it."

I excuse myself and stumble into the street. I'm required to conduct a short SDR back to my hotel. It's irritating this late at night, but it's a fully graded part of the exercise. Like everyone else I can now do it sleepwalking. No surveillance. I'm alone. The problem is, he's right. I *do* have a report to write. Several, in fact. I have to write up my meeting notes on the information I elicited and e-mail it to him over the encrypted network for him to grade prior to our Friday meeting.

Unfortunately, I am comfortably drunk. Three beers, half a bottle of wine, and three or four scotches. Yep. That would do it. I make it back to my hotel, turn on my computer, and sit down at the desk. I pound furiously on the keyboard for an hour. I finally notice the bedside alarm clock reads 4:00 a.m. It's time to stop and tumble into bed. The alarm wakes me at seven to send my encrypted message.

The rest of the week is uneventful. I conduct a second bogus business meeting with the same results as the first. No follow-up expected by the company. I leave an encrypted diskette in a dead drop under a steel street plate on the edge of downtown. My signal site is an espionage classic: a chalk mark on the wall behind a Chinese restaurant. I can't help myself. The site and the irony are too perfect to pass up.

On my Friday meeting with Dale we meet in a safe house (my hotel room), and I successfully recruit him to work for the United States as a consultant. We toast our new relationship and fire up cigars before he calls the exercise to an end and tells me how well I did. He has only one question.

"How in the name of all that is good and holy did you write your reports after all we drank that night? I could have killed you the next morning. I had an exercise with another student at seven thirty, and I was hurting. Beer, wine, and scotch. Three great things that don't go great together," he says.

"I have no idea. I remember getting into the room. I remember powering up the computer. I remember waking up the next day. What happened in the middle is anyone's guess."

He helps clean the room. "Well, yours was one of the best reports I've seen in the whole class. You remembered every word I said, you properly questioned parts that were contradictory, and you outlined your plan for a postrecruitment handholding. It was a textbook piece of work."

He gives me the evaluation to sign. It's the best one I've received throughout the program.

"Are you sure you want to be a reports officer?" he asks. "You can lock and load with the best of them. We need case officers out there something fierce."

"Thanks. I appreciate that," I reply while reading. "But I think I'm a little old for some of the late-night carousing. You weren't the only one hurting the other day. I wrote till four, got up at seven, and ran full tilt the entire day. I finally slipped into a comfortable coma around eight that night."

"Well, give it some thought. You might want to change your career plans to being a case officer."

"Oh, I don't know. Seems to me the CMOs get the fun jobs. I like the massive amounts of reading and writing, and maybe working with liaisons. I don't think case officers get to do that."

"Despite what a lot of people will tell you, case officers are not illiterate knuckle-draggers. We're on the front lines, the tip of the sword. If you are single and enjoy long periods alone out in the world, being a case officer is the way to go."

Yeah. I think I'm sticking to my current role.

I fly back to the Farm in alias that afternoon and quickly switch documents to be me again. More important, I slip a certain band of gold back onto the third finger of my left hand. Just in case there's a roving roadblock to try to snare us with two sets of identification in different names as we go home for the weekend, I empty my car of anything not installed by the manufacturer. I return to Washington and to the wife I've barely seen over the past year.

We have a blast all weekend, largely forgetting the three additional weeks of testing to go before we are actually living together as husband and wife. She's put the miscarriage behind her, now able to talk about it without crying. We really want kids. Now that we'll be living together again, our chances for success should increase dramatically.

After the weekend everyone returns to the Farm and settles into our new offices. There are no real "work hours" when we are required to be in the office. It's assumed we will be here (report writing, map casing, etc.), so when something occurs "in-country," we can be part of it. If there's a walk-in, we'll pull on a disguise and interview him using a fake name.

Sometimes an agent from another country is in Winnebago and needs some servicing. We read the original case officer's files (provided by Bill) and meet the agent in his normal way. It keeps us on our toes. We know something happens to each of us every single day, but there's no way to plan for it until it actually happens.

There are numerous scenarios built into Testing Phase; five different case officer plans, three for collection management and two for desk officers. All of them end up cunningly interrelated, so piping up in our morning briefs is a necessity to survive. It forces us to get to know one another quickly. Perhaps too quickly.

On Tuesday morning Allen pulls me aside. A phone call he received earlier seems to have troubled him.

"Hey, Tom," he says, "can I ask a favor?"

"Sure thing. What do you need?" I reply, expecting him to ask for a map or an SDR timing sheet.

"Can you cover for me for about two hours this afternoon around lunch?"

"Cover you?"

"Yeah. I need to disappear for a couple of hours."

I don't understand his request. Apparently, I'm not supposed to.

"What do you need?" I ask.

"Cover me if Bill asks where I am."

A number of students have "hooked up" in the program. It's understandable. You can't date someone outside the program because they will ask way too many questions about where you are during the week. It makes for a long year of training for the single folks. Dating inside the pool, as it were, is the only option other than a cold shower. Allen, however, is married.

"Um, sure. I can take care of you if he asks."

"Thanks, man. I appreciate it. I'll be as fast as I can."

"Right-o! Well, have fun," I say. I'm not sure if I mean it or not.

Allen disappears and is gone for two hours. Bill never asks where he is, so I don't have to worry much about it. When Allen comes in later in the day he merely says thanks and never refers to it again. I guess we all have to do what's in our best interest.

After the station closes for the night (i.e., Bill goes home), Allen leans over from his desk.

"Got dinner plans?" he asks.

"No. I was going to go test an SDR for tomorrow."

He nods. "Yeah, I was planning to do the same. But I talked to Marty a minute ago. He says there are surveillance checkpoints all over the place outside. Most major freeway access ramps and malls are being watched. He thinks the SPOs are signaling the surveillance teams by radio when we leave. This may not be the best time."

Damn. I want to check this route out.

"Great. Well, I guess I have no plans. You want to duck into the BBQ joint real fast?"

"Yeah, I was thinking we could hide in a booth. It's past dinner rush hour, so it should be quiet in there. I need another favor. An off-the-record favor."

"Sure."

The BBQ joint is a small mom-and-pop restaurant barely a thousand yards from the front entrance to the Farm. It's not directly in the line of sight but is so close that it's declared a safe zone. We can't use it operationally for meetings or SDRs. It's an oasis from the Farm's limited chow and a nice way to get outside the fence for a break. Allen drives out the front gate and starts talking.

"My wife and I are trying to have kids," he says. "We've been working on it for almost two years but were not having much luck."

"Being down here probably doesn't help your chances much," I volunteer.

"So we are learning. We're using a fertility clinic in DC, but of course, they don't know where I work. So they tell Janet, my wife, to start doing all this stuff. Timing her cycle, taking her temperature, all that jazz to make sure we know when she's, you know, ready. Then we're supposed to go at it like drunken teenagers on prom night. But we can't do it unless she drives down here."

Aha. The other shoe drops.

"Like, if she calls you in the morning and says it's the right time? Where can you meet?"

He nods. "Yeah, well, in theory it works out real well. We've been meeting for a couple of months now. She calls. I slip out and make a quick hotel stop while I'm doing my casing. We're real careful. We park on opposite sides of the hotel so no one sees us together. All the hotel records are on her credit card, which is still in her maiden name. That used to bug me, but it's come in handy now."

"So, you're having an affair with your wife?" I ask.

He looks up. "An affair? Who said anything about an . . . oh. Yeah. I guess from your perspective it did look like an affair. That's funny."

A future Spy Kid in the works!

EVERY MORNING we are treated to WNN, Winnebago National News, a custom-made television news program generated by the staff of the Farm's large television studio facility. The images on today's broadcast are grim. Attacks overnight killed seventy-five people. Guerillas crossed back into an allegedly neutral third country to evade military forces. There are calls for the use of nuclear weapons. There is great political dissent in the country. A coup could occur at any time. We must be prepared.

Another day in the paradise of Winnebago.

Bill tells us that additional security precautions must be taken. A Marine Corps lieutenant comes in to describe how to conduct an emergency evacuation of the station. Preparing for any eventuality, we are told how to access the roof for a helicopter escape (à la Saigon) or to use the back loading dock door and slip into a specially equipped Marine Corps LAV (Light Armored Vehicle). What we must first do is prepare the office to be shut down.

In high-conflict areas around the world CIA stations maintain a readiness so the entire facility can be shut down (abandoned) without compromising secrets or leaving behind items that could embarrass the U.S. government or compromise national security. We must destroy anything not absolutely essential for our day-to-day operations. The subterfuge is designed to force us to clean out our desks and remove our personal items from the office. In short: maintain your testing demeanor, but clean the joint up in preparation to be finished and out of here. I have never cleaned a room with such enthusiasm in my life.

Part of the process of cleaning out our files involves going over each of our cases to see where we might be interfering with one another, or somehow able to assist one another when someone needs additional help.

I've had several meetings with a Russian émigré who claims to have sensitive information about his government's support for the guerillas. He is willing to give us the keys to the kingdom but only in return for asylum and relocation to the United States. I'm not keen on the idea.

"I don't know. I don't like the guy's story," I tell the group.

"What don't you like? It seems straightforward to me," Bill says.

"Yes. It's too straightforward. This guy is a textbook walk-in," I say. "It's a red flag."

Annie doesn't see it my way. "Why can't you accept he wants to defect?"

"Oh, I don't doubt he wants to defect. I just think he's hiding something," I reply.

Marty's eyes narrow to troubled slits. "What do you think his motives are?"

"Let's be honest, here. Do the Russians have a vested interest in this country?" I ask. "No. So why is he even here? He's supposed to be a trained intelligence officer, but his tradecraft is lousy. He insists on using his meeting places, not mine. I don't like it. He calls on an open phone line, yet tells us the intelligence services monitor our phones. He's either incompetent, or he's not who he claims to be."

Bill says nothing, but has a bemused look on his face. I'm either overanalyzing or right on the money. Annie still doesn't agree.

"I think you're making this too complicated. He brought you good information. It turned out accurate. Why pick a fight over it?"

"He brought us good information, all right. It was the same material we saw on WNN during the morning brief. He had nothing credible to add. He had conjuncture, opinion, and analysis but no additional raw information. I think he was just marking time. Maybe he's not trying to defect so much as trying to probe."

Marty bolts up in his chair. "Do you think he could be doubled? Playing you to get to one of us?"

I consider the possibility. "I don't know. I haven't thought about it. Why?"

"What area of town are you meeting in?"

"South side, but north of Camden Street. Why?"

He settles down but still looks rattled.

"I've got a meeting over there. Tonight." He looks at Bill. "Could a walk-in be testing our methods in order to learn which areas of town we are most familiar with? Learn our methods, our jargon and tradecraft, so they could grab one of us?"

Bill shrugs his shoulders. "That's happened before, sure."

Caroline jumps in. "I don't get it. Why involve us? We aren't support-ing the uprising. We are trying to stay out of the situation, not inflame it," she says.

"Right," Marty says, to himself as much as to us. "So far we've stayed out of this fight officially. The guerillas are losing ground. They don't have the money, technology, or the balls . . ."

Bill clears his throat and scowls.

Marty starts again. "Sorry, *brains* to effectively pull off a successful coup. They need access to American money and military hardware, some-thing we have officially banned."

"So what?" Bill says.

"So kidnap or kill a U.S. diplomat, and the U.S. will pay attention. Our blood spilled in-country will create an American response, officially or otherwise."

We all turn to Bill.

"So," he says, "you might say your meeting is an elevated threat to the officer."

Marty's eyes widen. He's got a high-threat meeting.

A high-threat meeting is where the case officer has an elevated chance of being the focus of violence or discovery by a hostile service. It's not some-thing taken lightly, and it's not done alone. The entire office forgoes all other activity to plan the meeting.

Marty's agent cannot be contacted, so we are forced to either cancel the meeting altogether or change the conditions under which it will be con-ducted. Keeping in character, Bill says canceling the meeting is not an option. So we change the conditions behind a veil of backup officers and contingency plans.

Marty creates a large map of the mall where the meeting will take place. There is a phone booth outside a department store where the agent is to be met. He shows us where he will pick the agent up and where he plans to take him for debriefing. Though the agent will not know Marty's plans, there are only a few locations around this mall for a private car conversation. We identify three sites. All three are easy to ambush. We need a new plan.

Caroline takes Marty's case file and reads it from the opening cable to the most recent meeting, taking a few notes and interrupting our map session with an occasional question. She has a suggestion about how to shake the guy up from the start. The case file says he's a ladies' man. Marty confirms that the guy's a big-time skirt chaser. Caroline says fine. She will be the one to make contact with him.

I don't like the idea, and make my point directly. "Bullshit. If we are expecting something nefarious, the last thing we are doing is putting you out there as an appetizer."

"Why? Because I'm a woman?" she asks.

"Of course because you're a woman. It's not safe."

"That's so sweet, you wretched chauvinist. I'm a case officer, no different than you. I do the same work you do day in and day out. I'm making the initial bump. You can't exclude me because it's dangerous. Bullets kill men and women equally."

She turns to Bill for support, but he's already talking. "She's right, guys. No special treatment for being the fairer sex, no offense."

Marty and I exchange glares. We don't need this. Even though the agent will not be expecting it, who's to say Bill won't tip him off beforehand? What did we learn early on? Trust no one, confirm everyone.

I look at the mall brochure that Marty has in the file. Several major department stores. Some boutiques, a handful of kiosk-based specialty stores. Some restaurants and bars. Then I notice it.

"A ladies' man, huh?" I ask.

"Yeah," Marty says, "so what?"

"Well, if we can't minimize Caroline as a target, let's at least give her some competition."

"Meaning what?" Marty asks.

"Meaning let's hide her among peers. An attractive woman walking up to him will be obvious, unless she's surrounded by attractive women."

I point to the mall diagram. Marty breaks into a smile.

"Brilliant. Think they'll give us a uniform?" he asks as we both turn our heads to Caroline.

She looks over my shoulder.

"Oh, now that's an idea," she coos. "I'll go for it if they will. We could totally put him off guard with this. Can we do it?" she asks Bill.

He comes around the table and looks over the map.

The Hooters restaurant logo is prominently featured on the mall map. The company's signature waitresses in tight orange shorts and T-shirts would be sensory overload for Marty's agent.

"Your assessment is duly noted," Bill says, "but in the interest of time and long-term locality, I think it best we not go that far undercover."

The unspoken advice: It's a good idea, but the potential blowback of an Agency training operation at a Hooters restaurant near the Farm is too risky.

I look at Caroline. "Oh, well, the concept has potential."

Let it never be said the fairer sex isn't also the smarter one. She knows this would not just work, it would be completely over the top, something the instructor—or an actual hostile agent in the real world—would never suspect.

"All right," Marty says. "You're doing the initial bump in street clothes. You hand him a piece of paper telling him to walk around outside to the other end of the mall. I'll pick him up there."

"Good. How do you want surveillance?" she asks, getting back into the game.

Marty returns to his map. "Annie will watch from the parking deck. Stay out of sight. When you see him reach the phone booth, you radio Caroline. She walks up and hands him the paper with my instructions. Caroline, you keep walking and go back through the restaurant into the mall. He can't do anything to you if you're in the mall. Go down to the next store and exit to the parking lot."

Caroline looks over the map. "OK."

"Drew, you're on the bottom floor of the garage. When you hear Annie give the signal, make your way around the corner. You should hit it at the same time Caroline is handing off the note. You've got a nice long dragway here. If there's no problem, continue around the corner and pick her up. If there is, you are the first guy on the scene."

Drew nods to Caroline. "I've got your back."

Marty looks at me. "Tom, you're in another car staked out around the corner. If Annie sees trouble, she's going to call you in. Otherwise when this guy turns the corner, you've got the eye. Got it?"

"Got it. You want static, or do you want me to move with him?" I inquire.

"Static. We've dropped our pants once Caroline gives him the note. He'll know there are more people involved than me. I don't want him to know *how many* more until much later. Jim will be on the top floor of the mall, in 'God's position.' There's a pedestrian walkway there. It gives you a good view of the area. When everyone else is on the move, you stay perched. If you see anyone else moving, you sing out on the radio."

He ponders for a moment, getting into the scenario he's crafting.

"Now, if there's a shitstorm we don't want anything in public. We'd end up on WNN tomorrow. The abort code word is 'Tabasco.' If you hear it, everyone bails. Jim gets Caroline inside. I'll meet you both in the food court. Anyone stuck on foot meets us there. Annie, you go down the back staircase of the parking lot. Allen will pick you up on Sullivan Street. Tom will come get us in front of the movie theater. Rally point is back at Hooters exactly one hour later for a relaxing adult beverage."

Bill pipes up. "Actually, if something goes haywire, you want to get it reported ASAP. It might even need to be in flash traffic."

Flash traffic is received at the headquarters watch office in Langley twenty-four hours a day. If we need the Marines sent in, they put in the order.

We sit in the office practicing our radio chatter, with Allen and Marty taking turns playing the part of the agent. Everyone takes extra batteries for their radios, and Caroline compiles a list of cell-phone numbers in case the radios mysteriously don't work. We split up for a few hours to relax before meeting at five at the mall.

At the mall I realize how much we have probably been under similar static surveillance the entire time we've been at the Farm. Movement and multiple sightings dictate surveillance detection. Take away those two characteristics, and substitute good placement, adequate communication, and a bit of experience—detection is virtually impossible. We've been fish in a barrel since the day we arrived.

Annie reports to Caroline that the agent is in place. Per Drew's wise suggestion, she gives us a blow-by-blow description of everything going on. Drew will take over if anything happens. Now the rest of the team, who are too far away to see things directly, will know what is going on.

Caroline is wearing a stunningly short miniskirt. She calls it a "dressed to thrill" outfit—a nice play on words. She hands the agent the note and continues inside the building. He doesn't follow her. Annie reports that he neither signals anyone nor makes a phone call. He turns in the proper direction and starts walking around the mall. Drew spots him walking the length of the building until he turns the corner. That's when I see him.

It's Gavin. Apparently the separation of students and instructors from the same training office no longer applies. He should be an actor, not an intelligence officer, as I can see he is enjoying his part immensely. Marty better have every contingency planned out. Gavin won't tolerate slacking off. He's firm but fair, a real pro.

He is glancing across the parking lot, but no more so than anyone else does with speeding traffic only a couple of feet away. He navigates the entire perimeter of the mall and stands where the note dictates. He sees a phone booth and is probably expecting us to call with additional instructions. Not the plan.

"He's there," I call on the radio. "He's alone. Drew, do you see anything you don't like?"

"Nope. It's all rock-and-roll to me," he says.

"Marty, I think we're good to try this. Are you ready?"

"Yeah. But circle around the opposite way from what we discussed."

He's changing a plan already under way?

"You sure you want to change something?" I ask.

"Yeah. It's not major. It occurs to me you should approach from the op-posite direction so he's on the passenger side of the car. You and Drew need to flip directions. That's my fault. I should have thought of it."

We all should have. We've all done car meetings.

"No sweat. Drew, do you copy? Switch direction around the mall."

"Copy that. Annie, if I'm coming your way, I'll pick you up at the ground level of where you are now."

"Copy that," Annie replies.

Marty jumps back on the radio. "Sorry for the switch, guys. I know it's a pain in the ass. My bad. We have everyone accounted for, right?"

Drew has Annie. Allen and Caroline will exit together and set up a hun-dred yards down the road. They will survey us from ahead. Jim and Jed will be in the store behind the agent to make sure that nobody is lying in wait. They will come up behind us as trailing surveillance. Everyone is accounted for. Everyone is ready. Marty and I move in to pick up Gavin. Marty is one cool customer under pressure.

"Hello, Hector. How are you?" asks Marty as he comes out of the store behind Gavin.

"What's all this walking around bullshit?" Hector/Gavin asks. So much for small talk.

I pull up before Marty can complete his answer.

"Taking a few precautions," Marty says. "I told you your safety was im-portant to me. I wouldn't want you to think *we* aren't prepared." Marty opens both passenger-side doors on my car.

"Who is this guy?" Hector/Gavin snarls at me.

"One of my associates. He's going to drive us so I can give you my undivided attention."

Gavin stands outside the car looking in at me.

"I don't like the looks of him. I want someone else."

"Sorry, Hector. This is all we can do right now. Do you want to stand here on the street and debate it for the whole world to see, or do you want to talk about your money? It's a lot of money. I'd hate to see someone else get it."

Damn, he's good. Put the benefits at the front of the conversation. It distracts the agent from any legitimate concerns he has or a nefarious deed he may be planning. Hector/Gavin finally gets in next to me. Marty climbs into the backseat.

"This is One. We're mobile. Turning right onto Constitution," I say into my radio.

"'This is One, we're mobile.' Great. I've got Hawaii Five-O here. Are you talking to Danno?" Gavin retorts.

"Aw, come on. We're all friends here, right?" Marty calls.

"Yeah, sure. Whatever," Hector/Gavin mutters, looking out his window.

"Good. Since we're such good friends, you won't mind me patting you down, right?" Marty asks as he moves forward on Hector/Gavin. "Are you carrying a weapon?"

"Yes."

I didn't expect this. Marty checks both of Hector/Gavin's coat pockets to find a snub-nosed .38 Special. It's a dummy gun with a solid barrel and REPLICA stamped on the side. Nevertheless, it looks, feels, and nerve-racks like a real weapon. I wonder what else Gavin has planned, or who else might be with him.

Jim and Jed are in my rearview mirror. I can see Allen and Caroline up ahead. Nothing else looks out of place. No surprises.

"What's this? I'm bringing you money. You don't need to rob me for it," Marty says, placing the gun in his pocket.

"It's dangerous out here. I told you the guerillas will kill me if they know I'm talking to Americans. I need money to get out of the country."

Marty continues his debriefing, talking Hector/Gavin down from the original hundred thousand dollars he originally demanded to ten thousand dollars. They work out how and where the money will change hands. Hector/Gavin tells Marty about a plan the guerillas have to kidnap an American diplomat. They hatched the plan with help from a rogue Russian who claims to be a former spy, but they no longer believe his story. They are going to kill him today.

Our team surveillance bubble continues to rotate around us. Hector/Gavin notices the familiar faces. We've made the point that we're not alone.

"Stop here," he says, opening his door. "I've told you more than I planned to and agreed for less money than I want. Watch the news tonight, tomorrow at the latest. Check into this Russian. That should be enough for the rest of my money."

He slams the door, then taps on the window for Marty to roll it down. A school bus pulls up behind us.

Hector/Gavin eyes the bus disgorging kids to their waiting mothers. "Never mind," he says, and walks away down the street.

When we get back to the office, there is a note on my desk from a station desk officer (Bill). A dead Russian was found in the river a couple of hours ago. Isn't this the man I was scheduled to meet with? Yes, it is. Hector/Gavin's information checks out.

Though we all play a part in it, Marty is the only student to receive an evaluation on the exercise, since the key role-player is his. (My dead Russian was a textbook walk-in, all right. He was a throwaway character, included as one of a cascading set of options built into a very complicated exercise. Even the instructors don't know how it will ultimately play out—there is no set ending. When a character such as this Russian doesn't successfully pull a team together, instructors will introduce others to test how well students are sharing their cases. It's a test of teamwork and cooperation as much as tradecraft.)

Gavin gives Marty kudos for integrating Hooters into our plans, since the agent is a reputed ladies' man. That said, he also points out that there aren't too many Hooters restaurants in Iraq or Afghanistan. So while the idea has merit for the graded exercise, in the real world it might be considerably more difficult than this.

It turns out he had a surprise in store for us as well: It wasn't a mass-kidnapping plot with multiple players. Hector/Gavin was going to do it himself to get the full hundred thousand dollars he wanted. Marty's evaluation was stellar, with only one small learning point to darken an otherwise perfect meeting. Gavin had been carrying a second weapon.

He had another pistol hidden in an ankle holster. It is human nature, he tells Marty, to stop looking when you find something. So he left something for Marty to find, expecting he would then lean back and begin the meeting. Had Gavin been a real bad guy, he could have reached down and pulled the gun out, killing either one of us. He didn't pull it out when he got out of the car because of the school bus. Otherwise he would have waved it around to make his point.

I SEE GAVIN the following morning at the third SOTC fitness test, which this time is at a reasonable hour. It's a moot point, given there is no longer any jump school, but it's now a matter of personal pride. I am on task for sit-ups and push-ups, followed by the two-mile run. But it isn't all work and no play. I see Daryll for the first time in a long while, and we catch up. He's not the only one here, though. Once again, my old office shows up to support me.

The whole team is in running attire. I drop down and pound through the push-ups, throwing on a few spare until Daryll reminds me that I'll need the energy later. He holds my feet while I do sit-ups. My suspected hernia doesn't like them, but I've decided I'm not listening to it today. I've got a run to finish, SOTC or no SOTC.

We stand at the starting line. I set a comfortable pace on the opposite side of the road from the other runners. I don't turn around to look, but one by one they come up behind me. Coach is first.

Adam and Travis, then Mike and Dave follow. Ahead, Terry and Wendy smile at me from the roadside. They fall in as we pass. All eight of our original Farm team members together again. It's a beautiful summer day, a week before the program ends. Though my abdominal anomaly starts to burn, I ignore it. I'm with my team.

I complete the run with considerable time to spare. I'm barely even winded; the morning runs with Coach and Mike have paid off. I pass the exam and earn the right to attend SOTC.

Adam and Coach are trying to maneuver the group to dogpile on me, but I keep cutting around other students. I'm evading a third attempt when I run into Daryll. He points at my sweaty, conspiring teammates.

"What are you, royalty? You had an honor guard with you."

Indeed I do.

ALLEN INSISTS we go out for a drink. I'm tired, have a mountain of reports to write, and have generally had a long day. I only comply when he grabs me by the arm and growls, "Please?" This is apparently not another booty-call discussion. I take him out to a biker bar I'd found, confident we'll have no student or instructor interference. He orders two double scotches. Neither is for me.

"I had police trouble this morning."

Oh, crap! I order a drink before he starts. "What? Too much noise in the hotel room?" I ask.

I'm making light of it, though things apparently went south pretty bad.

"Janet calls this morning and says it's the right day. I figure, bada-boom, we hit the hotel for an hour and I'm back here right after lunch, right? Same drill as always."

"Right. So what happened?"

"So this morning Bill taps me on the shoulder and takes me across the hall to an interrogation room. (Course Chairman) John and (Farm Site Manager) Tom are there. I'm thinking, 'What the hell?' Right?"

"Yeah. What happened?"

"Janet's been arrested! She's a couple of miles from the Farm, speeding through town to the hotel. She hadn't called yet, so I'm still working and waiting for her."

He takes a long gulp.

"Janet is flying down the road when she's tagged by one of the locals. Not a highway patrol officer, one of the local sheriff's guys a few blocks from here."

"So? Speeding tickets aren't a big deal. What else?" I ask.

"She gives the officer some crap about being in a hurry. Could he speed things up? He says something about her already being speedy this morning, yada-yada-yada. Next thing she's talking shit—wants his badge number so she can report him. 'You can't do this to me! My husband works for the . . . ' "

The sentence dangles in the air.

"Yikes! Please be kidding," I venture.

"No, I'm not! The guy not only makes her get out of the car, he puts her on the ground. She starts raising hell. Her four-hundred-dollar Versace jeans are getting dirty; who the hell does he think he is? All this other shit. The woman's lost her mind!"

I'm laughing. "Holy mackerel."

"She doesn't shut up!" He lowers his voice before continuing. "The cop gets tired of her mouth and cuffs her. He locks the car and hauls her to the office and books her. She's arrested!"

"The sheriff called over here?" I ask.

"Yeah. I get reamed by John with instructions to bail her out, then get her out of town."

"So?"

"I can't bail her out with the cash I've got on hand."

"You can't use your ATM or credit cards anywhere near the Farm, or you've broken cover," I recall.

"Yeah. So I get to drive all the way out there, get her credit card, and drive out to a bank to get the money to bail her out. I could just kill her."

I pause a moment before asking. This could be touchy. "Did John make any comment about this interfering with your career? Your wife talking smack to a local cop is going to make them think she's a security risk."

"I know," he says, burying his face in his hands. "I know. What am I going to do?"

There's no good answer. At a minimum, Janet being arrested during a conjugal visit is guaranteed to memorialize Allen in Farm folklore for the next fifty years.

IT'S THE MIDDLE of the afternoon. Caroline is consulting with Marty on an SDR. Annie is revising a report. Jed is helping Allen with pictures for a new dead-drop site. We are neck deep in planning meetings and conducting the real day-to-day logistics of espionage. That's when Bill simply walks in and tells us it's over. We're through.

No more meetings, no more SDRs. Testing Phase is finished. No coup by the local guerillas. No insurgents storming the building. No evacuation by helicopter. The impact is like a horse's kick to the solar plexus. Silence crushes us, the room an implicit vacuum as this carefully crafted world suddenly implodes. The anguish is overwhelming.

We want closure. Does anyone use nuclear weapons? Does the United States intervene at all? Bill only smiles and says the scenario has enough built-in flexibility to insert all of these issues and many more, depending on how the team is progressing. There are so many built-in variables, the instructors don't even try to guess how things end up. No two teams in any class end the same way.

As far as resolution, there isn't any. Every CIA office around the world deals with the constant churn of modern humanity. Station officers and support personnel come and go daily. Some arrive for a two- or three-year assignment while others are on a two- or three-day Temporary Duty (TDY). It all depends, Bill says. It depends on our ability to correctly gather the information necessary to forecast world events. That's the reason we've been trained. Don't look for an end. There isn't one. There is always another tomorrow to prepare for.

Even on September 11, he says, after the initial shock wore off, everyone got back to work. There were meetings to attend, agents to be managed. While the United States took a few days to grieve, the Clandestine Service had to carry on the business of espionage. The regrets, remorse, and recriminations would be dealt with later. However, here and now for Class 11, there is only rejoicing.

We escape into the hallway as every office receives similar news. There are shrieks of delight, mountains of paper thrown into the air, and rounds of hugs and handshakes. A year. An entire year is closing on this day. Many of us can't get past all the advanced planning we have already finished in preparation for future meetings. The celebration spills out to the front courtyard of the building into a spectacular Virginia afternoon.

We spend the rest of the day cleaning out the offices. All classified materials must be shredded into tiny confetti. Our computers will be wiped clean by technicians after one more check for inappropriate Internet content. Not much chance of that. Who had time?

I look over the vast amount of exercise materials we have churned through. Entire forests of paper, a schoolhouse of chalk, and more Power-Point presentations than the Big Five consulting firms combined. The building, and the campus at large, no longer has any restricted areas. We are equals in the eyes of the instructors and staff.

I keep a few mementos. My alias business card. My dead-drop container. I also pick up a coffee mug from the base store. It's not flashy, but flash is not part of the job. We avoid flash; we hide from it. My souvenirs are for my recollection, not for showing to others. They couldn't possibly grasp what it means to be part of this group. Class 11 is ready. We will embark on the world. Unfortunately, the Farm does not have a souvenir from us.

Dropping the Class 11 coin idea was a grave mistake. We should have fought more for it. Instead, the walls of the instructors' areas are filled with commemorative items from other classes. Some are formal, created by local trophy shops. Others are casual, everything from puppets to shadow-boxes to retail spy toys mounted on plywood. Each class has memorialized itself in one form or another. How will Class 11 be remembered? I guess our reputation will have to suffice.

Personally, I'm glad there's no kitschy toy or whimsical knickknack bearing our name. We are a different class from the youngsters who usually depart these hallowed halls. We were midcareer professionals before join-ing the Agency, possessing a quiet maturity that many instructors were un-prepared for. We learned a lot from the Agency, but we also gave it a lot. The Agency gave us *credentials,* and in return we will endeavor to restore its *credibility*.

These people—athletes and bankers, cops and chefs—were at the top of their professions. Our age, maturity level, and real work experience is something new at the CIA. We've bucked the system in many ways, but overall the impression I have is that most Agency personnel are happy with this change. We proved ourselves in the unforgiving crucible of life, carving out our own little niches in every corner of this great nation. We produced our own results, and thus were selected as the best representatives of a na-tion that demanded results after 9/11.

The finality is sinking in. Training is over. The reality of this profession is upon us.

GRADUATION IS HELD in the Farm's airplane hangar, the only building large enough to hold the entire class plus staff and instructors. It's an Agency-only party; spouses and parents are not allowed to attend. In keep-ing with its Ivy League fraternal origins, the Clandestine Service is a secret society that doesn't allow its ritual initiation to be attended by outsiders. Secret it will remain.

That same afternoon, Dottie hands out our assignments in individually addressed envelopes. But it's not a happy end to the day's celebration. A few who had begged for Middle East duty are working domestically. Others who had no intention of leaving the United States are going overseas in as little as three weeks. There appears to be little logic applied to the decision making and even less attention paid to the wish lists we crafted. Many students are raucously angry and take Dottie to task, wanting to change their assignments.

The location and specifics of each officer's job is classified, but I am one of the students who does not get the assignment they selected. I consider this more an annoyance than anything else. I have no plans for living overseas and am flexible on just about any domestic assignment. It's the surprise coming after all the training and planning that I find disquieting.

For many who joined the Agency to track down those responsible for killing family, friends, or colleagues, their assignment is paramount. They want to work in counterterrorism to the exclusion of all other tasks. Several threaten to quit immediately if their assignments do not change. The responsibilities are important; several are in fact vital to U.S. national security. However, these are not the roles promised during recruitment; it is not the reason they joined the CIA. To these zealots, it is Bin Laden and al-Qaeda or nothing at all.

Once we return to Washington DC, our other priority is reclaiming the lives we suspended twelve months ago. Working hours often ran late into the night, especially toward the end of the program. I can't get used to not needing to *be* somewhere. There is an odd feeling of emptiness. We had been in training for so long, our normal lives don't feel normal anymore. Television shows I used to watch regularly don't have the same allure. My home computer holds an assortment of e-mail from friends and family who didn't receive a reply to their previous correspondence. Unread magazines are piled in a corner.

After a year of being alone, it takes a while to adjust to sleeping with my wife again. In our first year of marriage we have lived together for all of nine weeks. It's been a lot of pressure on her that nobody knows about. As far as family and friends are concerned, we are a happy newlywed couple enjoying our lives together in the nation's capital.

After a couple of days Cathy and I double-date with another Agency couple, Chris and Patty—two couples out on the town. We don't tell the ladies where we are taking them. They are stunned when we arrive in front of the International Spy Museum.

It had opened the same week we entered on duty last year. It's the only museum in the United States dedicated to the tradecraft and history of espionage. Not affiliated with any U.S. or foreign government agency, it houses the largest collection of espionage paraphernalia on public display anywhere in the United States. After the year we've had, it only seems fair to take our wives through the multitude of exhibits.

The next morning Cathy sits down at the breakfast table and shares with me some messages that have been piling up the last couple of weeks. The first one has her vexed.

"Last week you got a call from someone named Toni saying 'The dragonfly program has been declassified and your bug will be on display in the museum.' You gave some woman a bug?"

"It's a long story," I say. "What else?"

"You had a call from another woman too. She called a few days ago. A woman with a strong Southern accent."

"And?"

"It's on the machine."

I play the message. I haven't heard that voice in two decades.

My twentieth high-school reunion is scheduled for the end of the month. Twenty years? I can't be that old! Cathy says she has the perfect outfit for my reunion. Pulling a box from behind the couch she whips out a new Tommy Bahama September 11 shirt to replace the one stolen at the Farm.

"I think you'll look great! Should we start making travel plans?" she asks mischievously.

Somehow, I don't think I'll make it to the party. Even if I could tell them what I'm doing, no one would ever believe it. I haven't kept up with a single person from high school, but you can never tell. Some of my old friends might ask questions. That could be tough. Who knows where we'll be in a couple of years? The past year is a blur. So are the nineteen preceding it. Besides, I have a fresh set of classmates to keep up with now.

Walking the halls of Langley I feel a conflicting sense of eagerness and uncertainty. The sentiment is particularly strong when I walk down the corridor to the Wall of Honor. The wound of freshly carved granite is clearly evident; Helge Boes was recently honored with the eightieth star. Mike Spann's inscription was similarly raw when we began training. How many more stars will be added in the weeks and months ahead?

Mike Spann. Helge Boes. Captain Beaupre and hundreds of other military personnel. That fateful Tuesday in September keeps claiming more victims. The country as a whole lost part of its national character: Confidence. Tolerance. Patience. The thousands of Americans who applied to the CIA in those first terrible weeks sought to regain what we as a nation lost. The officers of Class 11 bear the responsibility to recoup this loss on behalf of every U.S. citizen. That we must do so in secret is an unfortunate part of the package.

We are embarking on a career path few people will ever have full knowledge of. As the Book of Honor starkly demonstrates, even in death, secrets must be kept and protected. CIA employees respond daily to thousands of different priorities: delivering intelligence, preparing analysis, and planning collection assignments. These are dedicated people, doing a very difficult job; their successes are undisclosed but their failures are front-page news. September 11, 2001, will be remembered as the greatest of those failures. But it will also be known as the trigger for change in the Agency.

Standing between the American and CIA flags in front of this revered wall, I recall what Winston Churchill said a year after the December 7, 1941, attack on America.

It was following the battle of El Alamein, 150 miles west of Cairo. Churchill was justifiably proud of the outcome, a pivotal British triumph against the German Afrika Korps. But, as with Pearl Harbor, he understood the heartbreaking reality of an individual victory: At best, its effect is a perfunctory annotation in the time line of war. Sixty years later, his words are hauntingly prescient for the war on terrorism. He observed:

> *This is not the end. It is not even the beginning of the end. But it is, perhaps, the end of the beginning.*

Deployment

NEWSPAPERS ACROSS THE COUNTRY laud the graduation of the first 9/11 spy class, the largest in CIA history. We are now the talk of *every* town. We save local newspapers, including *The Washington Post* and *The Washington Times*. But our excitement over the media's acknowledgment of our accomplishment is tinged by sadness. Things are different. There is a distinct feeling of change and loss. We've lost our strength in numbers. We've gone our separate ways.

We exchange cell-phone numbers and e-mail addresses, promising to keep in touch, but we know it will be difficult. We just don't see each other anymore. Knowing what Ahmed is up to requires asking Wendy, who heard it from Jed. We are no longer a loud and boisterous group on the second floor of the cafeteria.

Gone are the days when everyone acquiesced to our presence. Class 12 is on our heels, another fresh group of faces at the Farm. Class 13 is starting their training here in Washington next week. The big blowout party we'd planned on having after returning home never happened, our tight-knit class overtaken by the needs of a nation at war.

Families now feel the true effects of life in the Clandestine Service. Spouses quit jobs. Children feel the sting of inoculations to protect them from a wide variety of exotic illnesses. Cars and homes are sold; possessions packed for shipment to faraway locales. Such extensive preparation is not just for those with families. Unmarried officers have their own measures to take.

Daryll fires up his Harley-Davidson and takes an extended trip through the Shenandoah Valley. After he returns, he drains the remaining gas and prepares it for long-term storage. The bike will remain on U.S. soil while he is out of the country. The unavoidable separation of man and machine is quite moving. "Live Free or Die" never had a more confident personification.

Many other former students take time off for Caribbean cruises, golf vacations, or simply time with their loved ones. As difficult as the past year has been, the real work is only now under way.

Some officers go immediately into language training for areas of the world where English is not just uncommon, it's unwelcome. Learning complicated tongues such as Farsi, Arabic, or Korean, they will go overseas for up to three years. Those heading for hard-target countries like Russia receive supplemental training for coping with the particularly harsh living conditions.

Others leave for weapons training, learning how to safely carry, conceal, and fire the Glock pistol and the M-4 assault rifle—standard issue for Agency officers in the Middle East. Many of the younger, unmarried members of Class 11 are demanding an opportunity to join the fight. We needn't worry about missing any of the action. There appears to be plenty left over.

Coalition forces in Iraq are hit with an average of thirty attacks a day. The military is clamoring for qualified intelligence personnel to help locate and hunt down the insurgents. A number of Class 11 officers go on temporary duty to Baghdad, Basra, Tikrit, and Mosul. Deployments range from three weeks to nine months. Duties include searching for weapons of mass destruction, interrogating Iraqi detainees, and working in the Coalition Provisional Authority Fusion Cell.

Other graduates pound ground in Afghanistan, looking for Osama Bin

Laden. The Taliban has mounted several surprise attacks after marshaling their forces in the mountainous border region near Pakistan. Disguise gear is nearly impossible to use, given the austere environment and body-armor issues. Several officers decide to "go native," letting their hair and beards grow to blend in with the local population. They haunt secondhand clothing stores looking for foreign styles and labels—anything to make them look less American. For them the war on terror is about to take on an all-new meaning.

Only a year ago we were told that we would soon be on the front lines. But the memories of why we came to the CIA are ever vivid, perhaps more now than at any time. We are a different group of people from a year ago.

Our attitudes are changed, as are our expectations and hopes. Some changes are good. Allen's liaisons with his wife were successful. At the time of this writing, she's pregnant with their first child. Other changes are bad. Several members of Class 11 found the strain on their marriages too powerful and are divorcing.

A number of students had found solace in the arms of their colleagues; there are five engaged couples from the class. But even with this many changes, Class 11 is, was, and will always remain a family first, a class second. Like other families, we worry about those in harm's way. But it goes much deeper than such simple platitudes. This is dangerous and difficult work, but it is the life we have chosen. Or did *they* choose it for us?

Terrorists attacked our overseas embassies, military installations, and naval vessels. When the United States didn't respond, they brought the fight to our doorstep, striking our national icons of commerce and defense—cornerstones of democracy respected the world over. By creating civilian casualties on U.S. soil, they thought we would surrender. As thousands of military personnel have shown, they were mistaken. Al-Qaeda should have studied *our* motivations, understood *our* values and beliefs, before making such a judgment. Now we shall show them our resolve.

Class 11 marks a new cadre of spy, an officer so versatile he or she defies stereotype. Our enemies will never see us coming. We can blend into any crowd, disappearing before their eyes or hiding out in plain sight. Our voices are lost in the background noise of markets, mosques, and Main Street.

Terrorists turned to new tactics to achieve their objective. Well, two can play at that game.

It's *our* turn now.

Afterword
December 2004

'M SITTING in a foldout chair in my wife's Arlington, Virginia, hospital room. Cathy and my newborn daughter sleep in the bed next to me. Like any new parents-to-be, we've been preparing for Sarah's arrival. In the quiet period of the past few weeks, I've had time to stop and consider just how much has changed over the past two years.

The 9/11 Commission was visceral in its recently published report, particularly against the Clandestine Service. A separate presidential commission delivered a report equally damning on the Agency's analysis of weapons of mass destruction in Iraq. Once again, the CIA's worst enemy is its own results.

George Tenet has stepped down as the Director of Central Intelligence, followed by Jim Pavitt retiring from the position of Deputy Director for Operations. Congressman Porter Goss has taken over. One of his first acts has been to sheke up the upper echelons of CIA management. His mantra seems clear: Status quo is no longer acceptable.

Deputy Director John McLaughlin retired November 12 after a series of reported confrontations with the new leadership. Stephen Kapps, who had replaced Jim Pavitt as Deputy Director for Operations, resigned on

November 15 along with his deputy, Michael Sulick. Both men reportedly clashed with Patrick Murray, the new chief of staff. Critics howl that the Agency is imploding.

But the CIA is larger than any one person. It is larger than any four—including the top four. In accepting his new role, Porter Goss made it clear he would force the Agency to confront many of its most-prized tenets. He is cleaning house, and sometimes that means getting rid of treasured mementos of years past. So be it. A new generation, an experienced generation, will enthusiastically rise to the challenge.

In the eighteen months that we have been deployed, Class 11 officers have witnessed unparalleled events abroad and at home. Every member of the class volunteered for duty in the Middle East. Taking turns from our assigned offices, we work ninety-day rotations, giving in-country officers a chance to return home for some precious family time. Afterward, we return to our assigned countries (including the United States), picking up family and workload where we left them three months earlier.

A few Class 11 officers were in Indonesia when the tsunami hit. Others reported the genocide in Sudan's Darfur region firsthand. One Class 11 officer was gravely injured during a firefight in Afghanistan. He was evacuated to a hospital in Europe and transported home to convalesce. As soon as he could walk, he demanded to return to Afghanistan. Where do we find such men and women? Why, after such an injury, would he so adamantly return? Quite simply: The work isn't done.

Osama Bin Laden is still out there, taunting us with his continued freedom. Though he has a respectable lead, I have no doubt we'll catch up with him eventually. We are building our numbers up over time just as he did. That said, there are still more FBI agents in New York than there are CIA case officers worldwide. It will require many more Americans to "answer the call." But together we will bring this man to justice. In the meantime, many of the events that transpired during training have now come full circle.

The trials of Washington DC snipers John Allen Muhammad and his teenage accomplice Lee Boyd Malvo have finished. Both men were convicted, with Muhammad sentenced to death and Malvo receiving life in prison.

The young Pakistani girl raped by a tribal order has also had her day in court. An antiterrorism council convicted six men, but a higher court later overturned the conviction, releasing the four who carried out the attack. Mukhtaran Mai not only refused to flee her village, she skillfully focused international pressure on Pakistan President Pervez Musharraf to ensure the tribal court systems no longer operate in the shadows.

Press reports indicate that Zacarias Moussaoui is prepared to plead guilty to being the intended twentieth hijacker on September 11, 2001. He is the only person to face prosecution in the attacks on America. But the hunt for others continues. Though our fight with the Taliban has only recently started, a number of Class 11 officers have received promotions for exceptional service.

Once again our skills and drive serve us well. Prior to 9/11, these officers were tops in their fields of expertise, whether developing far-reaching technologies or creating the new business models of the twenty-first century. Spymasters? Not yet, but we have experience in producing *results*. Isn't that what everyone wants from the CIA?

I believe that our private-sector experience will ultimately benefit the Agency in the most unanticipated of ways. Intelligence is like other information-based professions such as law, accounting, or medicine. Practitioners operate from a body of common skills, yet there are numerous areas of far-reaching specialization within each profession. This characteristic makes them prohibitively expensive to maintain, giving rise to the growing wave in outsourcing. Intelligence, perhaps, is just now reaching this point, with mixed results.

The independent contractors provided to us in training were the result of haste, urgency, and shortsighted decision making. The CIA simply did not have enough instructors for the number of new employees it was training, and quality was sacrificed for expediency. These independent contractors had no real management and little oversight; their failure was a virtual certainty.

In stark contrast to this is In-Q-Tel, a venture capital fund created by the CIA to sponsor new technologies that benefit the Agency and the greater intelligence community. It is a private, independent, and nonprofit company, operating as a commercial partner to the federal government. With more than one hundred successful projects to its credit, it's a model for other organizations, including the FBI, NASA, and the U.S. Army.

Private firms are now firmly entrenched in the war on terrorism, developing the systems used for text mining, link analysis, financial traces, language translation, and communications intercept. All of these firms require employees with firsthand knowledge of the intelligence community and high-level security clearances. Some members of Class 11 are entering this rapidly growing area, pleased to combine our government training and commercial experience.

Whether as government officers or private contractors, Class 11 continues to hunt down the man responsible for September 11, 2001. The passage of time has not dampened our desire. Osama Bin Laden will be caught. This simple mantra is the motivation for the careers we have chosen. Most members of the class cannot envision leaving the profession until he is captured or killed. That feeling is shared by thousands of other CIA personnel in every directorate, in headquarters, and in the field.

Bin Laden. He is our singular obsession—the one man who shook Western society unlike any other before him. This is the reason we scour the Pakistani mountains, interview thousands of Afghan tribesmen, and elicit nefarious individuals in the dusty hinterlands of the Middle East. We cannot stop. We will not stop. Joined now by graduates of Classes 12 and 13, our network grows as Bin Laden's withers. Like every tyrant before him, now that a superior rival has emerged, his fate will be sealed in a simple matter of time.

The "Greatest Generation" liberated the world from tyranny by stepping up to the challenge of World War II. The CIA is bursting with innovative new officers who have sacrificed for the opportunity to serve their country in the war on terrorism.

Just imagine what this "Experience Generation" will do.

AUTHOR'S NOTE

THIS BOOK IS NONFICTION, and the events represented herein are re-created as accurately as the passage of time and one man's narrow perspective will allow. Does it encompass everything that happened to Class 11? No, of course not.

I changed dates, names, times, destinations, activities, and sequences of events to mask their real identities. I had to omit many of the more extraordinary parts of the training. To give out too much information would weaken the program, putting officers and the agents they supervise at risk.

I will do nothing to put my friends in jeopardy, nor will I give our nation's enemies the luxury of a warning. They have infuriated the most talented and capable class of spies this country has ever produced. Perhaps God will show them mercy in His final judgment, but only after Class 11 has hunted them down to the far corners of the earth.

Ask any former student what he or she remembers about our experience, and you'll get more than a hundred uniquely different answers. While we took the same classes, performed the same exercises, and traveled to the same destinations, every student's viewpoint is individually unique. That's something few people understand: Facts are universal, but truth is individual.

The perspectives on the things we saw and learned are viewed through my recently married, corporate-grown, thirty-seven-year-old eyes. The other former students, looking at the same scene, will see an entirely different picture. As a result, this book is based on the rantings and ravings of a single person, but it is no less a collaborative effort. The parts you liked were due to other's people's hard work. Any inaccuracies or omissions are completely the fault of the author.

I thank my patient and long-suffering wife, Cathy, who allowed me to disappear into my cave to write when I should have been making up for the time we have already spent apart. The book would not exist if literary agent Joe Veltre had not taken a risk on an unknown author and an uncertain clearance process. Mitch Hoffman, Erika Kahn, and the entire Dutton publishing team accomplished remarkable results, given my conflicting desire for thoroughness and concern for protecting my colleagues. I'm deeply indebted to their patience and professionalism.

I am grateful for the considerable assistance of the CIA's Publication Review Board and the Directorate of Operations for allowing me to write such an extensive summary of Agency doctrine and training.

I express my sincere gratitude and thanks to Gavin, Dale, and Nick, three exceptional instructors at the Farm and some of the best talent in the intelligence community. I regret that preserving their cover prevents me from fully praising their contributions. I also thank Steve, who headed up our training in the Washington DC area, who helped me quietly escape to Florida when Cathy needed me. You will always be off the "Steve-Scale" for your assistance on that difficult day.

I salute my part-time officemate and full-time partner-in-crime, Daryll. He is the undisputed favorite son of Class 11, a standout gentleman in a class full of outstanding people, and now one of my closest friends. I also pay humble homage to my officemates at the Farm: Wendy, Mike, Terry, Dave, Coach, Travis, and Adam. You watched my back then, and you watch it now. Where would I be without you?

I am grateful to the many Class 11 officers I came to know and respect, including Jed, Mary, Duke, Kirsten, Hal, Tim, Annie, Betsy, Zoe, Cameron, Ahmed, Sean, Melissa, Nicole, Sara, Kim, Brandon, Jamie, Chris, John, Caroline, Marty, Marcus, Rick, Brian, Kevin, Frank, Melanie, Chip, Bryan, José, Amy, Jay, and Mike.

Be careful out there, guys.

—Florida Tom

ABOUT THE AUTHOR

Prior to joining the CIA, T. J. Waters was a vice president of a private consulting firm specializing in intelligence collection and training.

He is currently a CIA and DOD contractor in counterintelligence.